In Search of Safety

*Confronting Inequality
in Women's Imprisonment*

Barbara Owen,
James Wells, and
Joycelyn Pollock

UNIVERSITY OF CALIFORNIA PRESS

University of California Press, one of the most
distinguished university presses in the United States,
enriches lives around the world by advancing scholarship
in the humanities, social sciences, and natural sciences. Its
activities are supported by the UC Press Foundation and
by philanthropic contributions from individuals and
institutions. For more information, visit www.ucpress.edu.

University of California Press
Oakland, California

Library of Congress Cataloging-in-Publication Data

Names: Owen, Barbara A., author. | Wells, James,
    author. | Pollock, Joycelyn M., 1956– author.
Title: In search of safety : confronting inequality in
    women's imprisonment / Barbara Owen, James Wells,
    and Joycelyn Pollock.
Description: Oakland, California : University of California
    Press, [2017] | Includes bibliographical references and
    index.
Identifiers: LCCN 2016040309 (print) | LCCN 2016043723
    (ebook) | ISBN 9780520288713 (cloth : alk. paper) |
    ISBN 9780520288720 (pbk. : alk. paper) |
    ISBN 9780520963566 (ePub)
Subjects: LCSH: Women prisoners—United States—
    Social conditions. | Prisons—Social aspects—United
    States. | Women prisoners—Violence against—United
    States.
Classification: LCC HV9471 .O94 2017 (print) |
    ISBN HV9471 (ebook) | DDC 365/.60820973—dc23
LC record available at https://lccn.loc.gov/2016040309

Manufactured in the United States of America

25 24 23 22 21 20 19 18 17
10 9 8 7 6 5 4 3 2 1

This book is dedicated to John Irwin.
We honor his contributions to prison sociology
and his unwavering insistence that we must
recognize the humanity of all imprisoned persons.
We, and the field of criminology, miss him.

Contents

Acknowledgments   *ix*

1. Intersectional Inequality and Women's Imprisonment   *1*
2. Pathways and Intersecting Inequality   *19*
3. Prison Community, Prison Conditions, and Gendered Harm   *42*
4. Searching for Safety through Prison Capital   *68*
5. Inequalities and Contextual Conflict   *93*
6. Intersections of Inequality with Correctional Staff   *135*
7. Gendered Human Rights and the Search for Safety   *169*

Appendix 1: Methodology   *187*
Appendix 2: Tables of Findings   *205*
Glossary   *223*
Bibliography   *227*
Index   *247*

Acknowledgments

Based on almost ten years of fieldwork, this book traveled a long and interesting road. After the passage of the Prison Rape Elimination Act of 2003, Anadora Moss, president of The Moss Group, asked James Wells and Barbara Owen to collaborate on a national study of staff perspectives on sexual safety and violence. We are very grateful to Ms. Moss for her work on improving operational practice in women's prisons and for introducing James and Barbara to this compelling area of study. Through this work, James and Barbara developed their initial approach to gender issues surrounding sexual safety in prison. We then received funding from the National Institute of Justice (NIJ), through the Research on Violent Behavior and Sexual Violence in Corrections Program, 2006 (Award #2006-RP-BX). Our qualitative work, from which the narrative data were drawn, and the initial development of the survey instrument were supported by NIJ, under the stewardship of the late Andrew Goldberg. The final phase of the research, the *PREA Validation Project for Improving Safety in Women's Facilities,* was funded by the National Institute of Corrections (NIC) (Award #10PEI34GKB6). At NIC, we thank Dee Halley, Chris Innes, and Maureen Buell for their support of our project and women's services.

Points of view expressed in this book are those of the authors alone and do not represent the official position or policies of the U.S. Department of Justice.

As in all correctional research, we depended heavily on facility staff throughout the country to complete our work. In every site, we received excellent cooperation and support. Facility managers and line staff assisted us in far too many ways to mention here. We are particularly appreciative because we know research projects often compete with the demands of daily operations and can challenge staff in accommodating the requests of outside researchers. We are grateful for their help and hope they hear the ring of truth in these pages.

We also had excellent support from many research associates. We thank Bernadette Muscat, Janet Mullings, Ashley Blackburn, Shondra New, Adam Matz, and Stephanie Fratto Torres for their expert interviewing and note taking skills. Ms. Torres deserves additional mention for her painstaking coding of over eight hundred pages of focus group transcripts. Jennifer Leahy provided expert research assistance and insights into the experience of women in prison. James S. Parson was a full partner in every aspect of this research.

Many dedicated research assistants accompanied us on our many site visits. Hannah Robbins, Veronica Oropeza, and Marisa Baumgardner endured long days collecting data at facilities, followed by long nights cleaning data, while traveling with us around the country. Appreciation is also due to Norma Vidal, Carlos Del Valle, and Ivette Nurse for their professional and expert skills in translating our survey documents and protocol from English to Spanish, which allowed us to capture the perceptions of a very vulnerable and often invisible population rarely mentioned in correctional research.

We had excellent support from our data entry team, consisting of Millicent Wells, Robert Davidowski, Patricia Miller, Earl Angel, Kelle Parson, and Emily Wells.

Thanks are due Kevin Minor, Eric Lambert, Jill Farrell, and Vince DiCiccio, who served as subject matter experts and reviewers in several phases of these studies. We acknowledge the valuable contributions of Allen Beck, Mark Fleischer, Paige Harrison, Chris Innes, and William Saylor to our work.

Appreciation is also due to the staff of Just Detention International for helping us understand many of the intricacies surrounding these issues and for access to their archives.

In 2006, Barbara Owen was invited by the Kingdom of Thailand to participate in the development of the Bangkok Rules as a subject matter expert. During this work, she began to recognize the significance of the human rights approach and its absence from the U.S prison system. We would like to offer a special acknowledgment of the work of the Thailand Institute of Justice and the unwavering support of Her Royal Highness, Princess Bajrakitiyabha of Thailand, and her particular interest in reforming women's prisons and ongoing efforts to champion these human rights standards.

Barbara Owen would also like to thank Barbara Bloom, Stephanie Covington, and Nena Messina for their insights into the imprisonment of women. Brian Powers continues to be an essential colleague and friend. Allison Cowgill provided wonderful library support.

Tamie Fields Harkins was a true heroine in helping us shape three overlapping studies into this book. Her guidance on digging deeper into the data helped us find the story embedded within. We also appreciate the indexing excellence of Victoria Baker.

At the University of California Press, we were supported by Maura Roessner, acquisitions editor; Jack Young, acquisitions assistant; and Claire Renzetti, series editor. We very much appreciate the opportunity to tell this story.

We thank our long-patient spouses:

Barbara's husband, Vince DiCiccio, for keeping home life (and her) together during this long adventure.

James's wife, Brenda, and daughters, Emily and Millicent, for their patience and understanding.

Joy would like to thank Eric for all he does, as always.

Finally, we are very thankful to the women in prison and the staff members who participated in the focus groups and surveys. These participants were true partners in this work.

I

Intersectional Inequality and Women's Imprisonment

When most people think about prison, they think about men. And this makes sense: men make up over 90 percent of the prison population in the United States and in most countries around the world (Walmsley 2015). In 2014, women comprised just over 7 percent of the prison population, 112,961 of the 1,561,500 prisoners in the United States (Carson 2015). As Britton (2003) argues, prisons are deeply gendered organizations. We build on this insight to employ an intersectional analysis (Potter 2015; Joseph 2006) in describing the gendered harms embedded in the contemporary prison. In documenting women's experience with imprisonment, we argue that threats to safety are bound by multiple forms of inequality within the prison itself. Women's lived experiences while locked up, we assert, reflect the multiple and cumulative disadvantages that condition their pathways to prison and continue to shape their choices and chances in the total institution of the prison. In confronting these inequalities, women negotiate myriad challenges to their safety inside prison by developing forms of prison capital. This capital can protect women from the threats in the carceral environment, in their interaction with other prisoners, and from the staff employed to protect them. Learning how to do time, we find, is based on leveraging prison-based forms of capital that can protect women from the harms of imprisonment.[1]

---

1. While our data and our interest lie in articulating women's experience with imprisonment, the concept of prison capital is equally applicable to the exploration of violence

Multiple forms of inequality and disadvantage find direct expression in women's pathways to and within prison. While racial and class inequities constrain the life chances of many before they land in prison, understanding the experience of women requires a separate examination. In their examination of "gender-specific explanations of prison violence," Wooldredge and Steiner (2016, 12) find: "Although incarcerated men are disproportionately drawn from more impoverished populations, incarcerated women tend to be even more disadvantaged and face multiple deficits in social capital (inadequate job training, spotty employment histories, and economic marginalization)."

Our analysis builds on the intersectional inequalities that increase women's vulnerabilities to crime, violence, and imprisonment (Belknap 2015; Crenshaw 2012; Pollock 2014; Potter 2015). For women whose pathways lead them to prison, such disadvantages are replicated and often magnified inside prison, which, in turn, increases the threats to their already tenuous sense of safety and well-being. In addition to gendered disadvantage, our analysis introduces the notion of prison capital. We define *capital* as any type of resource, or access to a desired resource, that can keep a woman safe while she does her time. In addition to prison forms of social capital (who you know) and human capital (what you know), other specific expressions of cultural, emotional, and economic capital provide the foundation for the search for safety as women do their time. In the context of irrationality and inequality, women navigate these challenges embedded in prison life by marshalling their stores of prison capital. Women who develop and deploy their stocks of prison capital survive, and sometimes thrive, as they serve their prison sentences. Most can do their time safely by gaining economic capital, earning the cultural capital of respect and reputation, increasing emotional capital, and developing social capital through connections with nonthreatening and supportive prisoners and staff.

In documenting women's experiences with incarceration, we explore the ways these multiplicative and cumulative disadvantages create the

---

and safety in men's prisons (de Almeida and Paes-Machado 2015). We support further study of the utility of the concept of prison capital across all carceral settings. While the term *gendered* often indicates a study of women, there is much utility in looking at the gendered experience of male prisoners as well. We encourage investigations of men's gendered pathways to and within prison, as in the work of Sabo, Kupers, and London (2001) on prison masculinities. In the same spirit, an emphasis on the human rights of all prisoners is warranted, as guided by the recent United Nations human rights instrument, the Mandela Rules (retrieved 10/9/2015, www.penalreform.org/wpcontent/uploads/2015/05/MANDELA-RULES.pdf).

context for gendered troubles, conflict, and violence within the framework of intersectional inequalities and constrained choice. Reframing the lives of incarcerated women's lives in terms of the gendered harms of imprisonment directs attention toward the consequences of structural inequities and away from individual pathologies as explanations of prison conflict and violence.

Threats to safety and well-being are embedded in the world of the prison. Standard operational practice can threaten women's well-being through "gender-neutral" policies. Material needs and desires, unmet in the scarcity of the official economy, feed economic conflict and the subterranean economy through illicit trafficking and trading. Drug use and other risky behaviors inside also contribute to these potentials for prison violence. Relationships among women prisoners and with staff contain the possibility of risk, conflict, and violence. Prison culture may require women to resort to forms of aggression to protect themselves and their reputations as they do their time.

Women's safety is further compromised by the many contradictions embedded in the contemporary prison. We demonstrate how prisons manufacture risk and sustain unsafe conditions, contradicting the stated mission of "care and custody" of their prisoners. Existing prison conditions, such as inadequate housing, untreated disease, minimal medical care, and inferior nutrition create a context of risk and threat to women's well-being. Aspects of operational practice, such as gender-neutral classification systems and lack of women-centered services (Van Voorhis 2005, 2012; Bloom, Owen, and Covington 2003, 2004), also undermine women's ability to live safely inside prison. We claim these harms are unnecessary and constitute gendered human rights violations when viewed through the lens of international human rights standards for the treatment of women in prison. The United Nations Rules for the Treatment of Women Prisoners and Non-Custodial Measures for Women Offenders (2010), or the Bangkok Rules, serve as international standards intended to relieve the iatrogenic damage of imprisonment and better prepare women to reenter their communities. The Bangkok Rules, and other international human rights instruments, however, have gained little traction in U.S. prisons. We return to the promise of the Bangkok Rules in our conclusion.

GENDER AND IMPRISONMENT

The concept "gender" is used here as a sociocultural category, as opposed to the biological concept "sex" (West and Zimmerman 1987;

Belknap 2015). In summarizing work on gender as process, Wesely (2012) shows that gender is a socially constructed identity through social, cultural and psychological accomplishment. Gender is thus organized and managed within social structures and institutions (West and Zimmerman 1987; Belknap 2015). Wesely (2012, 11) outlines the ways gender socialization and different expectations of gender identity are "inextricably linked to unequal levels of social value, prestige, or advantage" in patriarchal societies. In challenging the assumptions of the duality of the social construction of "female" and "male," Wesely ties these artificial dichotomies to the assumptions of a patriarchal culture in which girls and women are subordinated, oppressed, and seen as "less than" boys and men. We see gender as "an ongoing and contradictory historical and interactional process, not as an attribution of individuals" (Martin and Jurick 2007, 29).

The concept of intersectionality (Potter 2013, 2015; Crenshaw 2012; Joseph 2006) informs our work by underscoring the overlapping inequalities of race, class, gender, and sexual orientation and identity that underpin women's status in the free world. Women's prisons provide a stark example of these intersecting and hierarchical forms of discrimination against women, the poor, and communities of color. Richie frames this argument precisely.

> I cannot imagine a place where one might stand and have a clearer view of concentrated disadvantage based on racial, class and gender inequality in the country than from inside the walls of women's prisons. There, behind the razor wire fences, concrete barricade, steel doors, metal bars, and thick plexiglass windows, nearly all the manifestations of gender domination that feminist scholars and activists have traditionally concerned themselves with—exploited labor, inadequate healthcare, dangerous living conditions, physical violence, and sexual assault are revealed at once. That gender oppression is significantly furthered by racism and poverty is undeniable from this point of view. Women's correctional facilities constitute nearly perfect examples of the consequences of the multiple subjugation and the compounding impact of various stigmatized identities. The convergence of disadvantage, discrimination, and despair is staggering. In fact, it could be argued that prisons incarcerate a population of women who have experienced such a profound concentration of the most vicious forms of economic marginalization, institutionalized racism, and victimization that it can almost seem intentional or mundane. The pattern is clearly evident in almost every crowded visiting room, in every sparsely decorated cell, and in the stories of each woman held in degrading and dangerous conditions that characterize women's prisons and other correctional facilities in this country. (Richie 2004, 438)

THE CONCEPTUAL FRAME OF THIS BOOK

We draw on multiple, overlapping concepts to frame and present our data. The constructs of pathways, gender inequality, intersectionality, community, capital, prison culture, human rights, and state-sponsored suffering guide our analyses.

Expanding the Pathways Perspective

The story begins in women's pathways to prison. Deeply informed by feminist theory, the pathway perspective examines gendered experiences that lead women to prison. The pathways approach draws on life course and cycle of violence theories to trace, retrospectively, the paths traveled by justice-involved girls and women (Lynch et al. 2012; De Hart 2005; Belknap 2015; Pollock 2014). It focuses on the lived experiences of girls and women and their multiple marginality from conventional institutions, such as work, family, and school (Owen 1998), and the patterns of violence and victimization throughout their life course (Bloom, Owen, and Covington 2003; Pollock 2014; Belknap 2015). These pathways are often shaped by punitive policies toward women. Sharp (2014, xiii) locates the high incarceration rate of women in Oklahoma in the legal and social climate of "mean laws," arguing that "to truly understand why Oklahoma imprisons women at such a high rate, we must look beyond the women themselves." The mean laws that have propelled women into Oklahoma prisons illustrate the punitive nature of U.S. prison policies, with disadvantage, discrimination, and despair (Richie 2004) embodied in these pathways. As Enos (2012) and Sered and Norton-Hawk (2014) suggest, prisons have become the default system for managing marginalized people disadvantaged through intersectional inequalities.

The notion of agency is critical to understanding women's experience (Bosworth 1999; Batchelor 2005; Miller 2002). We offer the idea of *constrained choice* to describe the limited options available to many marginalized women and emphasize the cumulative disadvantage rooted in structural and historical forms of inequality that produce oppression, trauma and subsequent harm. We argue that the pathways and choices that bring women to prison continue to shape their lives inside.[2]

---

2. Nuytiens and Christiaens (2015) question the application of pathways theories to non-U.S. populations, given the societal differences between the United States and countries in other regions.

Gender Inequality

We also build on the definition of gender and gender equality offered by the United Nations in *Women and Imprisonment: The Handbook for Prison Managers and Policy-Makers:*

> Gender refers to social attributes and opportunities associated with being male and female, including socially constructed roles and relationships, personality traits, attitudes, behaviours, values, relative power and influence. Gender equality refers to the equal rights, responsibilities and opportunities of women and men, and implies that the interests, needs and priorities of both women and men are taken into consideration. (UNODC 2015, 12)

Gender inequality finds expression in all aspects of women's imprisonment. It is a critical component of their lives inside and out, a foundation for the punishment philosophy vis-à-vis women, and a significant source of threat within the prison community. Such inequality intersects with other identities and social positions, particularly those generated by racial, ethnic, and class oppression, reproducing disadvantage and harm in their prison lives. In or out of prison, women's experiences with interpersonal violence and victimization must be contextualized within the frame of structural disadvantage and intersectional inequality, rather than dismissed as individual pathologies. We reframe the discussion of women's pathway experiences into and inside prison through our understanding of intersectionality and structural inequality.

Intersectionality: Intersections of Inequality and Identity

We are guided by scholarship articulating the dimensions of intersectionality (Joseph 2006; Burgess-Proctor 2006; Crenshaw 2012; Chesney-Lind and Morash 2013; Potter 2015). Potter (2013, 305) offers this definition: "Intersectional criminology is a theoretical approach that necessitates a critical reflection on the interconnected identities and statuses of individuals and groups in relation to their experiences of crime, the social control of crime and any crime related issues." With roots in black legal scholarship (Crenshaw 2012), this approach establishes that women must be understood in terms of the multiplicative social effects of an individual's identity "and the social forces that generate crime and reactions to crime" (Potter 2013, 305). Potter draws on Richie's concept of gender entrapment to show how the linked stigmas of gender, race, and economic and social class are amplified by "being battered women, being criminals and being incarcerated women" (2013, 311). Salisbury and Van Voorhis extend this argument:

> Beyond the "triple jeopardy" many women offenders must face related to their race, class, and gender (Bloom, 1996), several unique experiences have been described by women offenders in narratives of their life experiences leading to continued recidivism. Among them are poverty-stricken backgrounds, lifelong traumatic and abusive events, serious mental illness with self-medicating behaviors as coping mechanisms, little social support, dysfunctional intimate relationships, and difficulty managing and providing for their dependent children. (2009, 542)

This notion of multiple stigmas and "oppressed and subordinated identities" (Potter 2013, 314) is central to our analyses. Understanding differences among women and critically analyzing the experiences of individuals based on their social positions is important to any study of women (Potter 2013, 316). As Georges-Abeyie (2015) further notes, communities of color should not be seen as an ethnic monolith. Women, too, must be understood in terms of their diversity, rather than heterogeneity. The intersectional paradigm unpacks the experience of women in prison by focusing on the multiplicative effects of these identities beyond a monolithic definition of gender. With real differences in women's lives mediated by social position, the additional subordinated status of "prisoner," "inmate," or "convict" adds another layer to women's oppressions and marginality as they do their time.

Potter's 2015 book, *Intersectionality and Criminology: Disrupting and Revolutionizing Studies of Crime,* extends the argument by saying that since "intersectionality is a practice of understanding and interrogating the role of identities, we must understand the social construction of major identities categorized within our societies" (8). For individuals "who hold multiple intertwined identities at the lowest end of the social hierarchy, discrimination, microaggressions, and bigotry are multiplied" (35). We argue these intersectionally informed experiences continue to shape pathways and disadvantage *inside* prison.

Chesney-Lind and Morash (2013, 292) agree that intersectionality is key to transformational feminist criminology, stating, "The feminist perspective calls attention to gender (and thus masculinity) as something that is enacted in the context of patriarchal privilege, class privilege, and racism." They remind us that feminist theory concerns gendered organizations of social control that are "clearly implicated in the enforcement of patriarchal privilege" (289). The prison, as the locus of social control, reinforces and reproduces gender inequality and other forms of discrimination against women of color, those without capital, and those with non-normative sexual and other disdained identities.

Connecting the Free World and the Prison Communities

The idea of community influenced our work in several ways. Examining gendered inequality in the community structures of women's free world lives reveals the depth of struggle they experience prior to prison (Sered and Norton-Hawk 2014; Baskin and Sommers 1998). We were particularly influenced by the work of Sered and Norton-Hawk (2014) and Lipsitz (2012) as they emphasize the role of a spoiled medical status and housing insecurity in undermining women's safety in the free world community. Their work led us to consider how these factors contribute to safety inside prison.

Clemmer's critical work, *The Prison Community* (1958), frames our examination of the social worlds of the women's prison.[3] Clemmer's study was "intended as a compendium to cover the formal and informal organization of a conventional prison" (1958, xi). In his foreword to the 1958 edition, Donald Cressey (who worked with John Irwin in developing the importation theory a few years later) writes, "Although the premise is unstated, the book deals with the prison as a social microcosm in which the conditions and processes in the broader society are observed" (vii). This is precisely our argument: we can understand women's imprisonment by examining gender-conditioned inequality and other forms of cumulative disadvantage in the wider community.

After our research revealed to us that prison living units make up different neighborhoods, some more risky than others, we gained a deeper appreciation for the notion of prison as community. Women and prison staff told us that some housing units produced more conflict and violence while others were relatively safer. Women often made comparisons regarding the relative safety and inherent challenges of differ-

---

3. The literature on the social organization of women's prison documents these gendered worlds. Representative studies are Bosworth 1999; Britton 2003; Carlen 1983; Chesney-Lind and Rodriquez 1983; De Hart 2005; Faith 1993; Feinman 1976; Fletcher, Shaver, and Moon 1993; Freedman 1981; Giallombardo 1966; Girshick 1999; Hartnagel and Gillan 1980; Heffernan 1972; Henriques 1995; Kruttschnitt and Gartner 2005; Mahan 1984; Moyer 1984; Owen 1998; Owen and Bloom 1995; Pollock 2002a; Rafter 1990; Rierden 1997; Ross and Fabiano 1986; Schneider 2014; Selling 1931; Sharp 2014; Watterson 1996; Young and Reviere 2006; Zaitzow and Thomas 2003.

ent living units. This insight guided us in our sampling strategy for the survey data in the second NIC study (Wells, Owen, and Parson 2013), where we attempted to measure perceptions of risk across these different prison neighborhoods.

Prison Culture and Prison Capital

Women do their time differently than men by constructing gendered social worlds through rules and requirements for living in prison. One version of prison subculture is known as "the mix" (Owen 1998), a set of norms that mediates women's behaviors inside. Women in the mix run the risk of troubled relationships, involvement in drugs, fights with other prisoners, "being messy," engaging in gossip, and generalized conflict. As we looked at our data on violence and safety, we realized the mix can be understood as one source of prison capital. As de Almeida and Paes-Machado (2015, 190) suggest, "In prison, this capital relates to the internalization of norms and rules that constitute . . . the prison's social order." We now see the mix as a cultural adaptation to the multiple forms of inequality in prison that provides guidelines for surviving, and sometimes thriving, while imprisoned. In the coming chapters, we describe the contradictory influence of the mix: it creates the potential for conflict and violence while also shielding women from some of the risks inherent in doing time. Prison capital is generated through this cultural context, contributing to conflict and violence as well as to striving and thriving in this community.

Salisbury and Van Voorhis (2009, 545) tell us that the social and human capital framework is essential to deciphering patterns of female offending behavior. As most women offenders come from backgrounds of limited social and human capital, these concepts also inform our analysis of women's lives inside, as we argue that prison capital is essential to safety. *Human capital* concerns an individual's personal resources, such as education, intelligence, psychological stability, resiliency, skills, and other abilities used to make their way in the world. *Social capital* involves relationships and connections with others, serving to improve an individual's resources by providing material and social support. These networks and systems of mutual aid connect an individual to desired resources in this world of intentional scarcity.

Women who lack capital in the free world are vulnerable to gender-based violence, subordinated relationships, economic discrimination, and other forms of disadvantage. Giordano et al. (2002), Holtfreter,

Reisig, and Morash (2004), Reisig, Holtfreter, and Morash (2002), and Salisbury and Van Voorhis (2009) collectively conclude that improving the social and human capital of women offenders improves their chances of desisting from criminal behavior in the community. In contextualizing conflict and violence in women's prisons, we realized these concepts connect directly to women's search for safety inside in explicating the role of prison capital in creating safety while locked up. In addition to the forms of human and social capital, our analyses of safety include forms of emotional, cultural, sexual, and material capital as they play out in the prison community.

Sexuality and Sexualization

Sexuality and sexualization are key gendered differences in the lives of women and men in most societies. We note here the restrictions of the gender binary and the importance of acknowledging the fluidity of sexuality, sexual identity, and other forms of gender expression. Covington (2008, 210) offers this definition of sexuality: "Sexuality is much more than sexual behavior. It is an identification, a biological drive, an orientation, and an outlook. Sexuality is physical, emotional, psychological, and spiritual." Healthy adult sexuality integrates these components into identities and ways of living and includes perceptions of self and others. In contrast to healthy adult sexuality, many girls and young women are sexualized into destructive sexual behaviors and identities.

The term *sexualization,* used in this context, denotes a "central aspect of gender socialization and 'emphasized embodiment' for girls" (Wesely 2012, 14). In contrast to healthy sexuality, sexualization entails sexual objectification and narrow definitions of value, self, and desirability often imposed on an individual (Wesely 2012, 14). Although much of this sexualization comes about through individual experiences with abusive or violent sexual behavior, women are exposed to public sexualization by the "pornified" definitions of female sexuality and attractiveness embedded in the patriarchal social structure (Wesely 2012; Chesney-Lind and Irwin 2008). Wesely's concept of the continuum of sexualization (2012) captures the range of sexual socialization, from typical or healthy development to damaging and extreme abuse and violence experienced by girls and women. Richie (2012) provides additional insight in describing the multiplicative harm of the overtly sexualized image of black women in American culture and its connection to violence against them in the free world.

For women in prison, both the individual experience of abuse and the structural contexts of objectification contribute to cumulative disadvantage. In their lives in the community and in prison, sexuality can be commodified as sexual capital. Trading sex for money, drugs, or other resources is a common option for women who are undercapitalized in the community (Wesely 2006). This survival option is present in their prison lives. Both staff sexual misconduct and intimate partner violence are tied to this gendered form of capital. Smith (2006) points to the need to rethink prison sex, making the connection between healthy sexual expression and safety behind bars. Controlling women's sexuality leads to controlling women's bodies (Bagley and Merlo 1995), a key feature of carceral spaces.

Many women and men enmeshed in the criminal system are further disadvantaged by a nonconforming gender identity (Smith and Yarussi 2015). Gender identity, gender expression, and sexual orientation introduce additional intersectional elements in the lives of those not conventionally gendered. Controlling sex and sexuality is damaging for all women, but the evidence shows that gender-variant persons experience additional threats to their safety inside. As Stohr (2015, 127) argues, "Because of the historical rigidity around gender issues and a basic lack of concern for those on the societal margins because of their gender identity, transgender women and men have existed in what must at times seem like a war zone in which they are the perpetual target of scorn, harassment and assault."

Human Rights in Prison

The Universal Declaration of Human Rights (UDHR), adopted by the United Nations General Assembly in 1948, is the foundation of the human rights approach, enshrining the rights of humankind around the world. It promotes and encourages respect for human rights and fundamental freedoms for all (Office of the High Commissioner for Human Rights 2012, 3). Grounded in the fundamental principle of nondiscrimination of any kind, Article 1 of the UDHR sets the stage by introducing the principles of dignity, justice, and equality. Although not a legally binding document, the Declaration has moral weight and is the basis for several human rights instruments relevant to prisons and jails that we review in chapter 7. The Declaration, through specific articles, outlines the human rights relevant to prison settings: the right to physical security; freedom from torture and other cruel and unusual punishments;

equal protection under the law; and a community standard of living, including food, clothing, medical care, and social services. In applying these moral principles to carceral settings, the 2004 Commissioner on Human Rights highlighted "the need for special vigilance with regard to the specific situation of children, juveniles, and women in the administration of justice, particularly while deprived of their liberty and their vulnerability to various forms of violence, abuse, injustice and humiliation" (United Nations 2015, 42). The Bangkok Rules provides this special vigilance and informs our perspective.

HOW DO WE KNOW? MIXED METHODS
AS FEMINIST METHODS

Mixed methods combines the strengths of quantitative and qualitative methods while minimizing the weaknesses of each (Brent and Kraska 2010; Jenness 2010). Burgess-Proctor (2006) notes that mixed methods provide the best approach to explicating intersectionality and other feminist concerns. We follow this approach in foregrounding the experience of women through interviews and surveys measuring their perceptions of danger and safety. In documenting women's experience with "disadvantage, discrimination, and despair" (Richie 2004, 438), we draw on data we collected over the course of ten years in three funded studies of women's prisons and jails (Owen and Wells 2005; Owen and Moss 2009; Owen et al. 2008; Wells, Owen, and Parson 2013).[4] In these overlapping studies, we interviewed over 150 imprisoned women and dozens of staff through open-ended focus groups, asking them to describe their experiences and perceptions of violence and safety in women's prisons. From the thick description (Geertz 1983) generated by these interviews, we developed a survey instrument to measure women's perceptions of safety and violence, validating the questionnaire with over four thousand women around the country. Our work was supported by the National Institute of Corrections and the National Institute of Justice. Details of our methodologies are found in appendix 1.

The Prison Rape Elimination Act (PREA) of 2003 provides the framework and funding for collecting descriptive data, improving policy and practice, and developing standards surrounding sexual violence in all correctional facilities in the United States. The act recognizes that gender differences between female and male inmates require specific

4. A critique of our approach can be found in Buchanan 2012.

attention to female facilities (Moss 2007). Our technical reports provide an in-depth description of our findings, with a focus on improving sexual safety for confined women (Owen and Wells 2005; Owen et al. 2008; Wells, Owen, and Parson 2013). These studies are summarized below.

Staff Perspectives: Sexual Violence in Adult Jails and Prisons

Our first study of prison sexual violence was conducted between 2004 and 2006 through interviews with correctional staff at national correctional conferences and, in the second phase, in twelve jail and prison facilities that housed women and men (Owen and Wells 2005; Owen and Moss 2009). Using open-ended questions, this study collected staff perspectives on the dynamics of sexual assault, staff knowledge of training and procedures, problems and successes in responding to sexual violence, and recommendations for improving this response in both women's and men's facilities. Owen and Moss (2009) found staff perspectives on sexual safety for women differed greatly from staff views in men's prisons. Such gendered differences included more discussion of the relational context of women's prisons and its influence on the complexity of sexual relations, touching, and other physical closeness. Some staff noted that women's histories of abuse and trauma influenced same-sex behavior while incarcerated (Owen and Moss 2009).

Gendered Violence and Safety: A Contextual Approach to Improving Safety in Women's Facilities

Following the *Staff Perspectives* study, we were funded by the NIJ to collect qualitative and quantitative data on the context of sexual violence in women's facilities (Owen et al. 2008). Between 2006 and 2008, we conducted over forty focus groups with imprisoned women and correctional staff in four states. The majority (twenty-seven) of the focus groups were conducted with women prisoners: twenty-one groups with women in prison and six groups with women in jail. The focus groups with prisoners were conducted in two sessions, resulting in four-hour interviews with each group.

We were particularly concerned about protecting our participants. Being sensitive to the possibility that the subject matter and the group setting would cause distress to the imprisoned women, we reviewed our protocol with a victimologist, asked women about the best way to protect them during the study in the pretest, and provided specific information on counseling for such concerns at each site. We also told women about the possibility of an individual interview with project staff should they feel more comfortable speaking in private. Very few women asked for these accommodations. Our methodology for this study is found in appendix 1.

While much contemporary scholarship on the correctional world relies on deductive survey research or secondary analysis of administrative data, the NIJ study began with an inductive, in-depth, qualitative investigation. We used focus groups to ask about the participants' knowledge of violence and danger in these correctional worlds. The focus group interviews began with four basic questions:

What do you know about violence or danger in this facility?

How do women currently protect themselves from violence in this facility?

What are some things that can be done here to protect women from danger and violence?

What else should we know about violence and danger here?

Our conclusion was based on our original hypothesis: Sexual violence is embedded in a broader, gendered context of violence and safety. Like all aspects of incarceration, violence in women's correctional facilities is markedly gendered and nested in a constellation of overlapping individual, relational, institutional, and societal factors. Violence, we found, is not a dominant aspect of everyday life but continuously exists as a potential, shaped by time, place, prison culture, interpersonal relationships, and staff actions. Ongoing tensions and conflicts, lack of economic opportunity, and few therapeutic options to address past victimization or to treat destructive relationship patterns—all contribute to the potential for violence in women's facilities. However, our findings did not suggest that women's jails and prisons are increasingly dangerous. While some patterns that shape vulnerability and aggression exist in any facility, most women learn how to protect themselves and do their time safely. We also found that most staff and managers are committed to maintaining a safe environment (Owen et al. 2008).

As part of the NIJ project, we also conducted a content analysis of letters sent to Just Detention International (formerly known as Stop Prison Rape). This organization generously allowed us to review and code over fifty letters they had received concerning women's experiences with sexual assault. Chapter 6 reviews these findings, and appendix 1 describes the data collection effort.

The Development and Validation of the Women's Correctional Safety Scales (WCSS)

Building on the focus group data collected in the NIJ project described above, we constructed a lengthy battery of instruments and beta tested it on almost nine hundred participants as part of the *Gendered Violence and Safety* study. The NIC then provided funding to develop, refine, shorten, and validate the Women's Correctional Safety Scales (WCSS), a comprehensive battery of instruments to assess prisoner perceptions of safety and violence in women's facilities. The survey was validated with data from over four thousand women prisoners in fifteen geographically dispersed federal, state, county, and private correctional facilities. In this survey, we measured the nature and levels of concerns imprisoned women have about all forms of violence in their prison lives (Wells, Owen, and Parson 2013). We draw on these survey data throughout the book. Appendix 1 contains details on our methodology and sampling approach; appendix 2 presents tables of findings.

A Note on the Sources of Narrative Data

All quotes and comments from women and staff were drawn from typed transcripts of the focus group interviews and written comments from all three studies. Many of the segments included here were also used in the technical reports. We introduce these narratives with randomly selected names to capture the vitality and diversity of the women who were kind enough to share their experience with us.

SO WHAT DOES THIS MEAN?

While the funded projects were designed to describe women's experiences and perceptions of sexual violence and safety, a second look suggested another story embedded in our data. We realized we had missed some vital components of safety and violence in our earlier studies of incarcerated women (Owen 1998; Pollock 2002). For example, Owen's description of the "mix" captured elements of prison subculture for women but did not fully explore the dynamics of conflict and violence in any depth. In our previous work, we argued that women's prisons and jails were less violent than male settings. This remains true: when viewed through a male lens, women's prisons and jails are indeed safer. Women in prison tend not to engage in the physical and sexual hyper-masculine violence observed in male prisons.

However, a deeper look at women's prison experiences from a gendered standpoint reveals more complex forms of conflict, danger, risk, and violence. Wooldredge and Steiner (2016, 211) suggest that gender differences in background factors of imprisoned women and men may be "more relevant than confinement factors for predicting victimization risk among women." We argue that women's background factors, articulated in the pathways perspective, shape women's responses to imprisonment, with the harms and threats embedded in the prison further reflecting the continuous cumulative disadvantage of their lives inside. In this book, we dig into our original data to describe a broader view of women's lives while imprisoned and focus on how the key elements of prison community, culture, capital, and conditions combine with pre-prison experiences to shape how women navigate this risky environment.

Women living in prison confront myriad harms throughout their incarceration, some through interactions with members of this locked world, others through prison conditions and policies. As we reexamined our data across all three studies, we realized a better understanding of inequality experienced by women in the free world and in the prison community was critical to a sharper analysis. While the gendered harm of women's prisons (Owen 2005) has been documented, here we take a more structural approach to understanding the context of risks to safety and the gendered strategies women use as they search for safety in the irrational world of the contemporary prison.

THE PLAN FOR THIS BOOK

This book has several overlapping goals. In addition to witnessing and documenting women's experience with imprisonment, we offer a new analysis of the contemporary prison by reframing the questions of trouble and violence as a further expression of broader societal inequalities and human rights violations. Combining this more structural critique with a human rights approach to imprisonment expands our understanding beyond individualized and pathology-based explanations.

Chapter 2 describes women's pathways to incarceration, focusing on the impact of intersectional inequalities in women's lives in the free world. We offer an expansion of pathways that emphasizes intersectional inequities and the historical and structural trauma that propel them into prison. This focus on cumulative and structural disadvantage moves beyond an individualized and blaming explanation of women's crimes in setting out the context of constrained choice.

Chapter 3 examines prison conditions and elements of the prison community that contribute to women's fears over safety while confined. Conditions of material scarcity, substandard living quarters, and few program and treatment resources are exacerbated by the crowding that characterizes contemporary corrections. In the early days of our interviews, we were surprised to hear that concerns about cleanliness, disease, and medical care were described as primary threats to safety. As we learned more, we came to understand how deleterious prison conditions represent a serious challenge to women's well-being. The physical plant, operational practices, availability of programs and medical and mental health services, housing configurations, classification, and staffing patterns all contribute to women's perceptions of safety and danger. Crowding, a feature of all contemporary prisons, aggravates the injurious impact of these minimal living conditions as they combine to create tension and conflict.

In chapter 4, we explore how women's prison culture reflects and responds to gendered inequalities. Prison culture mediates these inequities by mapping cultural routes to survival and safety while at the same time creating the potential for risk and danger. Inequality within prison—between prison staff and women prisoners and among confined women—is expressed in relations among all members of this community. This chapter also outlines the strategies and tactics women deploy in their search for safety. Even in the face of risk and trouble, women learn how to protect themselves from the obvious and subtle threats to safety and well-being. The search for safety is embedded in prison capital, which enables a woman to withstand material, social, psychological, and physical threats. Women learn how to protect themselves from all forms violence by managing situations and relationships that harm them. In some circumstances, women must resort to threats and push back verbally or physically. Some of these strategies involve rule-breaking behavior and dealing in prison contraband. These gendered strategies for navigating forms of violence and conflict specific to women's incarceration can prevail over the gendered inequality that jeopardizes their search for safety.

Chapter 5 explores the impact of inequality on women's imprisonment as it creates and sustains conflict. Individualized vulnerabilities and levels of prison capital combine to create this gendered context of trouble. This chapter provides a detailed description of the forms of gendered violence we did not sufficiently explore in our previous work. Troubled relationships reflect the overlapping pathways of childhood abuse and subsequent trauma, relationship dysfunction, and deficits in all forms of human and social capital as outlined by the pathway theorists Salisbury and Van Voorhis (2009). Much of the violence in prison is embedded in these conflicted relationships in the form of interpersonal or domestic violence.

Chapter 6 expands on the consequences of the obvious inequality between correctional worker and prisoner. Much of this inequality is routinely expressed in disrespectful and derogatory comments made by staff about women prisoners. We draw on our narrative and survey data to describe how staff sexual misconduct, and physical violence are relatively rare but are a serious concern in the women's prison community. The problem of staff sexual misconduct is not one of magnitude, as our surveys and Bureau of Justice Statistics data demonstrate (Beck, Harrison, and Guerino 2010; Beck et al. 2013). Rather, the fact that *any* number of staff employed to provide care and custody of women prisoners harm women through sexual actions should be troubling to us all.

In the closing chapter, we suggest that women's prisons, because they are unsafe, have become the site of state-sponsored suffering in reproducing and reinforcing multiple forms of inequality through the gendered harm of imprisonment. We argue that women's prisons harm women and their life chances in unnecessary ways. There is no doubt that all imprisoned people suffer by confinement. We have determined, however, that the overt gender discrimination in the wider society and within the prison adds another punishing layer to the gendered cumulative disadvantage faced by justice-involved women. A focus on human rights reframes the discussion and directs attention to both reducing women's imprisonment through noncustodial measures and incorporating a human rights approach based on respect, dignity, and nondiscrimination in the prison. The promise of the Bangkok Rules and other human rights instruments provide the way forward.

2

Pathways and Intersecting Inequality

We begin by discussing women's imprisonment in the context of contemporary public policy. Next we profile women in prison through a description of shared characteristics and clusters of common experiences. Expanding the framework of the pathways approach to include structural and cumulative disadvantage, we explore how these gendered inequalities shape women's experiences on their pathways to and within prison. These pathway experiences influence how a woman does her time and responds to challenges to her safety and well-being. While agency and choice are essential to explanations of women's crimes, we also assert that such inequalities condition and constrain opportunity and initiative. These shared experiences contribute to women's emerging strategies to develop capital in their search for safety.

IMPRISONING WOMEN

The United States incarcerates more people in prisons and jails than any other country in the world (Walmsley 2015; Barberet 2013). With just 5 percent of the world's population, the United States accounts for almost 25 percent of its prison population. The Brennan Center for Justice finds that, by all measures, crime in the United States has declined in the past twenty-five years: since 1991, violent crime has fallen by 51 percent and property crime by 43 percent (Roeder, Eisen, and Bowling 2015). While many theories have attempted to account for this drive to what has been called "mass incarceration" (Simon 2014; Travis and Western 2014), few theorists have devoted much thought to the particular case of confined women. In 2014, the U.S. prison population totaled 1,561,525, of which 112, 261 were women and 1,448,564 were men (Carson 2015). The exponentially increasing numbers have resulted in more Americans incarcerated—by far—than ever before.[1]

In the United States, the proportion of women in state and federal prisons ranges between 5 and 7 percent of the total correctional population. Although these numbers of women in prison are dwarfed by the staggering numbers of men confined in U.S. prisons, the *rate* at which women are being imprisoned outpaces that of men. The rise in the number of women imprisoned began with a steep upward curve in the 1980s, culminating in a peak high of 114,612 in 2008 (Carson 2014, 213). As noted by the Sentencing Project (2005, 2007; Mauer 2013), since 1980, the number of women in prison has increased at nearly twice the rate of men.

Mandatory minimum sentences for drug crimes contribute to the overwhelming numbers of both women and men in prison (Mauer, Potler, and Wolf 2000; Frost, Greene, and Pranis 2006). Over twenty years ago, Bloom, Chesney-Lind, and Owen (1994, 1) claimed that "the war on drugs has become a war on women," as laws made for male drug kingpins were affecting women involved in lower-level drug offenses in detrimental ways. Little did we know that the number of women in prisons in the United States and throughout the world would continue to climb over the next decade. Danner (1998) and Dodge and Pogrebin (2001) detail the deleterious impact of mandatory sentencing and Three Strikes laws on women. Even with some substantial changes in sentencing policy, the female imprisonment rate continues to grow, although at somewhat slower rates (Carson 2015).

Despite this downward trend in crime, prison populations have steadily grown during the same period. With some exceptions (see Mauer and Chesney-Lind 2002), most scholarship and policy work has focused on how these factors have caused dramatic increases in the overall prison population (Travis and Western 2014; Western 2006). While racial discrimination in criminal justice practices is now discussed more broadly (Alexander 2010; Potter 2015), there has been less atten-

1. Both the number of people committed to prison and the length of sentence for each person fuel prison populations. Under the punitive policies of the U.S. drug war, both the number of people sent to prison and the length of their sentences increased. Legislation establishing mandatory minimum sentencing and so-called truth-in-sentencing laws limited the prison system's ability to release prisoners through earning "good time" credits.

tion to the gendered effect of these public policies (Bloom, Owen, and Covington 2003). Much of the increase in women's prison populations has been caused by the "profound change in the manner in which women are treated within the criminal justice system" as "a result of more expansive law enforcement efforts, stiffer drug sentencing laws, and post-conviction barriers to reentry that uniquely affect women" (Sentencing Project 2007, 1). This change in policy has not been a result of dramatic increases in women's criminality. While both women and men commit similar crimes at the less serious end of the crime continuum, the gender gap expands as the seriousness of crimes increases. Pollock (2014, 23) summarizes national data, noting that women's crimes have been increasing slowly, as measured by arrest trends, since 1935. The increase in arrest rates may be due to reporting and system practice changes—that is, girls and women are more likely to be arrested today for the behaviors that did not result in arrest in the past (Pollock 2014; Chesney-Lind and Irwin 2008; Winfree and De Jong 2015). Steffensmeier and Haynie (2000) propose analysis of gender and structural disadvantage variables to fully understand women's rates of offending.

Overall, women represented 25 percent of all arrests in 2010, just over one-third (37 percent) of all arrests for property crime, and 19 percent each for drug and violent crime. Compared to men, women are more likely to commit nonviolent property crimes and drug offenses. The percentage of women participating in violent crime, such as murder, robbery, rape, and kidnapping, has been consistently low over time (Pollock 2014; Pollock and Davis 2005; Chesney-Lind and Eliason 2006). When women commit violent crimes, their victims tend to be family members, acquaintances, and intimates, especially in the context of intimate partner violence. For women who commit violence against someone unknown to them, their crimes usually appear to be embedded in cultural and economic demands of their communities (Kruttschnitt, Gartner, and Ferraro 2002; Sommers and Baskin 1993). The "war on drugs" accounts for much of the increase in women's incarceration and its disproportional impact on women of color (Bush-Baskette 2000; Frost, Greene, and Pranis 2006; Richie 2012; Belknap 2015). Drug offenses accounted for half of the increased number of women in state prisons between 1986 and 1996 (Sentencing Project 2007). Additional factors, such as punitive sentencing policies (Frost, Greene, and Pranis 2006; Brennon Center 2005), unequal policing in communities of color (Alexander 2010; Pettit and Western 2004; Western 2006), decaying communities (Clear 2007), eroded social services (Enos 2012), and high rates of recidivism (Deschenes, Owen, and Crow 2006), have also fueled the increase in the imprisonment of women.

Prison rates do not vary by crime rates alone. As Travis and Western assert:

> Over the four decades when incarceration rates steadily rose, U.S. crime rates showed no clear trend. For example, the rate of violent crime rose, then fell, rose again, then declined sharply over this 40 year period. The best single proximate explanation of the rise in incarceration is not rising crime rates, but policy choices made by legislators to greatly increase the use of imprisonment as a response to crime. Mandatory prison sentences, intensified enforcement of drug laws, and long sentences contributed not only to overall high rates of incarceration, but also especially to extraordinary rates of incarceration in black and Latino communities. (2014, 3)

Echoing the call to use intersectionality to parse the impact of multiple forms of discrimination and oppression on women, Kilgore argues that an analysis of gender and class would "enhance our understanding of mass incarceration," which

> has been an assault on the poorest elements of the working class, primarily residents of deindustrialized inner cities. This layer of the population has been driven into the category of "criminal" by a combination of economic necessity, social decay, media manipulation and, most importantly, harsh sentencing laws and intensive police repression inspired by racially-biased polices like "zero tolerance" and "broken windows." (2015, 286)

In her analyses of black women's struggles within their communities, Richie expands our understanding of the impact of unfair law enforcement practices and damaging policies on women of color in America's "prison nation":

> The notion of a prison nation reflects the ideological and public policy shifts that have led to the increased criminalization of disenfranchised communities of color, more aggressive law enforcement strategies for norm-violating behavior, and an undermining of civil and human rights of marginalized groups. A prison nation refers to those dimensions of civil society that use the power of law, public policy, and institutional practices in strategic ways to advance hegemonic values and to overpower efforts by individuals and groups that challenge the status quo. (2012, 3)

In her critique of the white feminist domestic violence movement, Richie argues that emphasizing gender to the exclusion of intersectional variables has disadvantaged women of color. While feminism begins with a focus on gender inequality, she suggests, it fails to examine experiences among women across other identity and status groups.

Unpacking Gender and Race in Imprisonment Rates

In the United States, imprisonment rates vary dramatically by geography, gender, race, and ethnicity. Imprisonment rates are typically reported "per 100,000" of the general population, indicating the number of confined people per every 100,000 adults in the specified demographic category. In 2013, for every 100,000 adults in the United States, 623 were held in some form of incarceration (Carson 2014). For state prisons, the rate is 417 per 100,000 adults nationally. Males are incarcerated at a much higher rate (1,191 per 100,000) than women, who are incarcerated at 83 per 100,000 people in the general population. Some states are much more punitive than the national average might suggest; Oklahoma has the highest female imprisonment rate, at 136 per 100,000 female residents (Carson 2014, 6).

Illustrating the fact that racial and ethnic discrimination is a key feature of America's prison nation, women and men of color are disproportionately represented in U.S. prisons (Richie 2012; Alexander 2010; Young and Reviere 2006). While African Americans make up about 12 percent of the U.S. population, black women make up 22 percent and black men over one-third of the prison population. Young black women are five times more likely to go to prison than their young white counterparts (Carson 2014, 8). Latinas make up about 17 percent of the general population and of the prison population. At 49 percent, white women make up the plurality of women in prison, just under their representation in the overall general population. However, in the past five years, the proportion of black women in prison has decreased as the proportion of white and Latin women in prison has increased (Mauer 2013). As Mauer (2013, 1) notes, variation in "crime rates, criminal justice policies, economics and demographics" accounts for much of the changing racial dynamic among women in America's prisons.

Women and men in prison differ widely by offense category (Carson 2014, 8, 15; Greenfield and Snell 1999). Almost two-thirds of women in prison were convicted of nonviolent crimes (28 percent of property crimes; 25 percent of drug crimes; and 10 percent "other"). In contrast, just over half (54 percent) of male prisoners were convicted of violent crime, 18 percent for property offenses, and 16 percent for drug-related offenses. Men are also more likely than women to be imprisoned for sexual offenses and robbery. These gendered offense patterns hold true when looking at countries outside the United States; drug use and other nonviolent crimes account for the vast majority of women imprisoned around the world (Barberet 2013; United Nations 2010; UNODC 2015).

SHARED CHARACTERISTICS

Belknap (2015) and Pollock (2014) offer comprehensive overviews of issues surrounding women's involvement in the criminal justice system. In this section, we examine these characteristics within our model of cumulative and structural disadvantage, arguing that they are direct consequences of gendered inequality and other discrimination. Compared to male offenders, women are more likely to be primary caregivers of young children, have an incarcerated parent, and come from a single-parent household. In terms of emotional capital, women in the criminal justice system have experienced multiple forms of victimization and abuse as girls and as women. Women in prison are more likely than imprisoned men to report substance abuse and mental health problems and to suffer from serious health problems. Poverty and other forms of disadvantage are prominent pathway experiences in the lives of imprisoned women who have less human capital in terms of lower education levels and skills. Most women in prison also have shorter criminal histories than most men in prison, as measured by number of arrests and prior prison terms (see Pollock 2014; Belknap 2015; Bloom, Owen, and Covington 2003; Chesney-Lind 2002). We assert that intersectional identities and social positions condition pathways and agency. Any understanding of women's pathway and prison experiences must be understood in terms of the structural disadvantages that shape women's behaviors and life chances rather than in terms of the individualized and blaming explanations of pathology, deficits, or unworthiness.

Family Life

As a primary source of capital, family life makes significant contributions to life chances. Women offenders are likely to come from disordered families with histories of substance abuse, mental illness, arrests and incarceration, family violence, and addiction (Bloom, Owen, and Covington 2003; Pollock 2014; Belknap 2015; Langan and Pelissier 2001). Bureau of Justice Statistics (BJS) data show women in the community are more likely to have family members involved in the criminal justice system than men (Glaze and Maruschak 2010). While imprisoned women and men report a similar likelihood of having an incarcerated brother (34 percent) or father (19 percent), more women than men report having a sister imprisoned. Just under 10 percent of the women reported the imprisonment of a spouse, compared to 2 percent of the men (Glaze and Maruschak 2010). Glaze and Maruschak (2010) also show that women in prison were more likely to have been placed in foster care or another state facility as children.

Sharp (2014) examined the family background of women in Oklahoma prisons, finding that many, particularly women of color, come from families undermined by multigenerational drug use and incarceration. These patterns differed by race and ethnic membership: compared to the 5 percent of white women in her study who had a mother who went to prison, almost 15 percent of the black women, 10 percent of the Latinas, and 10 percent of the Native American women shared this family background. Sharp (2014, 21) documents, too, the "intersection of economic disadvantage and childhood abuse" and differences among women across class, cultural, and racial and ethnic identities.

Before They Were Women, They Were Girls

A discussion of findings on girls and young women adds another dimension to our understanding of inequalities and pathways to justice involvement. A complete review of current research on experiences of girls and young women is found in the work of the Office of Juvenile Justice and Delinquency Prevention (OJJDP)–sponsored Girls Study Group (2008, 2010). We highlight the experiences that connect girlhood to women's adult lives in their pathways to prison.

Fitting the childhood victimization pathway suggested by Salisbury and Van Voorhis (2009), youthful female offenders are more likely than male offenders to have experienced violent victimization in childhood and much more likely to have experienced violent victimization than nonincarcerated girls and young women (Siegel and Williams 2003; Abrams, Teplin, and Charles 2004; Goodkind, Ng, and Sari 2006; Adler and Worrall 2004; Owen and Bloom 1995; Simkins and Katz 2002; Widom 2000). Widom has established the basis for our understanding of childhood abuse and crime in her ongoing research (Widom 1989a, 1989b, 1989c, 1991a, 1991b, 1995, 1996, 2000; Widom and Ames 1994; Widom and Maxfield 2001). She argues that childhood experiences of victimization contribute to multiple problems in adulthood, including lack of intellectual performance, inability to cope with stress, suicide, abuse of alcohol and drugs, sensation seeking, antisocial attitudes, and lower levels of self-esteem and sense of control (Widom 2000). This association between victimization and criminal offending seems to be stronger for girls and young women than their male counterparts (Wesely 2012; Chesney-Lind and Irwin 2008; English, Widom, and Brandford 2001; Belknap and Holsinger 2006; Makarios 2007; Teague et al. 2008). Simkins and Katz (2002, 1474) claim that the strong connection between victimization and subsequent offending criminalizes abused girls, stating that there "appears to be a significant link between the abuse and neglect they have experienced, the lack of appropriate interventions or treatment, and the behavior that lead to their arrests."

Delinquent girls and young women have disproportionate histories of dysfunction and disruption in family, peer, and romantic relationships (Wesely 2102; Maeve 2000; Girls Study Group 2008, 2010; Garcia and Lane 2010; Rosenbaum 1987, 1989). Family support is often weak or nonexistent for such girls, particularly when relationships with primary caregivers have been shaped by violence or exploitation. Their peer and romantic relationships may have also been subjected to such violence and disconnection (Chesney-Lind and Irwin 2008; Pleydon and Schner 2001; Batchelor 2005; Batchelor, Burman, and Brown 2001; Miller and White 2003). These disconnections often shape the relationships the girls and young women form later in their life course. At the same time, girls and young women place a high value on intimate peer relationships (Giordano, Cernkovich, and Randolph 2002; Miller and White 2003).

Experiences as girls and young women can influence how a woman does her time. Islam-Zwart and Vik (2009) suggest childhood victimization mediates women's adjustment to prison. Silverman and Caldwell (2008) found violence in custody could be predicted by the types of material and reputational rewards and the need to gain respect. The impact of victimization experiences and the primacy of reputation and respect continue to shape their lives inside.

Women Offenders and Their Children

Women in prison are more likely than imprisoned men to have children and to have more than one child (Glaze and Maruschak 2010). Almost two-thirds of all women in prison have children and were likely to live with their children in the year before incarceration. The majority (80 percent) of the children of male prisoners live with their mothers, but only about one-third of the children of female prisoners live with their fathers.

The children of imprisoned mothers are more likely to live with grandparents, and five times more likely than the children of male prisoners to be removed from their home and placed in foster care. BJS data show that about half of the women in prison have never had a visit from their children, and one-third did not receive phone calls (Mumola 2000). Under the Adoption and Safe Families Act of 1977, women in prison face the loss of parental rights when their children are placed in foster care during their incarceration. Children of women in prison also tend to inherit lives of cumulative disadvantage (Johnston 1995; Allard and Greene 2011; Nickell, Garland, and Kane 2009; Kempfner 1995; Gabel and Johnston 1995). Hagan and Foster (2012) found that prisons have become the major stratifying institution in America by creating and maintaining inequality down the generations and across families and communities.

Victimization and Forms of Trauma

By every measure, justice-involved women have experienced childhood victimization at higher rates than male offenders and have higher rates of adult victimization than the general population (Bloom, Owen, and Covington 2003; Cook et al. 2005; Covington 2012; Pollock 2014; Belknap 2015; Pollock 1998; Greenfield and Snell 1999; Chesney-Lind and Pasko 2004; McDaniels-Wilson and Belknap 2008; Marcus-Mendoza and Wright 2003; Mullings, Marquart, and Hartley 2004; Messina and Grella 2006; Harlow 1999). The National Center on Addiction and Substance Abuse (2010, 6) found that female offenders are seven times more likely to have experienced sexual abuse and four times more likely to have experienced physical abuse than males. Browne, Miller, and Maguin (1999), for instance, found in their sample of 150 New York female prisoners that 59 percent had been sexually abused and 70 percent had been physically abused as children; 49 percent had been raped as an adult; and 70 percent had experienced severe intimate partner abuse. Sexual victimization, in childhood or adulthood, has been correlated with future revictimization. Women and girls who are sexually assaulted are more likely than nonvictims to experience subsequent sexual victimization (Breitenbecher 2001; Messman-Moore and Long 1994, 2000; Tjaden and Thoennes 2006). Wolff and colleagues (Wolff et al. 2006, 2007), along with national BJS data (Beck et al. 2013) found that prior victimization is a significant predictor of victimization while in custody. Messman-Moore and Long (2000) tied past abuse to a greater vulnerability to sexual harassment and coercion from authority figures.

Other studies explore the cultural components of victimization in specific communities, such as Abril's (2008) study of Native American communities and Arnold's (1995) study of the nexus between victimization and criminality among black women. Sharp discusses victimization and adult criminality and its link to patriarchy and marginalization in her feminist strain theory:

> [N]egative emotions become traits rather than transient emotional states as she grows up, and she becomes more likely to normally respond to strain with anger, depression, or frustration. She then becomes caught up in a cycle of illegitimate responses to adverse events. The woman experiencing chronic strain may also find herself more often in association with others who are responding to strain in socially unacceptable ways. She may also experience gender discrimination and resultant monetary strain. This is particularly true among marginalized groups such as racial minorities and the lower classes (Agnew 2006). Eventually she may develop a belief system that supports criminal and deviant behavior, a sort of outlaw mentality, where crime is seen as not only justifiable but desirable (Agnew 2006). Furthermore her constrained social network, embedded in a society dominated by males, often places her in the position to experience more abuse. As her negative emotionality and low constraint lead her to self-select into abusive situations and relationships, this creates a downward spiral. (2014, 16–17)

Abuse and victimization reduce forms of human capital such as emotional well-being and physical health for women on the pathway to prison. Trauma reactions and other forms of "negative emotionality" (Sharp 2014) undermine women's ability to stay safe inside and out (Battle et al. 2003). Social capital is equally undermined by membership in families and communities eroded by economic oppression. Sexualization through victimization, as Wesely (2012) argues, essentializes women's sexuality as capital. While these experiences are often explained in terms of individualized trouble, we argue that the context of women's lives and their families and their communities must be understood in terms of cumulative structural disadvantage, mediated by intersectional issues of race, class, and sexuality. The cumulative nature of these events is explored by the Adverse Childhood Experience (ACE) Study.

Adverse Childhood Experiences

A research collaboration between the federal Centers for Disease Control and Prevention (CDCP) and the Kaiser Permanente Health Appraisal Clinic in San Diego, the Adverse Childhood Experiences Study is one of the largest investigations ever conducted to assess associations between childhood maltreatment and later-life health and well-being. The ACE Study (CDCP 2006, 2008) documents how certain experiences are major risk factors for the leading causes of illness and death and other aspects of poor quality of life in the United States. For women who have experienced both personal and structural disadvantage, these negative outcomes are magnified.

Messina and colleagues (2007) apply this analysis to justice-involved women, demonstrating how such adverse experiences affect adult lives in destructive ways. Women offenders experienced more adverse childhood events than men offenders and more often reported continued sexual abuse in adolescence and adulthood. In another study, Messina and Grella (2006) found significant effects of cumulative childhood traumatic experiences on the adult mental health of five hundred women parolees. Among this group, greater exposure to multiple childhood traumatic experiences was associated with histories of substance abuse, homelessness, adolescent conduct disorder, arrest at a younger age, and longer criminal histories. Women with five or more childhood traumatic experiences engaged in criminal behavior earlier, and reported an average of 22.9 prior arrests, compared to 12.8 prior arrests reported by those with no reported trauma (Messina and Grella 2006). These experiences contribute to a range of troubles that pave women's pathways to prison (Comack 2006).

Substance Abuse

Substance abuse is both directly and indirectly related to offending behaviors (Lynch et al. 2012; Langan and Pelissier 2001). Drug crimes, and crimes to obtain money to buy drugs, send many women to prison. Drug use, typically a way to soothe or numb trauma and other pain, and "la vida loca" of those women seeking excitement are significant signposts in women's pathways (Owen 1998). Among prison populations, women offenders are more likely than men to be drug abusers, to use drugs more often, and to use more heavily. Early initiation into drug use, often by family members; drug and alcohol employed in exploitative sexualization; and the use of illicit drugs to self-medicate mental health problems, are additional gendered aspects of substance abuse. Women are more likely than men to state drug use as a motivation for crime, and to be under the influence of drugs or alcohol at the time of the offense (Snell and Morton 1994; Pollock 2014; Belknap 2015; Bloom, Owen, and Covington 2003). Messina and colleagues establish that when childhood abuse and trauma are considered, women with such histories become involved with drugs and crime significantly earlier than boys with similar histories and girls without such histories (Messina and Grella, 2006; Messina et al., 2007).

Mental and Physical Health Problems

A "perfect storm" of "physical and mental health problems, trauma, poverty, plus numerous marginalization issues" collide in the lives of incarcerated women and girls (Belknap 2015, 242). Some of these medical concerns are related to lack of health care in free world communities; others are tied to risky behaviors, such as drug use, sex work, and poor health practices. Long-term complications from interpersonal violence also undermine women's physical and psychological well-being. Women in prison suffer from high rates of infectious diseases, including HIV, tuberculosis, sexually transmitted diseases, and hepatitis. Reproductive medical care, including prenatal and postpartum care, is substandard in most women's prisons (Belknap 2015; Pollock 2014; Bloom, Owen, and Covington 2003). Dental care, a need exacerbated by drug use and past physical harm, is equally inadequate (Belknap 2015).

Female prisoners are more likely than males to suffer from mental health disorders (Bloom and Covington 2008; Teplin, Abrahams, and McClelland 1996). Estimates suggest that between 25 and 60 percent of the female prison population require mental health services (Pollock 2014). Women who have experienced abuse are about twice as likely as those who did not to exhibit signs of mental illness (Jordan et al. 1996). Studies of women in jail report similar findings (Veysey 1998). For instance, Green et al. (2005) found that 98 percent of women in the jail sample had experienced trauma, 36 percent reported some current mental disorder, and 74 percent had some type of drug or alcohol problem. Lynch and colleagues (2012) assessed the prevalence of serious mental illness (SMI), post-traumatic stress disorder (PTSD), and substance use disorders (SUD) among women in jail. The Lynch study used a structured diagnostic interview to assess current and lifetime prevalence of SMI (e.g., major depression, bipolar disorder, and psychotic spectrum disorders), PTSD, and SUD. In this large jail sample, 43 percent of women met criteria for a lifetime SMI, and 32 percent met SMI criteria in the past twelve months. Over 80 percent of the sample met lifetime criteria for drug or alcohol abuse or dependence. Over half of the women assessed had lifetime PTSD. Women with SMI reported greater rates of victimization and more extensive offending histories than women who did not meet the criteria for lifetime SMI. Lynch et al. (2012) found that while experiences of childhood victimization and adult trauma did not directly predict offending histories, both forms of victimization increased the risk of poor mental health. Poor mental health predicted a greater offending history. Mental illness, they found, mediates the gendered trajectory into the justice system (Lynch et al. 2012).

Poverty, Education, and Employment

Most women in prison and jails are poor. In analyzing the role of poverty and opportunity prior to imprisonment, Rabuy and Kopf (2015) find incarcerated people had a median annual income of $19,185 prior to incarceration, significantly less than the median of nonincarcerated people of similar ages. This remains true when age, gender, and race/ethnicity are controlled. The pre-prison incomes of incarcerated women are concentrated at the lowest ends of the national income distribution: nonincarcerated people had an average income of $23,745; imprisoned women had an average income of $13,890.

Prior to incarceration, women offenders were underemployed or unemployed, working fewer hours and making less per hour than their male counterparts (Blitz 2006; Flower 2010). Women are often employed in nonpermanent, low-level or entry-level occupations with little chance for advancement (Flower 2010, 8). While women involved in the criminal justice system are more likely than men to have a high school diploma, they are less likely to report any earnings prior to imprisonment. Confirming our emphasis on gendered inequality, Flower (2010) finds that the lack of human and social capital compromises women's ability to earn more income in their economically disadvantaged communities. Work opportunities for women, she argues, are compromised by caregiving responsibilities for children and undermined by the demanding requirements by agencies of social control, such as welfare systems and community correctional agencies.

Shared Experience

As we have demonstrated, women in prison share many characteristics and experiences on their pathways to prison. They are poor, disproportionately members of communities of color, and likely to be mothers of young children. Living in communities of concentrated disadvantage, their well-being is undermined by unemployment, crime, and private and public violence. Women are also more likely to have a family member or friend in prison. They have experienced violence and other forms of victimization as both girls and adults. Mental and physical health problems, relationship dysfunction, and repeated victimization can be understood as consequences of these shared characteristics. We argue that gender disadvantage reduces women's abilities to obtain all forms of capital that would protect them from gendered violence and oppressive relationships in the free world. With little access to the protections of capital, women are vulnerable to harm throughout their lives. This structural disadvantage and subsequent vulnerabilities shapes their lives in prison as well.

THE PATHWAYS APPROACH: STRUCTURAL INEQUALITY AND WOMEN'S OFFENDING

The addition of an intersectional analysis to the pathways approach improves the analysis of women's experience through a focus on diversity among women and their social positions. These pathways are not only gendered; they are also shaped by multiple discounted identities embedded in race, class, and other forms of discrimination (Potter 2015). Attention to the contribution of differences in racial, cultural, sexual orientation, and other intersectional identities is necessary to further the utility of the pathways approach. As the foundation for pathways theories, gender inequality must be understood in terms of historical, social, and structural inequality. Understanding the many pathways women travel to prison brings us one step closer to understanding how they seek safety and manage conflict and violence while in prison. According to Salisbury and Van Voorhis (2009, 543), "The pathways perspective recognizes that various biological, psychological, and social realities are unique to the female experience and synthesizes these key factors into important theoretical trajectories that describe female offender populations." Below we summarize selected research on pathways in terms of their connection to cumulative and concentrated disadvantage. Belknap (2015), Pollock (2014), and Sharp (2014) give a fuller description of the development of this theoretical framework.

In one of the first descriptions of these pathways, Daly (1992, 1994) distinguished critical life events that propel women into crime. Her work established a foundation for a pathways approach to female criminality and subsequent imprisonment. Violent victimization is a key element of the pathways explanation, but we argue, like Kruttschnitt and Carbone-Lopez (2006), that victimization cannot overdetermine women's life chances. Agency also shapes these pathways, but choices are constrained by concentrated disadvantage and further undermined by gendered inequalities. *In the Mix* (Owen 1998) places the experiences of imprisoned women in the context of their spiraling marginality to conventional institutions. These experiences include a multiplicity of abuse, adverse events in early family life, disrupted relationships with children and others, "la vida loca," and street life. As Matza has suggested, "All of us have free will, but some of us are freer than others."[2]

Listening to women is a hallmark of feminist research. The case for the pathways approach was first developed through in-depth interviews and other qualitative approaches (Pollock 2014; Belknap 2015). The idea of gendered pathways to prison has been tested through quantitative techniques, specifying statistical relationships among women's experience and offending in larger and more varied samples than possible in qualitative work. Brennan and colleagues (2012) employed factor analysis to describe their offender typology, based on childhood and early family experiences, adolescent delinquency, mental health problems tied to abuse and neglect, degree of criminality and aggression, and social marginalization.[3] Undertaking further statistical analyses to isolate and identify statistical types, Brennan et al. (2012) tested gendered pathway variables, such as measures of intimate relationship conflict or problems, safe housing, family factors, indicators of anxiety and depression, and employment and educational history.

Using path analysis, Salisbury and Van Voorhis (2009) found three pathways to crime in their study of women on probation:[4]

1. A childhood victimization path that included mental illness and substance abuse;

---

2. David Matza, graduate seminar, 1983, Department of Sociology, UC Berkeley.

3. Factor analysis typically is used to reduce data from a larger, mostly correlated set of variables into a smaller set of variables in an attempt to identify both manifest and latent variables that help explain (predict) outcomes. Factor analysis can be exploratory or confirmatory.

4. Path analysis is a statistical technique that extends the logic of multiple regressions in measuring and estimating correlations among sets of variables. In this example, path analysis estimates the relative strengths of such variables as abuse, mental health, income, and other pathway concepts in predicting reoffending.

2. A relational pathway that included dysfunctional relationships, domestic violence, adult victimization, low self-esteem, current mental illness, and substance abuse;

3. A social and human capital deficit pathway that included very low educational levels and unemployment, along with deficits in social/family support.

Our analysis draws on the wider scholarship on pathways (Pollock 2014; Belknap 2015), with a focus on the three-category conceptualization of pathways offered by Salisbury and Van Voorhis (2009). Each of these pathways is grounded in gender inequality and disadvantage and argue that interpersonal experiences are mediated by structural inequities in both women's pathways to prison and in their lives inside prison. In this view, women's lives in prison are expressions of class, race, and gender inequalities *within* the prison in much the same way their lives were structured *outside* the prison.

Victimization, too, must be explained as another consequence of gendered inequality. As Sered and Norton-Hawk (2014, 24) write, "Sexual assault is not simply a deviant act by a deviant man against an exceptionally unfortunate woman. Rather, it is part of a social cycle in which systemic gender inequality produces gendered violence that then reinforces gender inequality." Richie (2012) provides a significant analysis of the structural and institutional factors that contribute to domestic violence against black women. She argues that violence against women of color has been ignored in the mainstream domestic violence movement because there "was no counter-narrative of how the combination of childhood sexual abuse, adolescent intimate-partner violence, racial stigmatizing, and social marginalization could turn lethal," resulting in young women's desperate feelings of hopelessness. She concludes that the "institutions that should have protected young women are not held accountable for their failure to intervene" (6). Harm against black women, she finds, is best understood by examining the experience of women who are similarly situated "in dangerous households, in disadvantaged communities, in neighborhoods in transition, and on contested streets" (12). She continues:

> The abuse they experienced takes many forms and happens in many contexts. It is likely to be physical, sexual, and emotional; it will happen across their lifespan; it will originate from different sources. The more stigmatized their social position, the easier it is to victimize them. The further a woman's sexuality, age, class, criminal background, and race are from hegemonic norms, the more likely it is that they will be harmed—and the more likely

that their harm will not be taken seriously by their community, by anti-violence programs, or by the general public. (12)

The experiences of girls and women are distinctively different from those of boys and men in similar class positions. Sered and Norton-Hawk (2014, 67) state that communities with high rates of unemployment, insecure housing, and formerly incarcerated residents tend to suffer high rates of street violence, thus increasing the chances that girls and women will be sexually assaulted. The lack of an effective community response to the troubles of girls and women, and the ineffective response by the police and other social service agencies in communities of color, is arrested justice, in Richie's (2012) terms. Winfree and De Jong (2015, 65) offer "evidence of a war on women" in their examination of criminal justice responses to offenses committed by women and police handling of crimes involving female victims, especially for crimes of rape and sexual assault. Chesney-Lind (2002) and Chesney-Lind and Merlo (2015) also argue that victimization is criminalized in the lives of girls and women on the margins of conventional society.

In making the case that gendered and other intersectional inequalities are the root of women's pathways to prison, we argue that these inequities and disadvantages can be framed in terms of capital: the human, social, and cultural capital that shape women's life chances and lifetime vulnerabilities. Women situated in these disadvantaged circumstances have limited opportunity to accrue any kind of capital, making criminal offending a reasonable survival option among constrained choices. Criminal offending entails a potential gain in some kind of capital. Property and drug sales result in material gain, with drug offenses having the added benefit of supplying desired commodities for users. Violence can be deployed for material gain, retribution for past harms, and enhancing one's reputation.

While we are committed to the concept of agency, we again want to point out that choice occurs in a structural context, sometimes a profoundly constraining one. Much like the idea of "funneling options" suggested by Rosenbaum (1981), multiple marginality propels women outside the protections of conventional life and makes crime and prison possible. Thus, in our understanding of pathways, women come to prison with multiple pathway experiences, each situated in the context of gender inequality and other forms of discrimination. Even women who enjoy some of the protections of class and race privilege find them voided by gender inequality.

Cumulative Disadvantage as Context for Women's Pathways

While individual traumatic experiences are a critical variable in understanding women's pathways to prison, they must be contextualized within the larger structure of lives constrained by systemic inequality and disadvantage. Such clusters of cumulative disadvantage can also be seen as clusters of strain (Agnew 2006; Sharp 2014; Slocum, Simpson, and Smith 2005). Building on the social and human capital deficit model, Owen's (1998) view of multiple marginality from conventional institutions, and intersectional criminology (Chesney-Lind and Morash 2013; Joseph 2006; Potter 2013, 2015), the concept of cumulative disadvantage draws our attention to the social and economic realities of women's lives. As Crenshaw states:

> The structural and political dimensions of gender violence and mass incarceration are linked in multiple ways. The myriad causes and consequences of mass incarceration . . . call for increased attention to the interface between the dynamics that constitute race, gender, and class power, as well as to the way these dynamics converge and rearticulate themselves within institutional settings to manufacture social punishment and human suffering. (2012, 1426)

Concentrated disadvantage leads to lives constrained by the cumulative effects of poverty, gender, and racial discrimination; limited educational and vocational opportunity; restricted access to health care of all types; and community and interpersonal violence. A deeper and more nuanced understanding of these intersections of inequality shifts the focus from an individual-level analysis of behaviors and responses to a more structural understanding of the physical and cultural spaces that reflect and reproduce cumulative disadvantage.

Historical Trauma

In analyzing the cumulative disadvantage women experience "out in the storm" (Caputo 2008), we have expanded our framework to include historical and collective trauma (Walters 2010; Morgan and Freeman 2009). Historical trauma can be experienced by "anyone living in families at one time marked by severe levels of trauma, poverty, dislocation, war, etc., and who are still suffering as a result" (GAINS Center 2001, 1). The GAINS Center suggests that historical trauma can manifest itself in multiple ways: historically unresolved grief, disenfranchised grief, and internalized oppression. Walters (2010) makes a compelling argument about the role of historical trauma and micro-aggressions experienced by those embedded in communities of disadvantage. Historical grief, also termed historical trauma, may be experienced by those whose current life experiences are shaped by unresolved grief over oppression and its ongoing consequences (Walters 2010). Those whose cultural history is ignored and dismissed by the dominant culture experience disenfranchised grief.

Gender and Race

A focus on cumulative disadvantage underscores the multiplying effect of gender and race in women's pathways to prison (Henriques 1995; Young and Reviere 2009). Richie (1996, 2001, 2006, 2012) stresses the critical variable of race in her theory of gender entrapment as she analyzes culturally constructed gender identities and women's participation in crime.

Quoting work by Lipsitz, Sered and Norton-Hawk (2014, 66) point out that "black women and Latinas endure injustice of their own, but they also suffer from neighborhood race effects and the collateral consequences of mass incarceration of black and Latino men." Lipsitz elaborates on the role of housing discrimination in compounding women's troubles:

> The injuries that black women and Latinas suffer at the crossroads of housing discrimination and mass criminality are intersectional: Their race, gender, and class positions all work together to create a cumulative vulnerability to the negative impacts of housing discrimination and mass criminalization that is related to, but also different from, the injuries endured by black men and Latinos. Women of color are especially vulnerable to class injuries because of their relationships to the housing market and the criminal justice system. For example, employment discrimination, the gendered segmentation of the labor market, and the grossly disproportionate gendered impacts that marriage, child rearing and even divorce have on women's work and wealth, leave women consistently earning less and owning less than men. (2012, 1557)

He continues:

> The incarceration of women of color today is partially caused and powerfully complicated by the housing discrimination that concentrates the dwellings of black women and Latinas in impoverished neighborhoods that lack employment opportunities. Criminal records and histories of incarceration produce additional forms of economic and social exclusion for already-marginalized women of color. Black women and Latinas not only compose a

disproportionate percentage of the total number of incarcerated women, but their criminalization and demonization as people with nonnormative gender roles contribute crucially to the concerted political attack on communities of color more broadly. The putatively nonnormative and allegedly criminal behavior of women of color helps fuel moral panics about crime, sexuality, and sloth that divert attention away from the cumulative vulnerabilities that women of color face as a result of systematic racial and gender discrimination in housing, employment, and education. (2012, 1753)

In their study of health care for poor women in the community, Sered and Norton-Hawk (2014) identify many of the components of cumulative disadvantage that limit women's ability to participate in conventional institutions. Their work informed much of our analyses. They, too, see differences in the pathways between the black and white women in their sample. The white women in their study seemed to fit the childhood victimization pathway suggested by Salisbury and Van Voorhis (2009), as "nearly all the white project participants narrated a path to pain, homelessness, and criminalization that revolved around childhood sexual abuse followed by PTSD and drug use" (Sered and Norton-Hawk 2014, 59).

In contrast, most of the black women in their study reported being raised in "respectable" working poor families. Abuse and resulting trauma is not a plot point in their stories. Unlike white women, it was "the outside world more than the domestic one that set them on the path to suffering" (Sered and Norton-Hawk 2014, 60). As they suggest, "For black women far more than white women, subpar schools, racially discriminatory hiring practices, and segregated and impoverished neighborhoods present insurmountable challenges to building the kinds of lives they want" (61).

The public health field term *weathering* describes the erosion of health and well-being by destructive social and structural arrangements. Geronimus (2001, 133) uses this idea to describe health inequality among African American women, stating, "Weathering suggests that African American women experience early health deterioration as a consequence of the cumulative impact of repeated experience with social, economic, or political exclusion." Historical and collective trauma within disadvantaged communities further exacerbates the effects of weathering and contributes to the context of gendered inequality.

Community

Social and human capital converge in communities, creating or denying opportunity (Clear 2007). Petersilia and Rosenfeld (2007, 68) refer to "community capacity" as the ability of a given neighborhood to provide pro-social support to offenders trying to reintegrate into a community after incarceration. Without access to conventional institutions and their positive impact on improved life chances, women have narrowing options. In neighborhoods suffering from disinvestment, work is frequently reduced to employment in drug markets, crime, and both expressive and instrumental violence that often leads to subsequent imprisonment.

Living in disadvantaged communities may also produce toxic stress for children, undermining their ability to develop into healthy adults. Situations that can produce toxic stress are extreme poverty; physical, sexual, or emotional abuse; chronic neglect; severe maternal depression; substance abuse; and family violence. Without the support of a caring network of adults, toxic stress can disrupt brain architecture and lead to stress management systems that respond at relatively lower thresholds, thereby increasing the risk of stress-related physical and mental illness (Middlebrooks and Audage 2008; National Scientific Council on the Developing Child 2005). The effects of living in such a community, we submit, produce a context of continual toxic stress, which in turn plays a key role in women's pathways to crime and prison. For the children of women in prison, multiple forms of this toxic stress are tied to parental incarceration (Allard and Greene 2011).

In line with our perspective, Sered and Norton-Hawk (2014) also see the life trajectories of women in poor communities as conditioned by the two powerful forces of gender oppression and economic inequality. They assert that institutions that manage the poor, the sick of body and spirit, and the criminal reinforce a cultural ethos in which "pain and misery are considered products of idiosyncratic experience, personal flaws, and poor choices. Prisons, welfare offices, and clinics, albeit in different styles, promote the canon that individuals can choose their health, jobs, luck, and relationships, that we are responsible for our own misfortune" (2014, 11). They note that many women have adopted the message of personal blame and fault from what they call the "institutional circuit" of welfare offices, homeless shelters, child protective services, and correctional systems. Women have come to believe

that their suffering is the result of the choices that they personally made: the wrong men, wrong education, wrong drugs, wrong beliefs and wrong relationships. Drilled in that message, the Boston women [in their study sample] typically describe themselves as "needy": chronically ill, physically, emotionally and genetically flawed; and as victims of specific men or particular, nasty caseworkers or parole officers—not as victims of gendered, racial and inequalities that do not serve them well. (2014, 11)

We agree with Sered and Norton-Hawk's claim that "the same social inequalities that poor and abused Americans encounter in their homes, their communities, and streets are replicated in the institutional circuit when formal and informal policies reinforce racial, gender and class polarization and conflict" (2014, 14). They ask a fundamental question about the marginalized and disadvantaged citizens that come to prison: Have prisons become the way America deals with suffering? We explore this question in more depth in the last chapter.

Baskin and Sommers (1998) situate the behavior of women offenders in communities of causality. Their study, which is not without controversy, offers a social structural analysis that "roots the violent crime problem squarely within the everyday life experiences of growing up in underclass communities" (Baskin and Sommers 1998, 13). Communities distinguished by "intensified economic and social dislocation; growing drug markets; demographic changes; and situational factors related to family, school and peer relations contributed to their participation in violent street crime" (13). Focusing on the drug market violence that characterized the mid-1990s, they examine how the "social and economic norms associated with these markets combined with other elements to institutionalize violence as a way of negotiating survival on this terrain" (13). These notions of negotiating survival and women-initiated violence are echoed in our work.

CONCLUSION

Before prison, most women lived unsafe lives, with their well-being undermined by the cumulative disadvantages of oppression and inequality and the lack of any form of protective capital. For many, threats to physical, sexual, emotional, and psychological safety might be found in their homes, in their neighborhoods, and, often, in their relationships. Women also experienced violence when engaged in risky behaviors, such as sex work, drug use, and street crime. Gendered violence, we assert, is a function of intersectional inequalities. Poverty, lack of housing options, and few protections against male violence among marginalized women are often connected to limited options in education, employment, housing, and well-being. Struggles to make a living, care for children, and attain safe housing and health care can overwhelm the material coping abilities of those of any gender. Victimization as girls and women, reduced participation in labor markets, and criminal behaviors entwined with substance abuse and mental illness occur in the context of gendered inequality, aggravated by cumulative disadvantage.

Our emphasis on gender status in the shared characteristics and pathways experiences of most women prisoners leads us to see intersectional inequality and oppression as significant contributors to women's criminal behavior. Women come to prison with a set of experiences and perspectives that shape their relationships with other prisoners, relationships and interactions with staff, and reaction to prison culture, conditions, rules, and procedures. In the chapters that follow, we show how these pathways continue to shape women's lives inside the prison community, structuring women's search for safety.

3

Prison Community, Prison Conditions, and Gendered Harm

We build on Clemmer's (1958) general construction of the prison community to examine the physical, cultural, and social dimensions that condition risk or safety. Prisons are also, as Goffman (1961) states, a perfect representation of the total institution: a place where people live under the formal administration of state authority, with set schedules, mass movement, and lack of individual choice or autonomy. For Goffman, the custodial regime is regulated and regimented, encompassing the whole being of prisoners, while undercutting individuality and disregarding dignity. Women sleep, work, socialize, go to school, and seek safety as they live with "like situated individuals cut off from the wider society" and lead an enclosed, formally administered round of life (Goffman 1961, 11). The nature of this cultural and physical space radically determines women's search for safety. And this makes sense: Everything happens somewhere.

Prisons for women are very different from those holding men. Often cast as "hyper-masculine" (Sabo, Kupers, and London 2001), the men's prison (and the male prison staff) is the dominant image of prisons and prisoners (Britton 2003).[1] Thinking about women in prison (and women

1. During a training on gender-responsive principles in a women's prison several years ago, a correctional officer asked, "Are they women, or are they inmates? They can't be both." Such a comment illustrates the dominance of the male definition of prisoners, even among those who work with imprisoned women.

workers in prison) leads us to different questions and, following Britton, establishes prisons as gendered organizations with embedded gender inequalities.

In this chapter, we examine the carceral space where women negotiate the prison social order. We summarize the history and architecture of women's prisons in the United States, emphasizing the role of gender and inequality in their development. We then describe features of the physical plant and the prison environment that threaten women's safety, among them crowding, unsanitary conditions, and unconstitutional health care. Elements of operational practice can also undermine women's sense of safety, further aggravating inequality within the prison community. The chapter concludes with a brief discussion of litigation over conditions of confinement, focusing on the failure of correctional systems to provide adequate medical and mental health care to women who deserve better.

PRISON PHILOSOPHY AND PRISON ARCHITECTURE

Prison architecture embodies specific principles and values regarding punishment and those confined and punished. Attitudes toward women in the free world shape attitudes toward women behind bars, which, in turn, are reflected in prison philosophy and prison buildings (Pollock 2014, 192–200). The evolution of these principles of punishment and philosophies is revealed by examining the history of gendered carceral space.

We begin with a discussion of the English prison system as it developed in the late 1700s. English law was "very clear that women and men were different and possessed different rights under the law" (Pollock 2014, 192). Fathers and husbands legally controlled every aspect of women's lives and could rely on the legal system to punish their daughters and wives when judged to be disobedient or unchaste. This system also functioned to control poor women by committing them to poorhouses when debts, family poverty, or the lack of a male provider rendered them penniless, with little human or social capital to survive on their own. Gender and overlapping forms of inequality then, as now, constrained women's ability to resist confinement.

Women's lives in the early forms of imprisonment, known as poorhouses or bridewells, also reflected their gendered roles in the free world. Women were "expected to do the cooking, cleaning, spinning and sewing required for the institution" (Pollock 2014, 193). Freedman (1981), Feinman (1976, 1983), and Pollock (2014, 193) describe the impact of the "cult of true womanhood," in which women were expected to be "pure, submissive, and pious." Women who violated this idealized version of submissive femininity were seen as more deviant than criminal men, since they were viewed as violating the natural order of society.[2] As Freedman suggests, women involved in criminal activities were seen to "threaten social order doubly, both by sinning and removing the moral constraints on men" (cited in Pollock 2014, 193). From their very inception, prisons have reflected the patriarchal dynamics of the larger society (Chesney-Lind 1991).

Traditional definitions of womanhood and femininity entail control of female sexuality and bodies (Smith 2005, 2006; Bagley and Merlo 1995). The inherent class, race, and cultural biases embodied in this idealization of womanhood were reinforced by the prison. Under this guise of "true womanhood," sexual behavior and sexual liaisons were punishable by the power of the State. Controlling women's sexual behavior, and punishing those deemed not worth saving, was an implicit function of early women's reformatories and prisons. As the pathways research directs our attention to women's experiences with sexual exploitation, inappropriate sexualization, sex work, and sexual abuse and assaults, these lessons from women's prison history provide another gendered frame for analyzing the contemporary women's prison.

In one of many paradoxes, women were often sent to these prisons because they were convicted of prostitution. To survive inside, women continued to use sexual capital to endure imprisonment, having forced and willing sex with staff and, in some places, with male prisoners. Women prisoners in the bridewell system in England leveraged this sexual capital to better their conditions while confined through trading sex for goods and other favors (Pollock 2014). As we describe in subsequent chapters, sexual capital remains in play in the contemporary prison. Another example of sexual exchange and exploitation is found in the English use of transportation to Australia (Hughes 1987). Under the transportation system, women were convicted in England for sex-related survival crimes, sentenced to prison, and then transported via prison ships to the Australian colonies. When women arrived on this fatal shore (Hughes 1987), they were once again exploited, both by the male prisoners and by the male prison staff. Sexual exploitation has

---

2. Of course, as in any society, these norms and values were most often celebrated among the upper classes. Most poor women, then as now, supported their families without the protection of these lofty ideals of patriarchy.

been a consistent refrain in the lives of women, both inside and outside prison walls.

From the late 1800s to the early 1920s, gendered punishment philosophies evolved in the Reformatory Era, as "the perception of female criminals changed from being seen as evil and irredeemable to a view that they were misguided and led astray by men" (Pollock 2014, 194). In 1825, the prison reformer Elizabeth Fry published the book *Observations of the Siting, Superintendence, and Government of Female Prisoners*, joining other moral entrepreneurs in advocating for separate facilities for "wayward women." Zebulon Brockway, an early proponent of the Reformatory model, called for reformatories for women that would re-create "family life," wherein women could be instructed in "intellectual, moral, domestic and industrial training," under the presumably benevolent and watchful eye of "refined and virtuous women" (Rafter, quoted in Pollock 2014, 195).

Although reformatories offered, for the time, an innovative approach to imprisoning women, those who were sentenced to them were from the "respectable" classes and families, and therefore deemed more worthy of being "saved." Women who were younger, native born, white, early in their criminal career, and overall "less hardened" were sent to reformatories. Women outside the protection of class and white privilege (Pollock 2014, 197), however, were sentenced to the more restrictive custodial prison. The custodial prisons, often attached to men's prisons, held women judged to be less redeemable and more criminal, and these women were usually nonwhite or non-native born. These intersectional differences among women replicated the disadvantage of race and class. The Reformatory movement, for women and men, was phased out in the late 1930s, when industrial and custodial models became the norm.

Excluding the American South and some of the West, these industrial and custodial models coalesced in the Big House prison, characterized by a castlelike facade, many-storied tiers, and a large main yard. As the dominant model for punishment, the Big House embedded a philosophy of punitive control in the physical plant and operational practices (Irwin 2005). In some states, women were confined in sections of men's prisons. In other states, philosophies about imprisoning women evolved into a "cottage" or college campus–style model, replicating the domestic virtues of a subordinate gender. In recent decades, new women's prisons (with some exceptions) have adopted the male-influenced warehouse model.

PRISON CONDITIONS AND HARM

Recall that we began our focus group interviews with women with four basic questions:

What do you know about violence or danger in this facility?

How do women currently protect themselves from violence in this facility?

What are some things that can be done here to protect women from danger and violence?

What else should we know about violence and danger here?

We purposely left the questions open-ended to elicit a broad view of women's perceptions of violence and conflict, anticipating descriptions of interpersonal harm from other prisoners or from staff.[3] At the beginning of our fieldwork, we were surprised when women answered the first question with long descriptions of the dangers posed to them by the prison's physical environment, the lack of medical care, fears about communicable diseases, and the inability to keep living areas clean. Across the country, women told us that they felt the physical plant and operational practices created significant risks to their safety.[4]

During our fieldwork, we visited prisons and jails of all types to collect the data reported here. Some were built in the Reformatory Era; others looked like the warehouse prison, built in the utilitarian era of the 1980s and 1990s (Irwin 2005). Still others retained the cottage-style buildings of a previous time, overlaid with "gender-neutral" operational practices. Some imprisoned thousands of women, far more women than the space was built to hold. Others confined a few hundred women. Some smaller, local jails held fewer than twenty.

Women live in many types of settings in U.S. prisons: cells, rooms, open-bay dormitories, or barracks-like settings. In some facilities, women are housed in rooms rather than cells. Those deemed to need more restrictive custody will typically be confined to traditional cells with very little time spent outside them. This group includes women

---

3. We remind readers of the utility of inductive methods. In planning for the overlapping studies, we did not consider the role of conditions of confinement in women's search for safety, assuming that interpersonal relationships were the most significant concern. The open-ended questioning allowed us to hear the women's concerns.

4. We define operational practice generally as including rehabilitation programs and services, provision of mental and physical health services, classification, disciplinary procedures, policy, training, and staffing.

held in more secure housing, such as administrative segregation (Torres 2007), or those in "close custody" for disciplinary reasons or mental health care. Women under death sentences are always housed separately. According to the Death Penalty Information Center (2015), fifty-seven women are awaiting a death sentence, about 2 percent of the total death row population of just under three thousand persons.

McGuire (2011) argues that the American punishment philosophy of incapacitation and retribution results in spartan institutions that emphasize security and heighten the punitive nature of the prison experience. He writes:

> After all, an institution whose purpose is to warehouse society's "trash" and to punish its miscreants is *supposed* to be bleak, harsh and unpleasant. Scarcity of material resources, degradation of the person and an almost complete deprivation of privacy are inherent in its penological approach. (McGuire 2011, 154; original emphasis)

The physical plant of the contemporary prison is deteriorating. Women told us that vermin, mold, air temperature, water pressure, temperature in the showers, quality of food, and noise in the living units created threats to their well-being. Particularly egregious conditions were described by Brown (2015) in a series of articles investigating conditions in a Florida women's prison. As reported in audits and other official reports, conditions were particularly horrible in the housing units.

> In June 2014, the Department of Corrections received several reports that there were worms crawling out of the bathroom sinks and toilets in Lowell's annex in two dorms, P and Q. According to FDC's inspection report, black larvae were found in the sinks, and the drains were "filthy" and filled with bugs and other parasites. On June 16, the prison inspector took photographs of the bug-infested conditions and told prison authorities that the water should be tested in all the dorms. (Brown 2015)

A former prisoner described such serious problems with mice in the kitchen that women tied the bottom of their pants legs or tucked them in their boots to keep the mice from crawling up their legs. She said she fed the mice so they would stop jumping on her (Brown 2015).

Many prisons we visited were old, reflecting years of too many bodies confined in too small spaces. Public spaces—gyms, kitchens, medical offices, visiting rooms, libraries, and classrooms—showed decades of wear and tear. Since most of our survey administration took place when we were free from our teaching obligations, the research team also experienced another feature of the aging physical plant: heat. On numerous occasions, our team felt the impact of intense heat in old buildings and had a brief exposure to the challenging conditions that prisoners and staff routinely experience in going about their lives inside.[5]

CROWDING

As the imprisonment binge expanded (Irwin and Austin 2001), crowding became the "intractable status quo" (Haney 2006) in America's prisons. With few exceptions, the prisons and jails we visited over our ten years of study were crowded, holding far more women than intended. In a review of the causes and consequences of prison crowding in general, Haney (2006) documents how crowding worsens the quality of life and increases the destructive potential of imprisonment. Crowding leads to an "organizational instability," which, in turn, undermines the delivery of effective programs and treatment services and aggravates dangerous and depraved conditions of confinement, contributing to the widespread use of force and other damaging technologies of social control (Haney 2006, 270). Haney describes the psychological and cognitive toll of crowding:

> Crowded conditions heighten the level of cognitive strain that prisoners experience by introducing social complexity, turnover, and interpersonal instability into an already dangerous prison world in which interpersonal mistakes or errors in social judgments can be fatal. Of course, overcrowding also raises collective frustration levels inside prisons by generally decreasing the resources available to the prisoners confined in them. The amount of things prisoners can accomplish on a day-to-day basis is compromised by the sheer number of people in between them and their goals and destinations. (2006, 272)

Crowding, Haney confirms, strains the physical plant, creates material shortages, and slows other processes of everyday life. Delays in processing mail and visitors, long lines in dining halls and at the canteen, waiting lists for program participation, and limited access to medical and other services contribute to feelings of unease and danger, as Cyndie illustrated: "Here, you have 80-something women to fight for commissary. You have to stand in line for six hours. Sometimes I've seen people

---

5. We experienced the lack of ventilation and the almost unbearable heat in many facilities. In one particularly degraded site, women begged us to help them make the case that such conditions were inhumane.

get into fights trying to get to the store. [The other women in the focus group laugh.] [We go] elbows to elbows to get shampoo."

Steiner and Wooldredge (2009) note that while few studies examine the effect of crowding on women's rule-breaking behavior, crowding may contribute to disorganization in prison. Crowding is an environmental stressor, further contributing to conflict and violence (Steiner and Wooldredge 2009; also see Wooldredge and Steiner 2016). McGuire asserts that the punitively overcrowded nature of modern warehouse prisons promotes violence among women prisoners:

> It is, therefore, not surprising that incarcerated women have developed norms that are particularly sensitive to encroachments on their material possessions, dignity, and privacy. Overcrowding in recent years has only exacerbated the situation by making resources, dignity and privacy even scarcer commodities. The continued mass incarceration of women promises to make the situation even more volatile in the future. (2011, 154)

Crowding has both subtle and obvious impacts on creating and sustaining risk in women's prisons. In one interview, Jessie talked about her experience with jail crowding: "There was overcrowding and lots of tension. A lot of people coming down fresh off the street mainly. Women were all together with different attitudes. There was not as much security as there is [here in her current prison]." Crowding also feeds staff shortages. In contrast to men in prison, some women are more likely to expect staff to help them with problems and respond to their concerns (Wooldredge and Steiner 2016; Kruttschnitt and Gartner 2005; Bloom, Owen, and Covington 2003). In our interviews, women expressed frustration when staff would not respond to their needs, describing many instances in which the lack of a response contributed to a dangerous or risky situation. This story from Carlie was one example.

> When I got there, there were four people in a room and then they activated the eight bunks and it was terrible. I don't think that race is an issue, but it is all about whom you live with. I think the officers play a big part as far as keeping drama started, or egging things on, or continuing the problem. If you have a problem and try to resolve it in the rooms, and then if you take it to the cops to let them know [you have a problem with a roommate], they don't do anything until someone gets hit with a lock.

As we elaborate in chapter 6, staff inattention to women's safety is a critical concern in women's prisons.

Crowding and Competition

Crowding creates competition for the limited capital available to prisoners. More women means more competition for the limited resources of the prison. In addition to waiting lists for programs and services of every kind, crowding pits women against each other as they struggle to meet ordinary needs. A long-timer, Furr, said, "You gotta try to get [inmate] Suzie-Q off your phone time or off your laundry or whatever [because there are too many women and not enough slots]." Later we explore the multiple approaches women develop to combat scarcity and economic inequality in the prison and how these iniquities threaten women's well-being. This competition over desired and limited resources is particularly aggravating for women serving long sentences.

> *Natalie:* We have been down, what, three decades? When I caught my case I was 21 and now I am 48 and it's the same things with these girls. We are trying to get the hell out of here, we are getting put in a . . . what is it called?
>
> *Tootie:* A pressure cooker.
>
> *Natalie:* Pressure cookers, yes.

A counseling staff member of a very large prison agreed that crowding contributes to increased conflict:

> [The women prisoners] are getting crowded and getting more violent because they are getting forced to be more and more in close quarters. They are forced to either let it [a fight] happen or be victimized. They are forced to let it go, or just deal with it right there. More crowding has caused more friction, and then more sparks, and then you have the boom-boom-boom.

Kandy described the difficulty of living with eight other women in a space designed for four: "You know, I have fifteen personalities of my own. Then I am in a room with seven other women and the crowding has to influence the violence here." In chapters 4 and 5, we examine how women learn these negotiated safety skills and develop protective reputations and relationships in this uncertain and dynamic terrain.

Prisons often run out of places to house prisoners. In several facilities, we observed the use of "ugly beds," typically known as the "boat" or "EZ bunks," plastic canoe-shaped "beds" placed on the floor when the number of bodies exceeds the number of beds. Gyms, program spaces, and other areas are often "bunked" with makeshift beds. In these facilities, women reported trying not to step on or bump into anyone as they move around. Problems with protecting property, privacy, and access to bathrooms and other troubles develop as a result. In a prison with many ugly beds, women serving long sentences described the complications of this crowding.

> *Jo:* It's just radical there, it's not good. They have officers, but there is so much crowding that you get away with more because the cops can't control all these women. They say they are so understaffed . . . there is absolutely no cops around.

> *Blair:* It is just not safe. You have all these women in the dayroom and you don't know what to expect when you step out of the door of the room and you might have a nut coming at you right out the gate.

Crowded sleeping conditions can be noisy, contributing to tension among roommates or "cellies." Snoring and other disruptive sleep issues can contribute to conflict in these living areas. Different work schedules mean different wake-up times, with women "tiptoeing around" their sleeping roommates at all hours of the morning. A woman who works night shifts may need to sleep when everyone else is getting ready for their programming day. The following narrative offered by Nena illustrates how such events are contested in such close quarters.

> I got in a fight with this one girl. I was really tired. I just came back from work and needed to shower. So I shower, then I was cleaning everything, and then I went to sleep. And she comes in, being noisy. I said, "Come on, you don't work. Let me just get some sleep." She was walking around with a sheet [shows how the sheet was wrapped around just above the woman's breasts]. Like I wanted to see you! [Laughter] I just stayed in my bed. And she was talking shit. I was thinking, "Just one more time [and something would happen]. Please just let me go to sleep. I was tired." Then I'm thinking, "You know what, I'm going to cut this bitch." [Here, Nena poses in the door like a model and mimics how the woman was standing in the door talking to other prisoners with her hands on her hips, which elicited laughter from the focus group]. I got in her face and hit her in the mouth. She bit me twice.

> So I got back on my bunk so she got me on the back. That was a mistake, turning my back to her. And so we start fighting again. The cops came down. She [the officer] said, "Handle your business." So I couldn't sleep all night. She was sleeping. I was awake. [Laughter] So I told her in the morning, "One of us got to go." I couldn't go to medical because I might get a case [new charge], but then I decided I got to see the doctor because of the bites. So I had to go to the major. She [the other woman] refused [to change] housing. Then she messed with all my property. Put water all over my things and shit like that. They tested for the bites. Gave me tetanus shots.

Crowding is often complicated by classification policies, which address the need to "classify" prisoners into specific facilities and within a given jail or prison. While modern prisons separate women from men and adults from juveniles,[6] women are almost always mixed together in one prison, regardless of how they have been classified. Van Voorhis (2005, 2009) has led the charge for a gender-responsive classification system by conducting extensive empirical investigations into the classification needs of women.[7] She also makes the point that while classification systems in prison might have a small effect on housing practices, overclassifying women restricts their ability to be placed in community programs or other programs requiring a low-custody designation.

Many states have only one facility for imprisoning women. Those with criminal records of varying severity, diverse offense backgrounds, lengths of sentences, and other variables that might require separation of imprisoned men are all housed together. In men's correctional facilities, separate spaces must be maintained to avoid violence and victimization: racial and ethnic strife is an organizing fact of prison life and is often the basis for housing assignments. Wooldredge and Steiner (2016) confirm race as a predictive factor for violence and victimization in men's prisons. Among women, on the other hand, racial issues exist as a subtext rather than an organizing principle (Owen 1998). Wooldredge and Steiner (2016, 231) did not find race a predictive factor for conflict and violence among women, which "could reflect differences in race relations among male inmates vs. female inmates. We observed far less self-segregation based on an inmate's race in the facilities for women in both states."

GOOD AND BAD NEIGHBORHOODS

In our interviews, women described the way in which the physical environment shaped their feelings of safety across different prison neighborhoods. Dani, a short-termer in a low-custody unit, said, "Every yard

---

6. Until roughly the early 1800s, men, women, and children were often confined together in large facilities under dangerous and unsanitary conditions in Western punishment systems. In our early work on staff perspectives, we heard a handful of terrifying, jail-based stories of women accidently left alone with male prisoners, usually in the course of some movement within the facility or during transit from one controlled location to another. In one large jail, we were told the story of a woman prisoner who was inadvertently left in an elevator that opened up to a floor of male prisoners. Here, a woman's gendered vulnerability exposed her to a risk that does not have an equivalent for male prisoners.

7. See Van Voorhis 2012 for a discussion of the significance of creating gendered classification and risk assessment instruments.

has its horror stories." She went on to say, "Violence can happen on any yard. I have been to the two worst yards, [and on the Honor Yard] you must be a bit more discreet because we think that is the good yard." Kazie, a long-termer, described some of the neighborhoods in her prison:

> There are differences in yards here. Blue Yard is the most calm. It has the most beautiful garden. There are beautiful roses and they have a little bit of shade. I was on another facility yard and there was bad grass and more dirt than grass. I thought to myself, "On this ugly yard, no wonder people are so violent."

As in any community, some neighborhoods in the prison were said to be safer than others. A good room, a good living unit, or a good yard is defined as one without conflict and violence and with a minimum of "drama." Tanesha, who lives in a "good" neighborhood, offers this insight:

> Years ago I was in another college program [in prison]. I did a study on how physical structure affects violence [and] asked women who went to [another large prison known to be more troubled] about their ideas about safety. Eighty percent of them had gotten into fights and these were women who did not bother anyone or get in trouble [when they were here] and they were getting in fights. [I concluded] the physical structure impacts fights. I have seen the gang bangers come here—gradually they calm down here. That kind of crap is not going to fly here—it is the psychology of the grass, sit in the open area, pet a dog and that calms you.[8]

Kiki, a woman with a high-custody classification and doing her second term in a cottage-like setting, explained how place has a real effect on her behavior:

> I think it [violence] just depends on who you are or who you run with. It could be just you running with just your friend or you could get in the mix and end up getting a lock or a cup to your head. It is a lot about who you are. For me I did thirteen months in [a treatment facility]. I was fighting every other day and here I just chose not to. I have learned about myself and my addiction to violence.

When asked to expand on this insight, Kiki responded:

> In [my former prison] there are no doors, no rooms. Just a hallway and six people rooms. You can run up on people whenever you want. The towers

---

8. In some prisons, women foster service dogs to be adopted by the free world community. In some settings, staff bring in their own dogs for grooming or "doggie day care." Women involved in these programs talked about the positive and calming effect of the dogs' presence.

and COs [correctional officers] cannot see everywhere. We all share one big bathroom and we used to go to the bathrooms and fight a lot. The COs are a lot different here. Here there is a lot more respect to the staff. Women are not as F-U—they are going to fight anyways and in the face of the staff.

The desirability of a prison or neighborhood may be based on the condition of the physical plant; the sense that the officers in that area are more professional and less threatening (or easier to "get around"); perceptions of other women's investment in violence; a reputation for ease or toughness on the yard; or actual location, such as proximity to work, recreation, or education spaces. Some prisons create "honor" or minimum dorms or cell blocks as an internal reward for conforming behavior; in these units some rules are relaxed, and staff are somewhat more supportive of informal programming or prisoner governance.

In one example of the contradictions of prison life, some women reject the honor blocks, choosing to live in more chaotic units where they can develop prison capital through hustles and the like; for others, avoiding interaction with staff is a motivation. Sally and Courina contrasted the types of yards in their prison.

> *Sally:* Yes, A2 and G4 were off the hook. It was baby Iraq, but in G4 because they have a lot of the [women who refuse to program] and the fuckups over there. Our yard is pretty good. We both live on P yard and it is pretty calm: the medical unit, workers, and those with outside work. The worst unit on our yard is G4—that is kinda ghetto out there.

> *Courina:* Basically, I feel the same as them; you know you are in a bull pen [bad neighborhood]. This is our survival. I have been down so many years that if someone touches me I am going to go off. There is always violence unless you are going to the convalescent home [the minimum security dorm] on K yard, you know.

Somewhat surprised that someone would not prefer to live in a calmer setting, we asked Courina about her preference to live in a rowdier neighborhood. She replied:

> I like living where I am. I know how to live around the violence. But there . . . I don't know how to react. Here I know if someone dropped dead, I am going to step over the body and then move on. Maybe there in the [minimum security dorm], they are going to try to patch them up and I wouldn't know how to do that.

In the next two chapters, we explore women's ability to normalize violence, avoid "getting in someone's business," and, sometimes, invoke violence as they seek safety.

In the NIC survey (Wells, Owen, and Parson 2013), we measured women's relative perceptions of safety across housing units. Through the Women's Correctional Safety Scales (WCSS) survey, we asked the over four thousand women who helped us by filling out the survey instrument to rank their feelings about physical and sexual violence in their current housing unit. We administered the survey to women living in housing units that were said, by staff, to be high-problem units ("bad" neighborhoods) and low-problem units ("good" neighborhoods). (Later in the fieldwork, we expanded the survey distribution to all units in some facilities, as we explain in appendix 1.)

Overall, most women indicated relatively low levels of perceived physical and sexual violence in their housing units. When asked, "How physically violent is this unit?," over one-third of the women indicated "1" on the 1 to 10 scale; that is, their unit was "not violent at all." For the entire sample, the average score was under 4, indicating a perception of lower violence in their units, with 71 percent of the women marking 5 or less. Just about one-fifth felt their unit was "more violent," and less than 10 percent marked 9 or 10. However, perceptions varied somewhat by type of facility and housing unit. Women housed in prisons reported slightly higher physical violence ratings than those housed in jails. Those housed in "high problem" units also reported higher physical violence ratings; about 40 percent of women living in "high problem" units rated the violence on their units at a level higher than 5 on a 1 to 10 scale. In "low problem" units, perceptions of violence were much lower. (See appendix 2, table 8, for a summary of these findings.) While these responses allow us to conclude that most women do not see their living units as violent, we want to note that it is the existence of *any* violence and its potential, rather than its magnitude, that can threaten safety.

Women reported lower perceptions of sexual violence in our WCSS survey. In every category, women ranked their units as less sexually violent than they indicated in the physical violence responses. Overall, the entire sample rated sexual violence very low, with almost 60 percent rating their perceptions of sexual violence at "1," the lowest indicator. A major difference was found in high-problem units, where 46 percent of the women indicated higher ratings of sexual violence. Less than 15 percent of the women in low-problem units felt sexual violence was a big problem. (See appendix 2, table 8, for a full discussion of these findings.)

Cleanliness

Again, we were surprised at the intensity of women's concerns about cleanliness and their frustrations over keeping their living, kitchen, work, and other areas clean. Cleanliness and tidiness in the increasingly crowded conditions of the contemporary prison were priorities for almost all the women who spoke with us. Women stressed the critical importance of keeping the cell or room neat, grounded in the value of personal cleanliness and hygiene. Women perceive those who do not maintain their living quarters as "disrespecting" their cellmates or dorm mates. As Kimee suggested, "You have a lot of fights because you have nasty roommates. They're on their cycle and they don't wipe the toilet seat." Chyna offered: "I think that disrespect could be a smell too. This chick was in our pod and she wouldn't shower and she smelled and then she was farting and it was stinking up the whole pod." Rosalinda added:

> If I live with a woman, and she is really stinky, I mean, really, really bad, you go to her nicely and you ask her to wash her ass. If she don't, you eventually want to roll her up in a mattress and all of us will put her in the shower. Then we get in trouble.

Many conflicts between women begin as a dispute over cleanliness. Medical conditions, such as HIV-positive status or other communicable diseases, are both common and feared. As Sammie expressed, "This girl got staph and there is blood. Get me out of here. That is an abscess that is airborne and bleeding all over the toilet and we don't have bleach, we don't have spray." Another way that cleanliness can contribute to danger is that staff will sometimes ask one prisoner to educate another on the importance of cleanliness, which places women in the unenviable situation of telling another woman what to do. Boa offered this example:

> We feel violent because there is an environmental cleanliness issue with different people, but then there is one more issue here. The staff will say, "Hey, you are a long-termer. Get her [new inmate] to clean." So now I have to choose to get her to clean or just put myself in a problem situation. This elevates the tension.

Room Politics

Typically, incarcerated women are assigned to a room or cell, with little choice in the matter.[9] Conditions in the cell, room, or dorm make a

---

9. "Bed moves," as we discuss in chapter 4, are one way prisoners can earn money in under-the-table hustles.

significant contribution to a woman's sense of safety and well-being. When women agree on the nature of their social and material relations; share standards of cleanliness, tidiness, and behavior; hold common values about visits from friends and sometimes lovers; and manage contraband and other illegal activities in similar ways, they are said to live in a "good" room. The informal rules about the room are embedded in cultural norms. Throughout the country, women described incidents related to crowding and "room politics" as potentially dangerous. Conflicts in the relative privacy of the room can escalate into more intense forms of violence.

Some women attempt to "control the room" by directing the activities, cleanliness, and occupants of their living quarters. Women who attempt to control the behavior of other women are sometimes called "shot callers," as Shawnie described:

> We do have violence here and all. I don't like violence in the room; with my room I am very territorial. But I am not the violent territorial type. There are types that won't let you come in the room all day long. They get the type of people that they can prey on. [The shot caller tells the women] they can't use the bathroom. They have to use the one in the dayroom. They would get socked if they turn the water on too loud; they get slapped in the head for sitting on the chair. They can't shower until a certain time. I don't like that.

Serious fights, particularly between intimates, are more likely to occur in these private and backstage areas. The location of an altercation can be determined by the seriousness of the fight. Women who only want to "make a point" may challenge another woman verbally or physically in more public spaces, assuming officers or other women will stop the fight before an injury occurs. Those who wish to do serious harm to others are more likely to attack in more private, backstage locations, like rooms and cells, or other spaces outside of public view. Ashanti, serving decades of time, offered this illustration:

> In the dining rooms, I see it as the most dangerous place in the institution because they know they have an audience and everyone is present. It's a show when they fight. Everyone is watching them fuss, there is a tray or a cup there to use to hit someone with and then they are pulled apart and that is resolved in the eyes of the institution. The rooms are where the real violence takes place. The rooms are private, there is no audience, people don't see what happened, and the staff are not there. In the rooms is where real predators victimize their prey. Then the prey are usually the smaller and shy women and they get picked on and they have this reputation or habit long before they came here and then they get involved with a predator.

Staff, too, recognize differences among prison neighborhoods. A non-custody worker said she sees "more fists flying" in the reception area where new prisoners are processed. "We don't even know who they are yet and they are getting sprayed with OC [tear] gas and still going at it." Another noncustody staff member added, "It's jumping off on all the yards now." Birdie, a "baby lifer," added:

> There is a lot of violence here and I have been here a year and half . . . I have been told that it is a good thing that as nice as you are, you are lucky to be on the yard you are on because you wouldn't survive on the other yards. [The difference is] the boundaries and people are different in other yards and it is alleged that the COs and counselors will put a white girl that is here for the first time with a lifer who is very territorial and she will become very violent with her. Then the COs will not come to the room even when they are screaming for help.

TeeTee talked about the role of staff in maintaining a good unit:

> The way that [staff] run the unit—they know what it takes to keep us in line. They give respect . . . I get along with my housing unit. Being part of a programming unit and part of structure, especially in the dayroom, because they know that I'm really structured. I get along with the staff on the yard. That is just me. Maybe some wonder, why is she getting something [extra from staff], but that is just me. I've never really had any problems. I've never had anyone say [accuse me of] kissing staff butt or saying something [telling on other women].

CONCERNS ABOUT HEALTH

Women in prison carry a disproportionate disease burden relative to male prisoners (Pollock 2014; Belknap 2015; Daye 2013). The profile of justice-involved women and girls indicates that physical and mental health problems of all kinds shape their pathways to prison (Brewer-Smyth 2004; CDCP 2008; Ross 2011; Faiver and Reiger 1998; Fogel 1991, 1995; Proctor 2009). Older women have particular health problems in prison (Krabill and Aday 2005; Leigey and Hodge 2012). The women in our studies were vocal and articulate as they traced the way inadequate medical care threatened their well-being, reinforcing feelings of vulnerability. Inadequate community health care, risky choices in sex and drug use, and the long-lasting damage of interpersonal violence or intimate partner violence (IPV) all contribute to serious medical needs among women prisoners (for reviews, see Pollock 2014; Belknap 2015; Bloom, Owen, and Covington 2003).

Seeking health care in prison is a problematic process. Sered and Norton-Hawk (2014, 13) suggest, "Medicalization and criminalization are two sides of the same coin, namely, the definition and management of suffering as manifestation of personal flaws." Any sickness and disability, whether physical or emotional, is another sign of a woman's failed responsibility to get well. The intersection of the identities "sick person" and "criminal" undermines women's abilities to be treated as deserving of care (Rizzo and Hayes 2011). Untreated medical conditions further reduce women's capital and their ability to fully function in this community. Through interviews with women about their health care needs, Rizzo and Hayes explore women's perceptions of care, finding these needs are often pathologized and dismissed. Women seeking care are regularly interpreted by prison staff as "seeking attention," "scamming for drugs," or otherwise "manipulating the system" rather than as human beings in need of care and compassion. One respondent told them, "I understand that we did something wrong and we're sentenced but they are giving us a double sentence when we get sick in here" (Rizzo and Hayes 2011, 3).

The Adverse Childhood Experiences Study, replicated by Messina and colleagues (2006) and referenced by Sharp (2014), confirm that adverse childhood events—which are experienced at a higher rate by imprisoned women than by the free world population—contribute to compromised health profiles throughout the life course. Given that African American women are both medically underserved (Geronimus 2001) and overincarcerated in the United States, racial inequalities in access to medical care in communities of color also contribute to high levels of need among imprisoned women.

We understand all forms of physical and mental health, and other forms of emotional and psychological well-being, in terms of human capital. In their search for safety, women attempt to find care for their medical and emotional conditions and seek out ways to improve their overall well-being. Women with challenging physical needs or those with mental and emotional health needs may be undercapitalized in their search for safety. We argue here that the common neglect of women prisoners' physical and mental health care contributes to the unnecessary suffering embedded in women's prisons.

Growing old in prison can jeopardize safety. Women are aging in prison, in part because of unnecessarily long sentences. Older women report they feel highly vulnerable to exploitation by younger prisoners. Their ability to protect themselves, we were told, can be compromised by the chronic diseases and limited mobility common to this imprisoned age group (see also Williams and Rikard 2004; Leigey and Hodge 2012). Older women were said to be especially vulnerable because of physical infirmities, as told here:

> Just yesterday morning, there was an elderly lady, she was walking down the yard and an inmate ran by her and socked her in the face, and her cane went flying. Why it was done? Who knows? So she went up to her and socked her and she socked her hard. She had the big gauze on her face from being hit. The youngsters have no respect for the little old ladies. The youngsters just knock them down.

The Harm of Prison Health Care

Crowding undermines the provision of health care in women's facilities and contributes to one of women's primary fears: catching a disease and dying in prison. Women expressed their fear of catching a communicable disease, while those with such diagnoses felt vulnerable or targeted because of the fear of the spread of disease in confinement. Women told us not knowing "who had what" created an undercurrent of fear. This comment from VJ, serving her time in the general population of a mid-sized, cottage-style prison, demonstrated the logic behind this fear:

> I don't know why they have the people with Hep C or HIV in here with us in the general population. That is a risk for us. She is not going to tell you she has HIV or Hep C [and we just don't know who has it]. There was an incident with one of my friends and she is housed with someone with HIV. She is fearful for her life because her and her bunkie get into it [fight] every day. Her bunkie started reading her personal mail and threatened to take her [parole] date and her life, so why don't they segregate and put them aside? Before they used to have them in [another separate unit], but why do they have them in general population?

While many prison systems have instituted health care information programs, including peer health education, with some success (Ross 2011), women have both realistic and fear-based attitudes toward disease. While many women told us they do not disclose their medical status to other prisoners, others were said to be "upfront" about their condition. In one jail focus group, Franny acknowledged her medical problem and how she manages it. She did not seem at all concerned she was discussing this in the public setting of our group.

> The jail here needs to do something with the training medical staff receive. I have boils under my arms. The nurse is not going to give me antibiotics till

[several days from now]. I read that it [staph] is really contagious. You [medical staff] are putting me at a very big risk and everybody around me. I don't want to feel guilty for giving it to someone. If I have pus on me, I don't touch people or things, and I go and wash my hands. I don't sit on the toilet. They [the jail] put up signs that tell us not to use the same towel, but I have had to use my towel for days.

In another focus group, Connie recalled a cellie who informed her roommates she was HIV-positive in a nonthreatening way: "She sat everyone down and told everyone in the room what she had. She was nice enough to do this. She was very nice not to leave anything on the sink or blood in the toilet." But Connie was concerned about not knowing about the medical status of other women:

I've been living in the dayroom for a year . . . and I just found out yesterday that someone lives two or three beds away from me and she has HIV. She was really sick and she was throwing up. It is shocking and scary. I don't think that they should be putting us with them so that we can protect ourselves.

Disease, pain, and discomfort contribute to the escalation into violence. As Silki noted:

People here have skin rashes, toothaches, and allergy problems. When you in a lot of pain, it makes people want to fight. It makes you have a spoiled temper. I almost got into an argument because I had pus sores on my legs. This girl in my cell kept telling me I was nasty. Eventually I will fight if you keep talking trash to me.

Facility Response to Health Care Needs

Claims that staff of any stripe "just don't care" about women's well-being were common throughout the country. Women voiced particular alarm that correctional and medical staff ignored their real medical needs. The inability to protect oneself from communicable diseases is aggravated by eroded confidence in the correctional medical staff, as suggested by Rosemary:

I think this is such a big deal because medical doesn't take care of your problems. And it is important about the hepatitis, and many women have never lived with other women, and this worries us because medical don't take care of us as best as they could.

This neglect is grounded in infrastructural and systemic inadequacies, such as long waiting lists, lack of gendered health care specialists, and few medical practitioners. At every site, women told stories of staff neglecting their requests for medical help. Sometimes they were told they had to wait until medical staff was on duty, and other times women said they were ignored without explanation. We listened to example after example of staff not responding to women's requests for medical attention, whether it was an emergency or a less immediate concern. We also heard multiple versions of the basic story described below, when women with complicated or emergency medical needs or in crisis were said to be ignored by custody staff. This story illustrates both correctional staff inaction and the lack of medical staff on duty at all times.

> [Back in] 1996, one of the girls was full-blown AIDS. Over the weekend the nurses are not here, but they said there is supposed to be a doctor or PA [physician's assistant] on call.[10] But this girl is so sick. We were doing all this for her. Bathing her and stuff. This was on a Friday, and they said she wouldn't see a doctor until Monday. She died on Sunday. When they finally took her to medical, they wouldn't tell us anything. We did what we could do, but if she had got some medical attention, she probably would have made it. She was just trying to get to the doctor or whatever. She's got full-blown AIDS and they refused her medical attention. Here we are bathing her and trying to feed her and take her to the bathroom. She was covered with sores and blisters. We didn't have no gloves or nothing from Friday to Sunday.

To be fair, women also told stories about staff who did help them with their medical needs, as Celestina remarked:

> I think that a lot of times they don't take into consideration that we are all going through something and if they are being insensitive, it could just set us off. I was sick the other night, throwing up. On the intercom, staff said, "Unless you are dying, don't push the button." I had to wait for the other shift and then the new woman officer told me, "Let's send you to medical and start the process." Then she told me that they [medical staff] are changing shift so we may have to wait but we will go through the procedure. She even came back to my pod later and woke me up to ask me if I still wanted to go to medical because she called me over the intercom and I didn't respond. I knew from her actions that she wanted to help.

Moe and Ferraro (2003) characterize the poor health care in women's prisons as malign neglect. An investigation into a Florida women's prison provides further expression of this neglect in the *Miami Herald*'s report, "Beyond Punishment":

10. Many correctional facilities rely on physician's assistants, nurse practitioners, nurses of all levels, and other medical assistants to provide health care.

The institution—the largest women's prison in the nation—also has a long history, documented in reports and medical audits, of alarming and even life-threatening deficiencies, ranging from failing to provide routine medications to delaying treatment for inmates with potentially fatal illnesses. (Brown 2015)

Being sick and asking for help is grounds for punishment in this world. As the *Miami Herald* investigation found:

Inmates told the *Herald* they are not only getting sick, they also are finding themselves cursed at for complaining—and punished for pleading with nurses and doctors for help. Even those with serious, visible health problems are sometimes thrown in disciplinary confinement for "disrespect" if they question their medical diagnosis, inmates said. (Brown 2015)

The *Miami Herald* series follows a former inmate, who said she was disciplined for asking a nurse to change her bloody gloves before examining her.

They do as little as possible and will go to the lengths of letting you die or misdiagnose you to save money. The inmates are animals to them . . . if you have bone cancer, they will tell you [that] you have arthritis and give you Tylenol. (Brown 2015)

Mental Health Concerns

The prevalence and severity of imprisoned women's mental health needs is well documented (for reviews, see Belknap 2015; Pollock 2014; Bloom, Owen, and Covington 2003). Prisons everywhere struggle with providing mental health services in the correctional environment. The prison environment re-creates dangerous and risky situations that trigger women's experiences with trauma and introduce new concerns, thus exacerbating their mental health challenges. While barriers to accessing mental health care are parallel to obstacles to obtaining medical and dental care, the search for mental health services has an additional twist. In an odd and inaccurate use of the psychological term *manipulation,* staff consistently report women are "manipulative" and their claims of psychological distress have no merit. Few staff members are equipped with practical knowledge about women's mental health histories, particularly behaviors related to trauma and other victimization. Rizzo and Hayes (2011, 13) suggest that women prisoners are caught in the fault lines formed by the fundamental conflict between the philosophies of medical care and those that govern correctional facilities. This is especially true when it comes to psychological services.

INSTITUTIONAL TRAUMA:·
OPERATIONAL PRACTICE AND HARM

The contemporary prison can be a trauma-triggering and trauma-inducing institution, causing unnecessary suffering among prisoners (Covington 2012, 2016a). The National Resource Center for Justice-Involved Women (NRCJIW) (Benedict 2014) suggests operational practice in the prison can both reinforce past injuries and create new risk for trauma. In arguing for a "trauma-informed" criminal justice system, the Substance Abuse and Mental Health Services Center states:

> The experiences that trauma survivors have in the criminal justice system, far from leading them to positive changes in their lives, often add new trauma and deepen their wounds. Many of these women will never be able to break out of the narrow trajectory that constricts their futures unless the justice system and their communities can help them to focus on the root problem: trauma, its lasting effects in human lives, and the need to begin the healing process. (n.d., 1)

The NRCJIW (Benedict 2014) describes routine practices that can both create and re-create the damaging experience of trauma. To start with, prisons are loud. Raised voices, clanging metal doors, loud announcements, alarms, barked orders, and other unpleasant noises shape this sonic environment. Elements of operational practice, such as strip searches, cell extractions, segregation, male supervision, and having to talk with someone who is unfamiliar can also threaten one's emotional equilibrium. These events and routines are often experienced as "triggers" and make it very difficult for the traumatized person's nervous system to reset itself. For example, a woman who has survived childhood sexual abuse is likely to have developed finely tuned neurophysiological patterns to help keep her safe. When exposed to similar experiences, or cues in the environment that re-create the experience, she will experience the same cascade of neurochemicals that were triggered during the actual event. This reaction is automatic, often unconscious, and governed by the brain's fear-response system. Many women are intensely on guard; their primary (instinctual) brain is constantly scanning for threat or opportunity; and they are frequently feeling and acting out of fear (Covington 2016a).

Because trauma survivors carry "sensations of constant threat" (Covington 2016a, 225), many of the behaviors women exhibit in prison are attempts at managing trauma symptoms.

> Drug use, self-harm, defiance, and other negative behaviors exhibited by women inmates may be better understood as trauma-survival behaviors that

alleviate deep sensory distress, rather than a blatant disregard for institutional rules. Common correctional routines and practices can worsen or alleviate the sensory distress that accompanies trauma. For women inmates, attempts to neutralize, escape, or protect can take many forms: bullying another inmate, forming inmate families, withdrawing from certain activities, nurturing with food, and countless other behaviors. In the absence of alternatives and living in a climate of fear, these behaviors offer a sense of control and provide psychological and physiological relief. (Benedict 2004, 3)

The NRCJIW (Benedict 2014) and Covington (2012, 2013, 2016a, 2016b) offer extensive guidelines for becoming more informed about trauma in order to create safer and more secure facilities.[11] Trauma-informed environments facilitate psychological and physiological regulation; prisoners who feel safe in their environment are less likely to be triggered into self-protective responses that complicate facility operations. In women's facilities, staff interaction with prisoners can either create more psychological and physiological stability or cause more instability (Covington 2013, 2016b). In Massachusetts, for example, work to develop trauma-informed correctional practice resulted in significant decreases in prison violence, as measured by 62 percent fewer staff assaults, 54 percent fewer inmate-on-inmate assaults, and a 46 percent reduction in inmate fights (Benedict 2014).

CONDITIONS OF CONFINEMENT LITIGATION

An examination of recent court cases in California regarding prison crowding illustrates modern conditions of confinement litigation. The California prison system, like those in many other states, has been under judicial review due to unconstitutional levels of crowding (Simon 2014). Following challenges to state prison conditions in terms of medical, mental health, and dental services, *Brown v. Plata* (2011) was ultimately decided by the U.S. Supreme Court. The Court found overcrowding in California prisons did in fact constitute "cruel and unusual punishment" (Owen and Mobley 2012; see Simon 2014 for a complete discussion of these events).

The lack of appropriate mental health care for all prisoners was a key part of the legal claims of the *Coleman v. Schwarzenegger* lawsuit. As

11. While the concept of trauma-informed corrections developed in the context of women's experiences, juvenile and adult males too have been exposed to violence and victimization in their life course and pathways to prison, which should be considered in developing male-based practice as well.

Simon (2014, 175) notes, the connection between the "assertive" imprisonment policies and the lack of adequate community mental health care has funneled many people with significant mental health needs into the prison system. While the settlement did not address women's needs separately (2014, 12–13), the Court found California's prisons lacked minimally adequate mental health care and had systematically failed to treat mentally ill prisoners, a situation that constitutes "deliberate indifference to the serious danger faced and posed by those prisoners and thus violate[s] the Eighth Amendment" (12). In *Mass Incarceration on Trial* (2014), Simon focuses on the "abysmal and dangerous conditions in prison" (7). Discussing the Court decisions in *Coleman v. Schwarzenegger* in 2009 and *Brown v. Plata* in 2011, Simon states, "These cases show that California built prisons heedless of the humanity of those it planned to incarcerate, recklessly accumulated people with chronic illnesses in these prisons and committed itself to an extreme penal philosophy" (2014, 8). As prison managers lost the ability to see prisoners as human beings with individual needs, imprisonment became a version of torture for those suffering from physical or mental illnesses by creating a level of neglect that was cruel and unusual as well as inhumane.

Even with the weight of the U.S. Supreme Court bearing down on the California prison system, medical care for women continues to be substandard. As part of a required health care audit related to the settlement agreement, an independent team found that a California prison for women was "not providing adequate medical care, and that there are systemic issues resulting in preventable morbidity and mortality and that present an ongoing serious risk of harm to patient" (Goldenson, Lamarre, and Puisis 2013, 1). Later in the report, the medical auditors state: "We believe that the majority of problems are attributable to overcrowding, insufficient health care staffing, and inadequate medical bed space" (5). While the California case is a "remarkable court decision" (Simon 2014), this "cruel and unusual" way of treating incarcerated women is all too common throughout the United States.

CONCLUSION

Threats to women's safety are entrenched in prison conditions and standard operating practice. The Commission on Safety and Abuse in America's Prisons (2006) notes many harmful operational practices within the prison system: overuse of solitary confinement, problems in staff culture, lack of oversight, and inadequate measures of safety and effectiveness. It also points out that issues of safety and abuse are likely to play out differently for women and men, supporting our argument that women have additional threats to their safety and well-being because of their gendered identity.

Living conditions in the prison mirror the substandard housing and decaying free world communities in which so many imprisoned women were raised. Women voiced extreme concern about cleanliness and conditions, framing their worries about their physical health in concrete terms. These worries feed conflict, as some women try to control their space and others' behavior. The daily round in prison is often detrimental to women's well-being, particularly those with trauma symptoms or other mental health conditions. Inadequate medical and mental health care are significant worries among women; inadequate services and, in some cases, criminal neglect of women's health are part of everyday practice. In upcoming chapters, we show how components of prison culture, including respect, reputation, and relationships, mediate the specific forms of gendered inequality that shape women's search for safety.

4

Searching for Safety through Prison Capital

In the women's prison community, challenges to safety and well-being come from every quarter. Yet, against the longest odds, women can successfully confront these challenges by marshaling forms of prison capital. As we found in our 2008 NIJ study, most women learn to survive, endure, and even thrive in their prison lives by developing strategies that counter gendered inequality and other disadvantages of the prison community.

Intersectional inequalities shape life and create risk in any prison. Most prisoners learn to respond to these risks by developing the skills, connections, and knowledge to do time safely—by developing prison capital. Women find safety by confronting inequality in their physical, social, and cultural environments and, equally important, by controlling their reaction to such inequities. Against this overwhelming imbalance of power and agency, women in prison develop a variety of strategies to confront these challenges to their well-being. In this chapter, we review how gendered forms of human, economic, social, and cultural capital guide women as they seek safety.

DEFINING SAFETY

Safety is more than the absence of violence or harm. We define safety in two ways: the state of being protected from harm, danger, and other threats; and the product of having one's needs met. People are unsafe when their environment fails to provide components necessary to fulfill their needs, creating unnecessary suffering and conflict over scarce or desirable goods or statuses. In chapter 3, we made the argument that prison conditions themselves are unsafe, specifically because of the damage to human dignity grounded in disdain for prisoners, crowding, and lack of medical and mental health care.

The search for safety is compromised and constrained by living in a community bounded by toxic living conditions, competition over scarce resources, the demands of prison culture, and the absolute power of correctional staff. Most public life is grounded in the official and published rules and the legitimate and illegitimate authority of the staff. At the same time, women must navigate the private and powerful informal world of the prison subculture as it articulates the ways status, resources, and power are obtained, contested, and distributed. Women make their lives within the tension between the formal and public rules and the informal and private normative demands as they attempt to resolve fundamental conflicts created by inequality. Prison culture also contains guidelines for censuring, shunning, and punishing behaviors outside this normative framework, further complicating the search for safety. The contradictions and constraints of the contemporary prison are arbitrated by this subculture, providing pathways within the prison for women to manage their capital, confront inequality, and develop individualized safety strategies. Finding safety in prison is particularly problematic for women who have experienced violence and victimization throughout their life course (Heney and Kristiansen 1998; Schneider 2014; Benedict 2014; Richie 2004; Comack 2006).

Shifts in prison equilibrium make safety a tenuous and fragile state. Prison conditions change with political and budgetary winds; major events can cause a crackdown in prison rules; the number of women confined varies; and administrators, with their different philosophies, move in and out. As Maritza said, "I don't feel safe here at all, I feel like everything is subject to change at any given second."

No Place to Run, No Place to Hide

We borrow the phrase "no place to run, no place to hide" from an article by de Almeida and Paes-Machado (2015), which describes how "socio-organizational processes and patterns of inmate victimization" are tied to inequalities in social, human, and cultural capital in prison. Although it is based on a study of imprisoned men, their analysis mirrors our own. They find that a complex of factors within the prison environment, "risk, power, and vulnerability," combines with individual and group strategies to create conditions of potential victimization. Vulnerability is determined by the "volume and composition of economic, social and cultural capital—or different types of power and possession" held by each prisoner (de Almeida and Paes-Machado 2015, 188). Human Rights Watch (1998) presents a similar image of "nowhere to hide" in its description of staff sexual violence and retaliation against women in the extensive staff sexual misconduct litigation in Michigan prisons. We review these examples of state-sponsored suffering in chapter 6.

One basic challenge to safety within prisons is the constraint on movement. McGuire (2011, 148) describes "the inherent immobility of prison life" and its "effect of freezing inmates in physical space." Deprivation of freedom is one of the key pains of imprisonment for both women and men. That prisoners have restricted movement in prison and may be confined to one area for long periods further limits the ability to avoid difficult individuals or situations. Within any prison, blind spots and other nonsurveilled areas create opportunity for harm—by both prisoners and staff. As we outline in chapter 5, when enmeshed in difficult and risky relationships, or ensnared in the debt and disorder of the mix, women can feel trapped, with little control over most aspects of their lives.

Another trap concerns privacy and the male gaze (Owen 2005). Women have a larger expectation of privacy than men (Bloom, Owen, and Covington 2003). While some modern prisons have acknowledged the need for more privacy for women when dressing and attending to personal needs, many facilities routinely expose them to the male gaze. In the crowded contemporary prison, privacy is a scarce resource. The lack of both physical and psychological privacy is a gendered pain of imprisonment. Some prisons are making efforts to prohibit or limit male staff from performing strip searches or working in the living units at night. International human rights standards prohibit male involvement in the living units (United Nations 2010, 2015; UNODC 2015). However, as we discuss in chapter 6, it is shortsighted to see staff sexual misconduct as a threat only from male staff. Female staff can also present significant threat to a woman's safety (Beck 2015).

HUMAN CAPITAL

While the term *human capital* typically refers to one's ability to earn a living, we expand this concept to encompass prisoners' access to resources that enable them to do their time safely and, sometimes, productively. Most women in prison arrive with diminished capital in terms of education, employment skills, and material goods. The poverty of their free world communities is mirrored in the scarcity of the prison community. Because of their individual and structural experiences with violence and trauma, fragile physical and mental health conditions also undercut their human capital.

Women's strategies for securing human capital in prison are grounded in a personalized definition of safety. Diamond talked about how she found safety:

> I am not really threatened or insecure [now because] I know there are situations [to avoid]. I am not a first-timer so I know there is a big difference. But my first time I didn't know what to expect or how things work. I just felt introverted. I didn't want to make any waves. With the time, you just learn how to respect. Now I am in a place where I am just over the whole thing . . . [This prison] is safer than [another in the state system]. [It's] the two-man cells, the staff, the access to more programming. Even staff . . . is a lot more positive. In fact, I was relieved to know I was coming here because my fears changed. I was thinking about not what someone would do to me but what if I fall back into what would keep me in bondage. Safety is what I do here. Don't get involved with women and don't get in the mix. I exercise. Keep yourself busy in the idle time.

As Diamond learned to do her time safely, she developed stocks of knowledge about prison life, the importance of respect, avoiding girl-friends, and staying out of the mix. In a jail interview, Cerise said, "If you play around, then it is on you to take care of yourself." In this worldview, safety "depends" on your own actions. If you feel unsafe, it's your fault. Mirroring the isolates in Kruttschnitt and Gartner's (2005) analysis, many women told us that "keeping to yourself" is the only way to ensure safety. Being a loner, or having a few close friends, is seen as a logical response to the threats of the prison community.

"It's on Me": Safety and Personal Choice

Like the women in Sered and Norton-Hawk's (2014) study who were held "accountable" for their troubles, the women who participated in our study felt responsible for their own safety. Ellie said, "Safety is on me," because, "I can choose my environment. I can pick and choose my 'safetyness.' I know it is not safe over there and that it is safe over here." Around the country, women agreed that they "put themselves" in trou-bled situations. This self-blame for problems translates into a highly individualized search for safety. Women draw on their stores of human capital from the free world (such as "street smarts," "knowing the game," and middle-class manners), or strive inside prison to obtain material, cultural, and social resources to keep themselves safe. Regardless of how a woman is situated by time or place in the prison community, almost all women felt it was their own responsibility to keep safe. Their lack of confidence in the prison staff to protect them is explicit. For women who may have had very little control over their lives prior to prison, developing some semblance of control over their bodies and selves is central to the search for safety.

These claims of personal responsibility for one's safety are an example of the agency and sense of empowerment that women develop as they improve their prison capital. Just as "doing gender" is a process (Martin and Jurik 2007), "doing safety" is a daily effort, which shields women from situational and structural violence in this community. "Doing your own time" means just that: negotiating safety by doing it yourself.

"How You Carry Yourself": Confidence

Throughout the country, women told us they could feel safe in prison despite the multiplicity of challenges and dangers. A common sentiment was that "prison is safer than the street" (Bradley and Davino 2002). Many women shared Sophia's view: "I feel safe in here because I know I am not doing anything wrong." Valeria provided a slightly different take: "I feel safe because I am a confident woman, I feel safe already because other people see that and don't challenge me." For some, confidence and self-assurance are forms of prison capital that can serve as protection from most threats. Mariana said:

> I think it is the way you present yourself to people. I am not going to alienate myself to the room. I walk like I am proud. People say that I walk like I run the prison. That is just who I am—I walk with my head up and shoulders back. I don't play the bitch game [calling women names]. I call you by your name or whatever you want to be called by. I am not a kid. I am a couple years from forty, and I am not about to play games.

Safety, as we heard from women everywhere, is "how you carry yourself." Carrying yourself with confidence, "sticking up for yourself," and not looking weak (like a "rabbit") were said to be essential to safety among women. Our sense is that while the threats to safety inside the prison are ever present, developing stocks of prison capital allows some sense of control over the risk in women's immediate life round. While some women attempted to physically control situations with threats and violence, "learning to stand up for yourself" and "how you carry yourself" were fundamental to the search for safety.

Looking Tough

Physical appearance can contribute to a woman's sense of safety. Some women may adopt severe clothes and postures, some of which can be seen as more "male-like," conveying an attitude of toughness and strength. Although such accessories vary around the country, "sagging" pants and "bonaroo G-ed up from the feet up"[1] are some ways women try to look like someone "not to be messed with." Suki agreed that a "more masculine" appearance is one way to find safety: "[Safety] depends on what you think of yourself. In a macho society [of prison], the masculinity is what you seek. I know many women who have that boy exterior because that is the only way that they feel safe." Maria said these outfits and attitudes are how women "portray themselves as hard." Tracy added, "That is safety for them. I have done that with the shades [sunglasses] and a different walk."

Another woman in the group, Cecilia, disagreed that looking tough is enough to keep one safe: "That is not true; I have tattoos on my neck, but it is all about how you carry yourself."

Advice on Seeking Safety

So how do women learn to "stand up for themselves" and do their own time? When women enter jails and prison for the first time, they have questions and fears about how they will fare in this new, unknown world. Like Diamond, most first-term women prisoners "don't know what to expect or how things work" when they first roll up to the prison gates. Because women commit fewer and typically less serious crimes than men, they may have no expectations about coming to prison, with less distinct cultural maps to guide them once they travel the pathways

---

1. "Bonaroo" is an old prison slang term thought to be a corruption of French *bon* (good). Generally the term can be used for anything good or admired; specifically, it refers to one's best set of prison clothes, usually very clean and creased and ironed. "G-ed up" references "gangster" styles, typically from the street. The phrase "from the feet up" concerns shoes.

to prison. In the formal orientation for newly arrived women, one custody staff member gave women this advice: "Do not involve yourself in any type of relationship here because most of our problems are from relationships. Do not borrow or lend or steal anything. Do not tell anyone the amount of money you have on the books. Stay out of the mix." Mary Anne recalled that one staff person "told us a few things" when she first arrived.

> He told us, "Make sure to keep your room clean. Keep it safe. Respect other persons in the room. Go to school, program, and find something to do." He also said, "Don't do no snitches. Don't be trying to get in a relationship with anybody. Mind your own business." I took his words to heart.

However, such official advice does not address all the questions and concerns of the "fish," those new to prison life. Women soon learn to rely on other prisoners for both formal and informal knowledge about how to do their time. When a woman who has little experience with being locked up arrives, she may have deep concerns about her safety. Over time, this fear dissipates as she learns how to take care of herself and avoid trouble. Mia remarked: "I was afraid of the sexual violence before I came here. But when I got here, I saw that it was different because no one bothered me. I think I was watching too many movies before I came here because it was different than the movies."

Most women said they did not give advice unless asked. Shanika said she would give this advice to a newcomer but only if asked:

> If you don't want to be in a wreck, don't get involved in anything. Stay out of politics, stay clean . . . don't have any crumbs/hair/anything dirty that will set your bunkie off. You need to keep yourself respected and respect others. Don't get involved with gangs and drug activities. Keep to yourself, respect other people, and keep your area clean. You can't be perfect all the time, but that is basically it.

The individuality of doing time is captured by Andie's advice: "Keep to yourself. You came here alone, and you leave here alone. That is what I do."

ECONOMIC CAPITAL

Some of us know what it's like to be poor in the free world: substandard housing, low incomes, food insecurity, poor schools, limited health care, and few opportunities for employment. Poor neighborhoods are more likely to be unsafe, particularly for women and girls. Surveillance by law enforcement and obligations to social service agencies also subject the poor to more social control than the nonpoor (Sered and Norton-Hawk 2014; Richie 2012). Prisons compound the poverties and disadvantages of women's free world lives, aggravated by the limits on educational and vocational resources, few opportunities for legitimate work inside, and the risk of sub rosa incomes.

Economic stratification exists among prisoners, creating a context for conflict as those without resources struggle to get by. The myth that prisons provide "everything" and that prisoners don't have an economic care in the world is unfounded. For women particularly, pursuit of goods outside what they are issued and "what they have coming" becomes a key part of doing time. Food, shelter, clothing, and some basic personal hygiene goods ("hygienes") are provided by the prison "issue," items a prisoner is issued by policy.[2] With few exceptions, material goods are fairly basic and in short supply. In the prison economy, anything outside "the issue" is a luxury. "Street" clothes, food and snacks, makeup, hair products, and anything not available in the commissary are not only desirable (women in prison are consumers too) but also a marker of status and economic prosperity.[3] "What you have coming," is a phrase used by staff and prisoners to establish your eligibility or worthiness to access anything desirable or deserved. "You don't have that coming," is a phrase used by prisoners and staff to deny this access and to denote someone undeserving of material and social aid. Women without other forms of prison capital, such as social status or respect, are likely to have nothing coming from staff or other prisoners.

Economic capital contributes to a woman's status inside but can also create vulnerabilities. Having legitimate access to resources, through a prison job assignment (having a "pay number" in some systems), the

2. Prisons issue sanitary supplies, but they are limited in amount and quality. In many prisons in the United States, women who cannot purchase sanitary supplies in the commissary must ask staff to obtain them. Often, this staff person is male.

3. Underclothing can be a problem for women seeking correct fit, and staff are in charge of ordering prison issue underwear. Briefs are almost always "granny panties" and white, and in some systems women are issued used and discolored underwear. Bras are quite problematic. They are often plain, white, and utilitarian, and fit is problematic. Women who need sizes outside the normal distribution have particular difficulty. Bras can also lead to conflict. There is a formal rule that women must wear bars in common areas. Women who do not conform to this rule can receive a disciplinary writeup. Women who do not identify with a heteronormative version of the female resist wearing conventionally female underclothing. Some women and twin-spirited persons prefer to bind their breasts. Others might prefer to wear a T-shirt rather than a bra. Many prisons now offer "sports bras" as part of the commissary and sometimes as part of the "issue."

allowed packages from the outside world, or funds placed on the books by family, friends, and the occasional trick or John, enables a woman to buy food and hygiene items, easing some of the deprivations of imprisonment. "Running your mac" is an example of trying to hustle others for economic gain. Those who receive material support from the outside are said to be "well taken care of." (We offer a reminder: Most women come from families for whom such support is a real struggle. For women serving long terms, social support erodes as friends and family age, get sick, and pass away.) For those without these material resources, the prison community provides alternate routes to economic capital, in the form of prison hustles, black market opportunities, exploitation of other women, and illicit exchange with staff.

Like communities anywhere, economic and material capital is distributed unequally. Women in the top-tier economic group receive money "on the books" for shopping in the canteen and, where allowed, packages sent by friends and family. Just like the upper classes in the free world, the well-off woman does not need to resort to stealing or other hustles to gain access to material goods. At the same time, she is vulnerable to theft, pressure, hustles, and exploitative relationships from those without such capital or those who choose to steal to get by. Women in this category can protect their assets by acquiring political and cultural power by "holding their own" when confronted by those who seek to exploit them. They also must learn to avoid romantic or sexual entanglement with prison "gold-diggers," known in some prisons as "canteen whores." Most women, however, do not have much support from the outside and must develop a range of strategies and tactics to improve their prison economic and material capital in this world of collective deprivation.

Women without any outside economic support must find their way toward developing capital while imprisoned. "Gleaning" (Irwin 1970), defined as taking every advantage of prison programming or studying on one's own, is a common strategy. Those doing time using the adaptive strategy (Kruttschnitt and Gartner 2005) seek scarce educational, vocational, and program opportunities. Winterfield et al. (2009) document multiple positive gains made by prisoners who participate in prison college programs.

A small number of women solve their economic problems by working in legitimate jobs inside the prison, often called a "state job." A job with a "good pay number," or wage, may enable a woman to provide for herself inside and perhaps save money for her future release. For many women, prison jobs and vocational training may be the first consistent experience with the demands of work. The positive benefits of prison work experience and training for post-release outcomes have been documented by Saylor and Gaes (1999) and Wagner (2013). Although they did not conduct a separate gender analysis of their data, Saylor and Gaes (1999) found that prisoners of color benefited the most from working in the prison factories and vocational training, as measured by lower recidivism rates, higher wages, and job retention.

But such jobs are few in the opportunity-scarce prison, and competition for the good jobs can be intense. Women with human capital and women with strong connections to the staff (a form of social capital) who make these assignments are likely to get and keep these desirable jobs. In jails, which in contrast to prisons typically hold both women and men, female prisoners usually have less access to desirable work, for example, as a trustee, because women and men must be separated. Although protecting women from risky situations is important, sex-segregated work disadvantages them. Over time, women with long prison sentences can climb to the top of the job ladder by obtaining the better paying and higher skilled positions.

In some prison systems, like the Federal Bureau of Prisons and the California Department of Corrections and Rehabilitation, prison industry jobs provide the best incomes. For nonindustry jobs, pay rates are astoundingly low. Wagner (2013) finds that while the pay scale for prisoners depends on the nature of the job, the average wage for nonindustry work is 93 cents per day. For women who have a "pay number," $20 a month has to stretch to buy hygienes, other toiletry products, foodstuffs, stamps, and other necessities. This is only an average: many women make much less than this, mirroring the low-wage jobs available to them on the outside. Like the working poor outside, they cannot make ends meet in the economy of the prison community.

Hustles and the Sub Rosa Economy

Hustles provide income for those without other means of support and a way to develop reputation and other forms of social capital. A woman working in the kitchen might leverage her access to food to sell to other prisoners to cook for themselves, or to share, earning her both money and some level of prestige. In one of the hotter prisons we visited, smuggling ice to sell in the housing unit was one hustle. Scarcity creates the conditions for a given hustle; in prisons where every women has access to ice, such a hustle would not exist. Hustles range from "slightly" illegal activities to full-on drug dealing. Stealing from the kitchen, a work site, or other public resources is common. Some hustles are nonexploitative, such as selling or bartering with art, tattooing, or "doing hair." In prisons that depend on prisoner labor to accomplish clerical tasks, women can sell or trade a spot on a desired program or housing list. Hustles are risky when they break prison rules, expose a woman to disciplinary action, or infringe on other hustles. Women have to manage this contradiction as they strive to improve their prison capital while avoiding risk of discovery from staff or being ripped off by other women.

Trafficking and Trading

Sometimes known as "trafficking and trading," dealing in contraband is a risky route to economic prosperity. While drugs are often the most extreme example, any item that is not formally "issued" is contraband. While the source of contraband is always in dispute, such commodities are brought in by staff, visitors, outside contractors, and delivery workers.

Tobacco offers a specific example. Until the 1990s, smoking was permitted in prisons, and tobacco products were available in the commissary. As health concerns about tobacco use increased, prison systems began to control tobacco inside and then banned it entirely. Always desirable, tobacco became contraband and another commodity for the black market. Some observers suggest that dealing in tobacco is more lucrative than drug sales because its "OK-ness" on the streets makes compromising an officer somewhat easier.[4] Seth Ferrenti (2003), writing as the "Gorilla Convict," describes this process in his prison:

> As tobacco bans have spread across prisons nationwide, cigarettes have grown into a contraband item of choice, rivaling illegal and illicit drugs in their availability and profitability on the black market.

> With tobacco products now banned by the federal Bureau of Prisons and the majority of state prison systems, the price of a single Marlboro inside now reaches twenty dollars. A policy intended to produce health benefits and reduce fire risk has created a cash cow for prison gangs like the Mexican Mafia and Aryan Brotherhood, and the guards willing to work with them.

> By utilizing the smuggling methods developed to bring in heroin and other drugs (and aided by the ease of purchasing cigarettes on the outside) the

---

4. In another study, a woman explained that once her mother became ill and unable to send her money, she developed a hustle selling cigarette lighters brought in by staff.

gangs ensure prisoners can get a smoke anytime they want—if they are willing to pay the price. A pack of Newports or Camels can cost $200 while a pouch of rolling tobacco, like Bugler, which sells for a couple of dollars in the free world, can earn an enterprising inmate hundreds.

The same hustle is found in women's prisons. Beanie told us, "The going price for a can of tobacco is $500 [worth of goods at the commissary]. Or she can give me a couple of $100 bills. There is no more cocaine or heroin; it's all tobacco. They fired a whole crew of administration workers [prisoners] for it. It's tobacco." Prices vary, but the penalty for not paying is the same. Lorrae said, "There is a lot of violence over a $100 pack of cigarettes. There is a lot of, 'Bitch, give me back my money for that cigarette, or I am going to kick your ass.'" Julia talked about the role of tobacco in the prison economy:

> There are more debts because of the tobacco. On the streets, you have the opportunity to get the drugs, to make the money for the drugs. When you come here, you cannot make that money so you don't do the drugs. But tobacco is a whole 'nother thing. Just like the drugs, it is the chase, the excitement, and the adrenaline—the whole thing. Women who would not have chased the drugs will do anything to get the tobacco.

While gangs may be less of an economic force in women's prisons, distribution and enforcement systems exist, informally controlled by "shot callers" and "big ballers" and their more loosely organized crews. We examine the contribution of economic conflict to producing violence in chapter 5.

EMOTIONAL CAPITAL

Women improve their ability to do time by shoring up emotional and psychological well-being. Like emotional intelligence (Goleman 1995), this form of capital prepares a woman to withstand the threats to her emotional equilibrium. Such threats to emotional stability are embedded in conditions of confinement, operational practice, and inequities among prisoners and with staff. These threats are magnified by individual and structural traumas experienced by the majority of imprisoned women (Negy, Woods, and Carlson 1997; Schneider 2014). Whether it is through formal and structured programming, prisoner-designed groups, or individual study, women seek safety by improving emotional capital. In prison systems with adequate mental health services, trauma counseling leads to this capital improvement. In similar ways, drug treatment programs and other therapies have been shown to improve women's overall well-being. This is particularly true for programs that use gender-responsive and women-centered programs (Messina 2011). Suzee, a low-custody prisoner, gave an example of improving emotional capital:

> A lot [of women] are really working on recovery and themselves. They have a different approach. We are taught to handle conflict, and if there is no way to handle it, we can go to our counselors. I have pretty decent housing staff. If it is something that can't be handled, they will make the move for you.

Greer (2002, 116) sees women do their time by walking "an emotional tightrope" and doing "emotional labor" to keep themselves safe. Because of the need to avoid any appearance of weakness, women in prison "may find that displaying feelings is not approved formally or informally" (116). She found the emotional environment of the prison to be capricious and unpredictable and, simultaneously, rigid and constraining. The women in Greer's study recognized differences in "the varying degrees of resources" they could marshal to manage their emotions: "Some of these resources resided within the individual while others were contextually limited or culturally grounded" (123). Greer argues that women walk the tightrope by seeking diversions from feelings, following spiritual pursuits, blocking and burying emotions, engaging in self-reflection, and expressing humor. Laughing, particularly, was seen as an asset used to diffuse tense situations, release negative feelings, and entertain others.

Recovery

Working on recovery is another route to increasing emotional capital. In their study of women and recovery in the community, Veysey and Heckman examine the "moments of personal transformation" that spur positive change among justice-involved women. They suggest:

> While each person's path is unique, each also shares common elements. As a whole, these women speak about three elements of change—a shift in the way they think about themselves or their lives; an external event or personal influence that gave them the motivation to change; and a concrete change in behavior. None of the individual elements alone was sufficient to make concrete and lasting changes. All of these things appear to be necessary. (2006, 26)

The women in the Veysey study had been trapped by the cycle of violence, self-harming choices, criminal and damaging behavior, and constrained opportunity. In recovery, they found a moment of transformation to move forward in life. Recognizing the consequences of trauma in their lives and their choices, particularly in relationships, was a breakthrough. Reframing negative definitions of self toward a healthier and less damaged identity was another form of cognitive transference connected to these transformations. Involvement in therapeutic and self-help programs was also said to help with the shift in thinking and behavior. The behavioral changes included "learning how to stand up for myself," seeking help for gendered treatment needs, and engaging in forms of self-care (Veysey and Heckman 2006).

Women in prison, too, can experience these moments of transformation, even within the threatening and harmful prison environment. Some women start their prison terms by "running the yard," fully engaging in the mix. Some women never participate in the mix, adapting to prison life by following the rules and keeping themselves out of trouble. Many move back and forth along the continuum of trouble and safety throughout their term. But for some, prison can be a place to strive and thrive. Women can make their own cognitive shift toward transformation, even in the face of seemingly impossible odds.

As women reimagine themselves, discarding the identity of prisoner or convict or victim, they also reframe their experiences with trauma and cumulative disadvantage by finding practices that heal and reset pathways away from prison. In striving to obtain limited resources, women who thrive learn to leverage their relationships with prisoners and staff; parlay the few therapeutic, educational, and vocational opportunities; and rise above the trouble and strife of the mix. The women in the Veysey and Heckman study (2006) said receiving respect and empathy from treatment and other authority figures was necessary to their transformation. As we discuss in chapter 6, prison staff have a fundamental role in ensuring or challenging women's sense of safety.

SOCIAL CAPITAL

Relationships contribute to all forms of social capital. Covington (1998a) draws from work by Jean Baker Miller and the Stone Center at Wellesley College (Bloom, Owen, and Covington 2003) in her conceptualization of "relational development." She argues that relationships and connections are primary to women's psychological development, as compared to men's tendency toward developmental independence from their families (Covington 1998). Many women who travel the pathways to prison have experienced disconnections in their free world lives, often related to trauma and violence (Covington, 2016a; Pollack 2007). Women's continued emotional development is dependent on healthy relationships. When women feel disconnected from others, Covington (1998) concludes, they experience disempowerment, confusion, and anxiety. Within the prison community, these relations contain the potential for striving and thriving as well as the potential for risk and violence.

Doing time is a relational experience for all prisoners. While human capital in all its forms is essential to women's safety, networking or social capital also keeps women safe. Social capital is the capacity of a person to call upon personal ties and social networking to advance a personal interest or goal (Clear 2007, 80). According to the Saguaro Seminar (2016), sponsored by the Harvard Kennedy School, social capital works through information flows and norms of reciprocity that support mutual aid. Collective action depends on social capital. As the Seminar asserts, broader identities and solidarity are encouraged by social networks that help translate an "I" mentality into a "We" mentality. Social capital refers to the collective value of all "social networks" (people you know and their combined resources) and "norms of reciprocity," an inclination to do things for others within the network. Social capital is one of the specific benefits that flow from the trust, reciprocity, information, and cooperation associated with social networks. Social capital creates value for the people who are connected within the network and, at least sometimes, for bystanders (Saguaro Seminar 2016). Social capital exists in the prison just as in the free world. Prison social networks facilitate access to all forms of prison capital.

Relationships and Connections among Imprisoned Women

Social relationships—with other prisoners and with staff—are fundamental to gaining the social capital necessary for prison survival. Women forge relationships that socialize them into the prison community, teach them the "game" of doing time, and provide needed forms of economic, social, cultural, and emotional capital. Friendships and other kinds of constructive relationships can guide women as they chart their strategies for doing time, creating safe harbor in the consistently chaotic world of the prison. As a custody officer in a prison known for its relative safety and programing environment suggested, these relationships can be constructive:

They go with someone who is not violent that they can be comfortable with. It may not be a sexual relationship—it may just be that they can share things. Not all of them end up in sexual relationships: you buy canteen, I buy canteen, and we share. There are some honest inmates out there.

Rachel and Phoebe, held in a high-custody unit, assert healthy relationships are possible.

> *Rachel:* I don't think a relationship has to be sexual here. Me and her [points to another woman in the group] are good friends, but it is not sexual. She keeps me balanced and this is healthy. Women want to have a title with everything. So now they go to the title of girlfriend . . .
>
> *Phoebe:* [A relationship] can be healthy if [they] push each other to improve themselves. But they are sneaking it. It is [unacceptable] conduct and you have to learn to follow the basic rules. You don't get written up for the relationships, but you get written up for how you flaunt it. Hickeys and black eyes and all that.

Constructive partnerships can be romantic and sexual, or they can be based on strong bonds of friendship and experience. Some of these are mentor-protégée partnerships. A more savvy woman may take a less experienced and naive prisoner "under her wing" and guide her through prison politics. Groups of loosely affiliated women—in a room, a work situation, or a programming group—can also act as mentors, teaching a woman how to build a life while avoiding violence and conflict. Similarly situated prisoners may also act as peer advisers to a woman trying to find her way. Lifers, for example, may adopt a "baby lifer" and school her in the ways of "doing" a life sentence. In a conversation that took place during Owen's fieldwork in 1998, Grey Eyes, a baby lifer who had "just rolled up" and received many incident reports in her first months, said that all this happened because she did not know how to do her time. She added, "I thought I came to prison to get in trouble. I didn't know I did not have to get in trouble."

Sisterhood and Solidarity

Orange Is the New Black (Kerman 2010), and the TV series based on Kerman's memoir, presents a pop vision of imprisoned women to a wider and more public audience. Although we disagree with the TV show's stereotypical views of women of color and non-gender-conforming women, and its one-dimensional view of staff, we welcome a public dialogue about prison that includes women.[5] Codianni (2015), a former prisoner represented as a character in the show, adds another critique:

> Neither does the series show the real solidarity among women behind bars. When a woman is called to see the chaplain, automatically women will drift to her, and walk with her as far as they are allowed, because they know she is going to be told of the death of a loved one. They will be waiting to escort her back to her bunk and will stay with her or give her the space she needs. Women risk being sent to SHU [disciplinary housing] for bringing back milk, fruit and vegetables from the chow hall to give to a pregnant woman. When the new mother comes back to the camp or prison without her baby, women are there to greet her with hugs. Women will carry an ailing woman up the stairs to the sick call room. There is a strong sense of sisterhood at Danbury that the series ignores.

We agree that women can and do create and sustain sisterhood, a gendered form of social capital. Prisoners participate in systems of mutual aid (Irwin 1970), sharing the little they have with other women within their networks. Contributing food to a meal is typical among small groups of friends, prison families, members of a good room, or other connections. The nature of these exchanges is grounded in relationships and trust rather than profit or commerce. In some jails and prisons, women will prepare a "welcome wagon" of hygiene and other items that ease a woman into her time. More seasoned prisoners, with their secure stocks of prison know-how and material support, "mother" a newcomer who does not know the traps (the crosses or trick bags) of prison life. Marlana, whom we interviewed in jail, told us how this works in her jail:

> There is a core group that kinda sets the pod environment. Then we see a new person and we mother them and [tell them] you need to be careful around that person [who might harm them]. You make your own judgments, you come to whoever. You identify who needs help [and which] person might prey on a new person. There is some kind of protective group who kind of sees what is going on.

Play Families and Intimate Relationships

In doing their time through relationships, women can develop play families and mentor relationships that provide a sense of belonging in this chaotic community. Such connections can be emotionally and physically intimate or based on platonic and deep friendships forged over

---

5. Owen consulted informally on the TV series and gave the writing team copies of the original technical reports on which this book is based.

years of collective struggles. Many women find safety in a prison family and small circles of trusted friends. In prison or play families, women take on extended kinship roles, including typical male roles, such as father or brother, and conventionally female roles, such as mother, daughter, or auntie (Owen 1998). Of course, some women are doing time with their biological birth family members. Although some contend that the play family is found less frequently inside today than in the past (Greer 2000; Alarid 2000; Kruttschnitt and Gartner 2005), we found that women continued to form families as a way of doing time by obtaining social and human capital.

Prison families provide friendship and material goods, as well as mediate disputes, shielding a family member from the negative actions of others. A woman without capital can improve her situation through membership in a high-status prison family. Prison families can also contribute to sanctuary by protecting family members from harm and providing emotional support and guidance. Conflict within families does occur, but it is usually mediated or "squashed" by the older or more powerful family members.

Some women do their time by forming intimate partnerships with other prisoners. These relationships take multiple forms and direction and must be contextualized by the confluence of experience, culture, and constrained choice. Women's attitudes about these dyads vary greatly—by individual values, by sexual norms, and by time spent in prison. We heard descriptions of healthy and satisfying relationships, as well as descriptions of harmful and hurtful dynamics of ever-changing connections among women. These relationships, in all their forms, are an acknowledged and accepted part of this community. Relationships can bring trouble when they threaten a woman's standing or incite jealousy, re-creating the cycle of violence inside prison. Trammell (2009) also sees that romantic, emotional, and sexual relations run the risk of intimate partner conflict and violence, as we discuss in chapter 5.

Other sources of social capital are found in organizing prisoner-led programs or social groups. Women are creative in modifying existing program materials and developing women-led groups of their own invention. Special interest organizations can be found in most prison communities, typically involving like-situated women; these include long-termer and lifer groups, battered women classes, 12-step and other recovery groups, spiritual groups, and the like. Such groups require staff sponsors, structuring positive interactions with staff and reinforcing reputations within this community of women.

Connections with staff personnel from headquarters, outside service or advocacy groups, or having a family member active in such organizations are additional sources of social and cultural capital. Women can become known to prison officials outside the facility, either through appeals, writing letters, being involved in some act that gains publicity, or by filing lawsuits against the prison. These high-profile women may get attention from decision makers within the prison system and thus expand their social and cultural value by leveraging connections from the outside. For women who are politically active in the outside community, connections with groups that advocate for political change in the prison system—some specifically for women—provide another outside source of social and political capital. In addition to participating in the political work of these organizations, women may work with journalists and other advocates to get the word out about prison conditions, sexual safety issues, and other grievances.

Juice

Relationships with powerful and well-connected prisoners and with helpful staff create and sustain prison capital. These connections and the ability to leverage them contribute to informal power, or juice. Women can expand their prison capital through connections to a decision maker, a big baller or shot caller, staff who control access to any commodity, or other keepers of scarce commodities (whether prisoner or staff). Being "in the know" about formal and informal prison rules, mastering the byzantine bureaucracies of prison life, and moving easily among the different groups are some ways women can acquire juice. Women navigate this social terrain, collecting information, forging alliances, and developing a reputation to "get things done," multiplying their own capital in the process.

Prisoners who "hang together" and have the same level of juice are said to be in the same "car"—prison slang for exclusive social networks and their attendant privileges. Having juice and being in the car can facilitate a better work assignment, desired housing, a move up waiting lists, and generally less hassle navigating the prison bureaucracy. Having juice protects women from other prisoners and, to some degree, from staff. Juice can also be gained from underground activities. Some women with juice can be running the yard in the mix and control access to the goods of the underground economy.

Juice is a social product. It can be generated by reputation, by becoming known as someone who "can get things done" in this irrational and bureaucratic community and is willing to help others. Engaging in the formal political order, such as running for office, designing and implementing self-help or other programs, and becoming an advocate for women through alliances with outside reform groups, is one avenue toward juice. Most prisons have some form of prisoner governance (typically limited in scope) that places individual women in contact with high-level prison managers when advocating for their community. Women on prisoner councils are typically allowed more movement throughout the institution to meet with their constituents which solidifies connections to other politically useful prisoners and staff. Women in these roles advocate for addressing shared grievances, improved programming, and organizing events and celebrations that benefit the entire community (such as Women's History Day, public holidays, Black History Month, or arranging in-prison sales of highly desirable goods such as free world food). In addressing the concerns of other prisoners, women build up stores of owed social obligation, somewhat similar to patronage systems in the free world.

CULTURAL CAPITAL

Pierre Bourdieu (1986) defined cultural capital as high cultural knowledge that ultimately rebounds to the owner's financial and social advantage. In Bourdieu's view, cultural capital represents fluency in a society's elite culture. In the prison community, "knowing the game," and leveraging this knowledge, contributes greatly to safety of all sorts. The mix (Owen 1998) frames the key norms and rules by providing a cultural frame for obtaining prison capital, particularly respect and reputation. Other norms, such as prohibitions against snitching and stigmatizing certain categories of offenses (e.g., "child" cases), make their own contribution to potential violence (McGuire 2011).

Components of prison culture are embedded in the "convict code," which shapes behaviors, status, and hierarchy among prisoners (Kruttschnitt and Gardener 2005; Bosworth 1999; Kruttschnitt 1981, 1983; Trammell 2012; Blackburn, Fowler and Pollock, 2014). Debates about the origin of prison subcultures have centered on whether they are "indigenous," responding to the deprivations and pains of imprisonment (Sykes 1958), or "imported," meaning grounded in free world values and experiences (Irwin and Cressey 1962). In Sykes's formulation, prison culture for men is a response to specific pains of imprisonment, offering strategies to lessen these pains. Pains of imprisonment, we submit, are alleviated by the development of prison capital.

These deprivations are gendered. Both women and men suffer from the loss of freedom and rejection by society but do so differently. The most difficult deprivations among men are losing the freedom to make their own decisions (particularly in following rules not of their making), loss of free world status and material possessions, lack of "normal" heterosexual relations, and fear for personal safety. Women share these concerns but have been shown to be more troubled about losses and pains related to their social worlds: loss of connections with partners, families, children, and friends and forced interactions with people not of their choosing, including staff and other prisoners (Pollock 2002b).

The classic formulation of the men's prison code, proposed originally by Sykes and Messinger (1960), conveys details about expectations surrounding the admonition to "do your own time." The core of the code is embedded in loyalty to prisoners, antipathy to staff (particularly officers), and privileging prisoners' views over others, even if it means bringing trouble on oneself by supporting the prisoner case against "the man." Being "tough," "cool," and "sharp" are further expressions of this masculine code. The importation approach argues that prisoners bring into the prison their street values, experiences, and definitions. Irwin and Cressey argued in 1962 that free world identities, such as "thief," informed men's prison culture. Fifty-some years later, we see prison culture as a combination of both.[6]

In their description of hierarchy in men's prisons, Sabo, Kupers, and London (2001, 3) suggest that "far too little consideration" has been given to the ways "manhood and the patterns of men's relationships with one another influence how men ended up in prison in the first place," how they function inside, and what happens upon release. Prison, they argue, facilitates "hegemonic masculinity" by accentuating male dominance and violence (5) and "serves to reproduce destructive forms of masculinity" (4). They conclude that "prison violence reflects and feeds wider patterns of male violence within the entire gender order" (8).

The prison code has not been found as plainly or unambiguously in studies of women's prison culture (Owen 1998; Kruttschnitt and Gartner 2005; McGuire 2011). Drawing a parallel between the "masculinity" of the men's prison world, which seems to drive violence, and the "femininity" of the women's prison community does not explain life in women's prisons. However, as cited in Blackburn, Fowler, and Pol-

---

6. John Irwin felt the distinction between these two approaches was artificial. He would agree with this combined conceptualization. Personal conversation, summer 1998.

lock (2014, 93), Giallombardo suggested in 1966 that "to live with other women is to live in the jungle," though she also asserted that women were more involved with relationships and generally did not take on the male proscription to "do your own time" in the same way. For women, elements of the code include "minding your own business" and less severe injunctions than for men against interacting with staff and participating in positive activities. As Owen (1998) and Kruttschnitt and Gartner (2005) find, the women's prison code continues to exhort prisoners to do their own time but offers a wider range of norms and roles disconnected from narrow definitions of masculinity.

Kruttschnitt and Gartner (2005) identified three strategies employed by women as they negotiate the prison world: adapted, convict, and isolate. An adapted strategy is used by women who have "figured out how to manage the contradictions and constraints of prison life" (132). In our view, these contradictions and constraints are the concrete expression of gendered inequality. Women following the convict strategy are invested in gaining and keeping the respect of a select (and small) group of like-minded women and avoiding interactions with staff. Kruttschnitt and Gartner define convicts as "women who watch out for themselves and their friends. They don't associate with others, especially correctional officers" (132). The isolate strategy is chosen by women who choose to do their time alone. Kruttschnitt and Gartner characterize the isolate style as "negative and singular" (133). Each strategy unfolds over time within the mix. We return to this formulation in chapter 5, showing how women leverage their forms of capital to conquer inequality and disadvantage.

The Mix

Owen's 1998 study identified the mix as comprising rules and expectations surrounding respect and reputation, involvement in the underground economy, relationships among women and with staff, and the use of violence (and its threat) as a way to establish control. The mix also contains specific prohibitions about "being messy," engaging in gossip about other prisoners, particularly with staff. Typically a source of trouble, the mix can be seen as continuing the behaviors that brought a woman to prison. Different dimensions of the mix are based on the types of capital women possess or develop to confront intersectional inequality. The "fighting mix" describes women who use the threat of violence and, less often, perpetrate violence in expressive and instrumental ways.

Women involved in drug sales and drug use are said to be in the "drug mix," doing time by chasing a high or the money surrounding this desired commodity. Esmeralda remarked, "The only violence that I see is people that get in the mix."

We today see the mix as a cultural adaptation to the multiple forms of inequality that must be negotiated in order to survive and be safe. The mix mediates the contradictions and constraints of gender inequality and its resulting deprivation by providing strategies and tactics for surviving and enduring time in prison. The mix is one source of prison capital. Chief among these is the primacy of respect.

The Primacy of Respect

Respect and respectability are highly valued capital in all prisons (Butler 2008; Fleetwood 2015). Crewe (2009, 248–49) explores the different meanings of respect in his study of a men's prison in England. First, respect "conforms to the Kantian notion that all persons are worthy of respect as a virtue of being human" (248). Respect is a human right in this view. Respect is also a "moral right," in that it entails an obligation to treat others well. Crewe states, "When prisoners talk of 'treating everyone with respect,' they are acknowledging the basic right of others to be taken into due consideration" (249). For Crewe, "prudential respect" is instrumental, as it "conveys an obligation to restrict one's behavior toward someone not based on moral considerations, but rather fear, awe, and other such sentiments. Respect of this sort is offered for self-protection" (249). "Appraisal respect" is based on admiration, regard, esteem, or veneration. Crewe notes that these forms of respect can overlap and serve as the foundation for status hierarchies within the prison community.

Respect in prison is a very serious thing. A woman can be respected for positive and negative reasons. "Standing your ground" when challenged, providing assistance and mutual aid to others, and learning how to work with staff to accomplish tasks are among the ways women earn positive respect. Respect can be earned through aggressive behaviors, including fighting, "holding the bag" (drug dealing), compromising staff into unethical behavior, being a shot caller, and other displays of prison capital. Relatedly, a woman's reputation reflects the kind of respect she earns (and gives) to other prisoners and staff. Disrespect refers to interpersonal behavior that impinges on another woman's status, reputation, sense of self, personal space, or rights of prison citizenship. Staff members are highly sensitive to being disrespected by imprisoned women. Perceived or intended disrespect provides fertile ground for conflict and confrontation throughout the community.

Do Your Own Time

Time is a fundamental concept with multiple meanings in the prison community. Prisoners often remark, "Do your time; don't let your time do you." "Doing time" captures the notion that living in prison is an active, fluid process of prisonization. A woman can do "hard" or "easy" time, depending on how she leverages her capital in the mix. Learning how to do time centers on grasping the ins and outs of the official requirements, responding to the demands of the prison culture, and developing a "program" that structures her prison sentence and her daily life round. Time can refer to the number of years she has to "do," the phase of her sentence (beginning, middle, and end), and prior prison experiences. The type of sentence shapes a woman's definition of "time." A woman serving a determinate sentence, with a specific release date, knows generally when she is going home. In contrast, a woman serving an indeterminate sentence—including a life term—does not have a release date and depends on keeping her prison record "clean" to improve her chances of "getting a date" for parole.

CONCLUSION

In this chapter, we examined the role of prison capital in mediating the gendered and intersectional inequalities of this community. These inequalities among women and with staff are a dynamic expression of the imbalance of power and lack of autonomy that play out in almost every aspect of daily prison life.[7] We then focused on components of prison capital necessary to women's search for safety. Stratification of prison capital among women creates and reinforces vulnerabilities grounded in inequalities. To stay safe, women must find ways to reduce their vulnerabilities to every member of the prison community by developing prison capital as protection. Some women leverage free world capital to build safe lives inside; other women actively seek out ways to improve themselves and their conditions while locked up; still others develop prison

---

7. While we do not explore this, it is clear that hierarchy and inequality shape the lives of staff as well.

capital by becoming big ballers on the yard, claiming their place in the prison world through aggression. But we also now know gender inequality and coercive power relations take a specific form in this world of women, creating troubles and violence between women and with staff.

Building on what we know about the destructive and deleterious prison conditions and women's past experiences with violence and other forms of gendered inequality in their pathways to prison, we contextualize women's safety in terms of conditions, experience, and culture. This context can serve to guide women to not only endure their prison sentence, but develop strategies and tactics to conquer this embedded inequality as they seek to survive and sometimes thrive in a community made up of "contradictions and constraints" in capital and conditions (Kruttschnitt and Gartner 2005). In the next chapter, we examine how deficits in prison capital contribute to conflict and violence and undermine women's search for safety.

5

Inequalities and Contextual Conflict

We now turn our attention to the contextual conflicts embedded in the women's prison community. Their prison lives are shaped by the same intersecting inequalities related to class, race, and gender positions that paved their pathways to prison. In the total institution, imprisoned women confront a physical, social, and cultural space where challenges to safety and vulnerabilities play out in a context bound by inequality.

In our earlier work (Owen 1998; Pollock 2002b), we argued that women's prisons are less violent than men's facilities. Indeed, women's prisons can appear to be less violent when measured by a male standard. A gendered perspective, however, produces a more empirically grounded and nuanced view. While women's prisons do not create and sustain the same forms of violence found in men's facilities, interpersonal conflict and violence in gendered forms exist. As a foreseeable consequence of inequality, this conflict takes two general forms. First, instrumental, or problem-solving, conflict and related violence is born as women struggle to confront inequalities in resources of all kinds. Vulnerabilities related to pathway experiences and intersectional identities contribute to this struggle. Ongoing tensions and conflicts with other women and lack of economic opportunity inside, combined with the demands of prison culture, structure trouble. Women with low stores of capital are further jeopardized by the damage of disadvantage inside prison. The second form of conflict is expressive, based on both the demands of prison cultural norms and intimate partner violence embedded in troubled relationships. We argue that all such conflict and violence is embedded in the inequalities reproduced in the prison community.

THE CONTEXT OF GENDERED VIOLENCE

As Wesely (2006, 306) notes, interrogating women's violence requires an investigation of "more intricate motivations" than that of men. Childhood abuse, a common pathway experience, has been correlated with adult violence perpetrated by women. Differences between those who commit violent and nonviolent crime have been found across multiple factors: women who engage in violence tend to be younger, more likely to be unemployed, less likely to have children, have longer criminal histories, and belong to gangs (Pollock 2014, 36). In documenting the free-world violent experience of young female prisoners, Batchelor, Burman, and Brown (2001) found nuanced and individualized definitions of violence. Certain behaviors or experiences, such as attempted rapes by acquaintances or physical fights with siblings, were not defined as violent, even though they would be so defined by others.

Like the reciprocity implicit in Daly's (1992) "harmed and harming women," using violence is one response to gender inequality and other challenges in women's free world neighborhoods. Chesney-Lind and Irwin (2008) introduce the idea of "horizontal violence" to examine violence among girls. In the context of male privilege, girls and young women direct harm toward other powerless individuals as a consequence of their own experiences with violence in their homes and communities:

> Such a perspective is puzzling, but the reality is that marginalized girls who have been the victims of male power often see that sort of agency [using violence] as the only source of power available to them. Most of the girls regarded their victims as "responsible" for the violence they committed, since they were acting as "sluts," "total bitches" or "assholes." Clearly, where these girls live, "you gotta watch your back because the world is a piece of shit." (Chesney-Lind and Irwin 2008, 119)

The girls and young women studied by Chesney-Lind and Irwin learned that violence was one of the few forms of power available to them in their communities of disadvantage. "Otherizing," blaming, and targeting other young women they see as a threat also contributes to the possibility of violence. Chesney-Lind and Irwin conclude that both violence against women and girls by women, and violence against women and girls by men, "are really the twin products of a system of sexual inequality" that valorizes male violence as agency (2008, 119). For some young women, valor is capital in their search for status.

Kruttschnitt, Gartner, and Ferraro (2002) examine factors contributing to serious interpersonal violence perpetrated by women, detailing the dynamics between personal characteristics and situational factors in a gendered context. They also note that few studies have explored intersectional factors, such as the impact of race and gender on women's violent behavior. In employing violence, some "women perceive their severe aggression as self-defense" (2002, 538). Other motivations for violence, they found, are protection of economic well-being, approval of violence within peer groups, and reacting to violence in interpersonal relationships. In fact, they suggest, the victim-offender relationship should be a primary focus of research "because the vast majority of women's involvement in acts of serious interpersonal violence takes place within an intimate relationship" (537). Male acts of lethal violence against women, they find, "may not simply be a result of a domestic argument but rather they reflect a male's calculated plan to control the behavior of a female" (539). Kruttschnitt, Gartner, and Ferraro assert that increased attention to gender inequality and gender status differentials is needed to better understand violence committed by women (544), arguing that "our knowledge about the situational nature of women's encounters with violence is particularly impoverished" (552).

Renzetti (1992) also explores the nature of violence in same-sex intimate relationships. High levels of didactic attachment and commitment, with an emphasis on monogamy and an interdependence or fusion of identity, can facilitate same-sex intimate violence, particularly among those without family or social support systems. Renzetti identified factors that facilitate, but not necessarily cause, partner abuse among lesbians, such as jealousy and distrust, imbalance of power, and substance abuse.

Van Dieten, Jones, and Randon (2014, 4) explore additional risk factors associated with female-initiated violence. In addition to demographic and environmental factors, they point to family history (e.g., witnessing violence in the home, parental substance abuse, mental illness, and incarceration); relationship conflict (such as high levels of discord, little relationship satisfaction, and mutual violence); and a range of psychological, emotional, and behavioral factors. Other motivational factors are self-defense, an inability to manage the expression of negative emotions, the desire to control, jealousy, and assuming a tough guise. Van Dieten, Jones, and Randon also examine additional motives for "proactive" violence: anger or frustration, jealousy, or attempting physical harm (2014, 11). These proactive factors, in our view, represent agency and choice, a key part of pathway theory. Again, we believe women do make choices about their behavior and actions, but choice is very often constrained and narrowed by structural and cumulative disadvantage in their communities and experience.

The complex context of women's violence has been considered by Wesely (2006). She, too, locates cumulative victimization in the context of cumulative disadvantage:

> The lived experiences of cumulative victimization [are] characterized by abuse and violence, economic vulnerability, gender inequality, loss and dislocation, degradation and social exclusion. This context severely constrains opportunities and choices available to the women in terms of livelihood, safety, coping and survival. The women engage in violence as a way of resisting and responding to their cumulative victimization, and this violence has multiple meanings and is manifested in different ways. (303)

Wesely further sees the influence of social exclusion and disadvantage as limiting life choices and shaping coping and survival strategies, which may include violence (304). Violence, in this view, is a response to structural and individualized disadvantage. She describes the multiple ways such cumulative disadvantage and the "accumulation of victimization they experienced . . . set them up for social, emotional, and behavioral deficits" (325).

In exploring women's use of violence, Kubiak, Kim, and Bybee (2013) compared differences between women who were incarcerated for assaultive offenses in an isolated instance to those who had a patterned use of violence. They measured levels of expressive and instrumental anger, impulsivity, and other risks to determine these differences. Levels of trauma, mental health, and substance abuse are linked to differences in women's use of violence. Women in the patterned use of violence group scored the most problematic on most measures. Babcock, Miller, and Siard (2003) also found differences between women who were involved with intimate partner violence and those who engaged in violence for more instrumental purposes. Makarios (2007) reminds us to consider the role of race in disentangling these patterns of gendered violence among intimates. McKenry et al. (2006) use disempowerment theory to explain lesbian and other same-sex partner violence, an approach similar to our emotional capital perspective.

While numerous studies make the connection between violence and victimization (Belknap 2015), we concur with Kruttschnitt and Carbone-

Lopez (2006), who argue that "essentializing" women's past victimization as the only explanation for women's use of violence is incomplete, deflecting our attention from other explanations. Our analysis parallels this reasoning: causes of violence in women's prison cannot be explained solely by individual trauma histories. We, too, argue for a broader contextual and structural explanation.

Causes of violence in women's prison have also been examined. Individual and environmental effects on conflict among women prisoners were studied by Steiner and Wooldredge (2009). While some factors were found to predict misconduct for both imprisoned women and men, mental health status, abuse history, and relationship status were more significant factors among women. In a more recent study, Wooldredge and Steiner (2016) explore the need for a "gender-specific explanation" of prisoner violence and victimization. The differences in carceral experiences among women and men, they suggest, may translate into different structural processes underlying victimization risk during confinement (Wooldredge and Steiner 2016, 210). They found comparable levels of assault victimization for women and men, except in terms of theft, as women were many times more likely than men to be victims of theft. Wooldredge and Steiner (2016, 232) "favor the idea that the risk of inmate victimization is gendered (to some degree)." Lahm (2015), too, found that a combination of gendered pre-prison and in-prison factors predicted both violent and nonviolent victimization in women's prisons. Race, a significant predictor for violence in men's prisons, was less significant in women's facilities (Carbone-Lopez and Kruttschnitt 2003). They, like Owen (1998), found "far less self-segregation" (232) based on prisoners' race in women's facilities.

These perspectives on women's use of violence confirm our analyses. Gendered risks for victimization are replicated inside, with the potential for violence embedded in the intersectional inequalities of the contemporary prison. Violence in prison can be contextualized in terms of cumulative disadvantage, aggravated by constrained choice. It can also be seen as one form of prison capital. This potential for violence can escalate in everyday interactions, as set forth by the escalation model.

The Escalation Model

In prison, violence can escalate from "anything and everything," as described in the escalation model proposed by Edgar and Martin (2003; see also Edgar, O'Donnell, and Martin 2003). The dynamics of interactions that lead to violence in women's and men's prison, they found, resulted from an interactive process between two prisoners and incorporates internal motivations and interpretations of the event. Edgar and Martin found fights, assaults, and other disputes can be analyzed in terms of the following variables: structural setting, interests, catalysts, interpretations, purposes, and power relations between prisoners. Interpretation by the participants is critical in determining if a conflict will result in physical violence.

More specifically, Edgar and Martin (2003) found that elements of the prison social structure created the potential for violence, including material deprivations, competition for scarce resources, restrictions on movement that inhibit one's ability to avoid other prisoners, and lack of privacy. Prison culture and its norms regarding respect and "not backing down" made additional contributions. Among women, Edgar and Martin found about half of the conflicts involved material interests, such as drugs, personal possessions, games, food, tobacco, and phone cards. In all incidents, nonmaterial interests, such as self-respect, honor, fairness, loyalty, personal safety, and privacy, underscore all violent exchanges (Edgar and Martin 2003, v). Multiple elements of prison capital are combined in this model. In our analysis, the everyday tensions and conflicts in this closed community of gendered inequality can spark a chain of events that escalates into violence.

Women's Perspectives on Trouble, Conflict, and Violence

When asked about the roots of violence in their prison community, women and staff agreed that jealousy, debts, and disrespect were the major catalysts. Combining pathway experiences with violence and the deleterious conditions of this closed community, these explanations for violence are grounded in inequality in prison capital with the potential for escalation. Troubles in interpersonal relationships replicate pathway experiences of violence and victimization, feelings of being trapped, jealousy, and other consequences of fragile emotional capital. Debts and other conflicts related to inequality in economic capital contribute to the use of violence. Contested cultural demands of the prison norms and values, particularly in terms of respect, also spark violence. This view is bounded by the cultural strictures to "do your own time" and "take care of business." McGuire (2011), building on Owen's concept of the mix, found that violations of the inmate code were a primary source of violence among women. As we also found, snitching, gossiping, commenting on others' time, and failing to maintain standards of cleanliness are "unacceptable behaviors that are likely to be sanctioned violently by other female inmates" (McGuire 2011, 145). Below we explore specific connections between individualized vulnerabilities and prison capital aid women's search for safety.

INDIVIDUALIZED VULNERABILITIES

While many explanations for prison violence focus on individual characteristics, such factors cannot be understood apart from the prison community context of inequality and prison capital. Those more likely to be targets of prisoner-prisoner aggression and vulnerable to staff misconduct were said to be "naive," to "act like a victim," or to "put yourself in that situation." These seemingly discrete and individual factors are, in our view, the consequence of lower stores of prison capital.

Women noted the duality of vulnerability. For example, age (young or old) was said to be related to both victimization and victimizing, again mirroring the duality of harmed and harming women (Daly 1992, 1994). We submit that this duality is mediated by all forms of capital. Any vulnerability to violence can be aggravated or diminished by prison capital. Below we delve into some of these individual vulnerabilities and how such vulnerabilities and risk are outcomes arbitrated by capital and culture.

Age

Age is one example of the dualities mediated by capital. Some women told us that the younger prisoners are more violent; others felt that younger prisoners are more vulnerable. Sally described how being young, especially of slight build, contributes to vulnerability.

> She is slighter and she is smaller and she is attractive. She is more of the physical type that they might try to bully. In the county jail, I had a cellmate who had been in prison. She was very little and she was very petite and she was here for a violent crime. So she was in our two-man cell and her bunkie tried to force herself on her.

In contrast, we also heard that younger women were more violent, sometimes victimizing older women. Steffi said:

> It is the maturity level, mental maturity. A lot of the women are still children when they come in here. They are women physically, but they are still

children in here [points to her head]. Common sense, goals, direction? They don't have any. They are just worried about music or movies instead of setting a life direction. What does this person have to offer? They don't know who they are. They are lost out there. Life is obscured with drugs and alcohol. They have no clear view. In here, some clean up, some see, but some are stuck in a time warp.

Maturity can be understood in the context of capital and community. Younger prisoners may feel the need to establish a violent reputation as a form of protective coloring in the uncertain world of the prison or jail. The following conversation examines the connection between youngsters and violence.

> *Beatrice:* The violence is here more because we now have the youngsters. Youngsters with a long time to do and no cares. They have no concept of what it is like to do a long-time term.
>
> *Rue:* A lot of youngsters who are coming in with a lot of time. They are pretty pissed off at the world out there. If you are coming in here with fifteen years or whatever, you have your whole life ahead of you and that is hard. It puts a chip on their shoulder.
>
> *Estella:* You have got this new breed that are just ruthless.
>
> *Dottie:* I, too, have seen a lot especially with the youngsters coming in with double life sentences and they have a mentality of nothing to lose. They are at a time when they will not listen to you.

A correctional officer agreed with this assessment: "The younger inmates are more prone to violence. I don't know if it is the makeup of the crowd or just youth. The combination of a lack of education with substance abuse could be a cause." When "youngsters" engage in more frequent or severe violence, custody staff may respond with force, accelerating tension and fears for all women who observe such actions. Nikki described this process.

> The youngsters fight and get sprayed [with pepper spray]. Everyone is more macho now. It is a whole buildup of attitudes. My coworker [another prisoner] got sprayed the other day when it wasn't necessary. Things got out of hand and he [the CO] decided to spray everyone in the building.

On the harmed side of the duality, older women were said to be especially vulnerable because of physical infirmities. On the harming side of the duality, we were told that some older women "were the ones to watch out for," indicating that age was not always a defining feature of vulnerability. We suggest that "Original Gangsters," or old-timers who have been in the game a long time, through their street life or by doing so much time, accrue forms of capital to rise through the prison hierarchy. Potentials for victimization, then, may be less influenced by age than by how one learns to behave in a way that avoids risky situations and risky relationships. Although age was mentioned as a vulnerability, it seemed to be less important than an individual woman's behavior and stock of prison social and cultural capital, as Santha suggests:

> Vulnerability is not an issue with age. It is who you associate with. If you associate with people that are like you in your same age group, you can be fine. I wouldn't limit [vulnerability] to older women. I would limit it to a certain sense of attitude of being vulnerable that streetwise women can pick up on.

Physical and Mental Health Vulnerabilities

While some mentioned the vulnerabilities of those with physical disabilities, the majority of the comments focused on the duality of vulnerabilities bound by mental health concerns. One staff person described a consequence of this vulnerability: "Some inmates have a lower mental health. They [aggressors] see that right away and the experienced ones want their canteen. We see that all the time." Just as age represented a duality of vulnerability and aggression, this same complication can be applied to women with mental illnesses or mental disabilities. That is, while some women suggested that those with mental health challenges may be hurt, the mentally ill are also likely to be violent, as expressed here by Lupe: "[The mentally ill] can be spontaneous. This one inmate got up in the dayroom to get something to drink. The next thing you know she is beating up an inmate based on something that happened a year ago." A custody staff member described these dynamics:

> I work with the psychologically and physically impaired. They have the same issues—girlfriends, debt payment, loans, commissary. They don't have the finesse, though. All weapons are of opportunity or convenience. Most of them [are more vulnerable than general population]. Not all of them, but most of them, I would say one-third are extremely street smart. They know how to carry themselves and manipulate. They prey on the others due to lack of education, and learning and language barriers. I'm getting more of those.

This finesse, we suggest, is cultural capital.

Women with mental illnesses can also be "aggressors" rather than victims, as described by Sally:

> They go nuts. They are crazy. They need to be in a special unit. They do something crazy to people. I had a roommate who is crazy and who is nuts.

She fought with my roommate one day and she is just nuts. They will whip some ass, they have this strength. I don't know where they get it from. They are just crazy bitches. Like the retarded ones, they have this strength. Like the women who are mothers, they have this strength to care for their kids.

Tamara described her response to an unprovoked assault: "A [mentally ill] woman came up to me and she smacked me in the face with a cup and I got a big old black eye. I tried to close the door and [staff] didn't come for me, so I will be real [and admit] I beat the shit out of her." Women with mental health issues are as likely to hurt themselves as well as others. Anya said that her self-destructive behavior of cutting and bleeding in her cell caused her roommates and staff members to be antagonistic toward her. Even though she said she "cleaned all the blood up with bleach," her roommates were hostile to her and wanted her out of the room. She also reported, disturbingly, that a staff person looked at her wounded arms and said, "You are disgusting. Get out of my sight," ignoring her obvious need for medical and psychiatric help. This remark was one of the stories that gave us pause.

While "doing your own time" may constrain intervention in other women's conflict, some can be moved to protect a vulnerable woman from exploitation by others. Cersei said, "If someone does try to mess with [the mentally challenged], then the others would just tell her to leave her alone." She described how she felt compelled to respond, even knowing it would leave her vulnerable to retaliation:

The fight I had was really behind another girl. She is really [mentally] slow. She don't think [giving oral sex] was not cool because she's slow. So I told her, "You can't be doing that." These older women have her in a cubicle. Having her doing oral sex on them. She'd do one, then another would say, "Do my friend." Then this one and then this one. And I said [to the dominant woman], "What do you want to do her like that for?" And then she went after me with the lock.

Language and Cultural Vulnerabilities

Vulnerabilities are compounded for women who are non-English speakers. A custody staff person remarked, "If you have no way to communicate, you can't ask for help. There is also no way to decide what their mental abilities are." Prisoners often serve as translators for non-English speakers. Tamika told us, "Officers need to speak both Spanish and English. I speak both, and when I tell the officer about an inmate's problem, [if] the officer doesn't like me [he] asks me, 'Why are you meddling?'" It may be that non-English speakers have diminished capital outside their cultural or language groups.

Prior Victimization and "Acting Like a Victim"

The link between past and present victimization is critical in creating vulnerabilities, as we explored in chapter 4. As Stassi said, "If you have been victimized, you present an aura that allows you to be victimized again, and bullies look for it." "Acting like victims" meant that women who acted afraid and passive appeared to be easy targets for economic and/or sexual exploitation by more aggressive women. Women who did not stand up to threats were likely to continue to be victimized. Yesenia explained, "Some people walk around with 'victim' blinking on their head." Shaina described a potential victim as one who is "walking down the sidewalk with the head down and terrorized inside. You can smell fear here; you can smell it, and you just know." Lorrae observed the cyclical nature of being exploited in the correctional environment: "Once you get punked, then you get punked every time you turn around. You gonna get your canteen taken. She is going to take it." A "typical victim" was one who was timid or showed her fear to others: "A victim is one that's real quiet and don't take any action. They [other female inmates] can tell you're afraid. Stand your ground, and nobody will mess with you."

"Rabbits"

In some prisons, a weak woman is known as a "rabbit," as illustrated in this exchange among correctional staff.

Officer Smith: Rabbits are weaker. They are not as intelligent. They are just terrified, which is a weakness.

Officer Jones: They are so desperate for acceptance so they are more willing to pay the price for the sexual favor or what have you, and they want to get under the wing of someone who is appealing to their weakness.

Officer Baker: They are stuck in the victim role. They are blaming everybody else and are big drama queens.

Officer Smith: Rabbits. Easy to spot. The inmates tend to talk in groups and say, "Oh, look at this one. She will last like five minutes." You see the body language: chin up is confident, and chin up high if you are challenging. If you are sitting like this [leans back with hands crossed] this is a shot-caller stance. Weakness is very bad in this environment and assertion of power is always incremental.

Officer Jones: I think there are less rabbits and more predators. More than half are neither.

Officer Baker: I would go less predators like 5 percent and more rabbits. Predators could have more than one rabbit. Rabbits: 25 percent. Seventy-five percent are in between.

Sondra added this observation: "There are three types of people. There are victims, victimizers, or observers. You don't choose, it is just your personality. I fall into the observer category and that keeps me out of danger."

Race

Racial oppression in the free world finds full expression in the prison. Isaac, Lockhart, and Williams (2014) examine violence against imprisoned African American women from a structural perspective. Paralleling our analysis, they argue that "the inequitable distribution of power, culture of degradation, imposed isolation, and other social conditions created by the prison environment combine to create conditions of violence" (134). Isaac, Lockhart, and Williams note the persistence of racial discrimination against black women throughout the criminal justice process and how this dynamic is complicated by black staff in positions of authority (132).

Racial tension is less definitive in women's prisons (Carbone-Lopez and Kruttschnitt 2003; Kruttschnitt 1981; Owen 1998; Wooldredge and Steiner 2016). There were few mentions of racial and ethnic conflict in our conversations. Since our focus groups were almost always composed of mixed races, like most activities in women's prisons, we do recognize the possibility that the sensitivities surrounding race may have dampened discussion. While the women's prison community is not shaped by the racial self-segregation of the male prison experience, this does not mean conflicts over race and ethnicity disappear entirely. Teresa suggested the "guidelines" for racial affiliations are different for women and men: "I am aware of a black gang thing. I ran into it yesterday with some of the behavior that they think is big and bad. But we don't hear about the BGF [Black Guerilla Family] and all that. Women's affiliations are different. Their guidelines are different." Lenora, whom we interviewed in jail, noted, "I came from a very, very racial town. A lot of fights that was there [in the jail] was behind the color of someone's skin. That was in 2002. A lot of the women's state of mind was, 'if you weren't white, you weren't right.' I saw a lot of violence against offenders because of the color of their skin."

Sandia, a woman of color, illustrates the dynamics of racial conflicts.

> One fight I got into was with this white girl. At first, we were kind of close. We shared. She was a Featherwood; you know, part of the Aryan circle. She explained to me they weren't prejudiced; they were just down for themselves. Down for their people, not against any certain race. I can understand being down for your color because I am. We never really talked about it. One day these other Aryans moved in. I was going to do her hair, braid her hair, and she wanted to pay, but I said no. This one time she got crunk on me because I was going to do [braid] another girl's hair first. She started screaming. I jumped up and got in her face. She said I was a black nigger and she did not want me to touch her hair. I punched her in the mouth. She was bigger than me. They said I was the aggressor.

As a subtext, racial and ethnic issues have some influence over women's interaction in the prison community. Kruttschnitt and Gartner (2005) tie racial and ethnic identity to forms of cultural adaptation in the prison, suggesting women of color are more likely to adopt the convict or isolate strategy for doing time. In a secondary analysis of our NIC survey data, Leahy (2014) examined the impact of race on women's perceptions of safety and problems in our nonrandom sample. Just under a third of the women completing our survey identified themselves as black. This subsample of black women indicated greater concerns about problems in their housing unit than did nonblack women who participated in our survey. They reported problems with debts and theft at somewhat higher rates than other women; and a larger number perceived problems with sexual aggression from other prisoners and even greater concerns about physical violence and aggression. The most significant difference between the two groups was in their treatment by the staff: black women were much more likely than other women to report problems of all kinds with staff.

By every measure, racial discrimination and other intersectional inequities are reproduced in the prison community. As the insights of the intersectional approach teach us, the impact of race and ethnicity is mediated by other factors, including stocks of prison capital.

Dynamic Gender Identity

Women who express a more fluid or nonheterosexual gender identity are particularly vulnerable to the harms of imprisonment, as argued here:

Jails are traumatizing and often dangerous places, especially for lesbian, gay, bisexual, and transgender people, and anyone who is gender nonconforming. In a country that incarcerates more of its people than any other in the world, LGBT people are more likely to end up behind bars, and more likely to face abuse behind bars. Being LGBT in a U.S. jail or prison often means daily humiliation, physical and sexual abuse, and fearing it will get worse if you complain. (Marksamer and Tobin 2015, 2)

Marksamer and Tobin (2015) and Smith and Yurussi (2009, 2015) detail the additional disadvantage faced by non-gender-conforming prisoners, offering policy guidelines for improving the safety of LGBT prisoners. The compelling evidence of increased vulnerabilities among LGBT individuals demonstrates the intersectional impact of sexual orientation, gender expression, and gender identity. LGBT people come into contact with a criminal justice system that does not accommodate their identities, often discriminating against them and exposing them to further risk inside prison and jail. LGBT persons are often poor, another intersectional inequality propelling them into prison at higher rates, as described by Marksamer and Tobin:

According to the National Transgender Discrimination Survey, 16% of transgender adults have been in a prison or jail for any reason. This compares with 2.7% of all adults who have ever been in prison, and 10.2% of all adults who have ever been under any kind of criminal justice supervision, including probation. Transgender people, especially poor people and people of color, report facing disrespect, harassment, discriminatory arrests, and physical and sexual assault by police at very high rates. (2015, 3)

Such cumulative vulnerabilities continue to shape their lives inside. Prisoners who present a nonheterosexual identity are victimized at higher rates than other prisoners (Beck, Harrison, and Guerino 2010; Beck et al. 2013). Marksamer and Tobin (2015, 3) find that LGBT prisoners face other forms of mistreatment behind bars. Humiliation and degradation from staff and prisoners is common. When victimized, they may be blamed by staff for their own victimization, believing they are "flaunting themselves," resulting in staff refusing to take grievances or reports of abuse seriously. As we have argued, operational practices undermine safety by not addressing all prisoners' needs and failing to protect all categories of prisoners. Alternative or fluidly gendered individuals are additionally disadvantaged by such practices as classification systems; housing assignments; requirements for traditional gendered clothing, makeup, or grooming items; and lack of appropriate treatment and services. In some systems, individuals are punished when they attempt to express gender identity contrary to the traditional female/male binary. The lack of medical and mental health services for this population is particularly harmful (Smith and Yarussi 2009, 2015).

As they do their time, women can express fluidity in gender identity, gender expression, and sexual orientation (Keys 2002). Some may come to prison having adopted a male identity, living their lives on the street and in prison as more male than female. Others, known as transformers (Owen 1998), take on transient aspects of a male-based role and modify their identities as they serve their time. Taking on a male-oriented identity in itself is not a marker for gendered violence between women prisoners. Our data on interpersonal conflict provide little description of the "maleness" or "femaleness" of those involved. We did not find that nonconforming identity or expression was a critical area of discrimination among the women, although it was said to be common among staff. While some of the women who spoke with us expressed disdain for women who were "gay for the stay," we did not find consistent evidence of higher levels of hostility to those with non-normative gender or sexual expression.

As we conclude this section on individual vulnerabilities, let us restate out premise: conflict and violence are a clear consequence of inequality within the prison. Violence in women's prisons occurs in a community context fueled by a combination of pathway experiences, living conditions inside, prison culture, and constrained choice. Those without the protection of any form of prison capital can be more vulnerable to prison violence. We now examine forms of gendered violence among women in this community.

GENDERED VIOLENCE IN A COMMUNITY CONTEXT

We found several types of gendered violence in the prison community: verbal conflict, economic exploitation, physical violence, and sexual violence. Given what we know about the escalation of violence, small conflicts can spiral into serious harm in the toxicity of prison conditions and prison culture.

Verbal Conflict

Verbal conflict over "anything and everything" was the most commonly reported form in our interviews. Verbal arguments can be placed in five general categories: (1) those grounded in the everyday tensions of living in close, crowded, and often uncomfortable surroundings; (2) those derived from other forms of conflict, such as gossip, debts, "room politics," or "disrespect"; (3) ongoing conflict in troubled relationships; (4) those based on establishing or confirming a reputation as "one not to be messed with" or protective posturing as a way of "standing up" or "pushing back" to a perceived threat; and (5) those that were an indirect means to another end. This last category can be seen as instrumental and includes "dry-snitching" (drawing unwanted staff attention without actually informing) as a means to obtain a desired outcome.

Sometimes the descriptions seemed stereotypical, as verbal arguments were often described by prisoners and staff as an example of the inability of women to "get along" or as related to the "female" nature. Unlike conflicts in men's prisons, where verbal arguments often lead to physical violence, most verbal fights remained unpleasant situational skirmishes. Threats of physical violence, however, often accompanied other forms of verbal intimidation, as in the case of "bullying" in order to control the room. Every argument has the potential to escalate into a more serious form of violence.

Most prisoners and staff routinely ignore this quotidian verbal conflict. These frequent arguments are seen as normal because, as many women said, "It is an everyday thing around here." This was particularly true of relationship-based arguments and those in which women were trying to "prove a point." Such verbal conflict was very often referred to as "drama," another stereotypical term that reduces women's experience to their "emotionality" and their presumed need to be involved in dramatic relationships. This term, we suggest, minimizes women's real concerns about their safety inside and undermines the ability to report their fears to staff, further isolating the vulnerable and undermining safety.

Although described as rampant in every focus group, we decided to exclude measurement of more generalized forms of verbal conflict in the NIC survey items as such conflict can be seen as a constant. Instead, the NIC survey asked about arguments as they are linked to the other forms of conflict and violence, such as debts and physical threats. In a separate question, just over 40 percent of women said verbal threats and pressure regarding theft was a concern. Verbal threats of physical violence were said to be a medium to very big problem for about 57 percent of the women surveyed. Tables 1 and 3 in appendix 2 displays these details.

Economic Exploitation

Economic exploitation includes stealing, "borrowing" without intent to return, or boldly commandeering a possession in direct confrontation. Some women avoid conflict by "buying their way out" of trouble, giving in to demands for goods or property. Extortion of women who were more materially advantaged and vulnerable can occur either through demands or through exploitative personal relationships. Verbal actions such as "begging," "sweet-talking," "pressuring," and "intimidating" another woman to give up her belongings, commissary purchases, or packages were frequently mentioned in our interviews.

Like verbal conflict, economic conflict has the potential for escalation to more serious forms of violence. Retaliation for theft, reacting to extortion, or settling debts can lead to verbal threats and physical violence. When verbal arguments arise over economic conflict, about half the women completing the NIC survey said physical fights over debts or theft were a medium to very big problem in their housing units. In contrast, the remaining half indicated that the use of threats, pressure, or physical force to steal from other women was not problematic. Appendix 2, table 1, provides more detail on the NIC survey findings regarding fights and debts.

Being "indigent," or without any other prison capital, undermines a woman's search for safety. In this stratified community, women without a way to provide for themselves can be seen as potential economic aggressors. Women who have a too visible means of support and "shop" either conspicuously or carelessly, those who "brag about how much money they have on the books," or those who are "well taken care of" by their families or others outside the prison can be targeted for economic exploitation. "Trying to buy friends" and "not keeping your mouth shut" can increase the potential of exploitation of well-resourced women. Stacy provided an example of this exploitation: "The first-timers do not know *not* to tell that she is getting boxes [packages from home]. People who have nothing take advantage of that. The staff are pretty good about protecting this type of person." While women can certainly respond with retributional violence, such reprisals appear to be less violent than in men's prisons.

Fraud and con games are other ways of getting desired goods and services in this world of scarcity. As Sally described, "But you know there's lots of criminals here and, well, you got people who want what you have, and con you out of it. Then that brings violence." The extortion process can be subtle and take time, as suggested by Aim.

> Of course, it's not like, "Give me that, or I'm going to beat you up." It's more like you befriend someone because they have money. Everyone is going to test to see [how she responds]. Sometimes you can get their whole [amount of commissary] this way.

Natty described one such theft and extortion.

> You have someone who says, "Ooh, I'd like to see that ring." And you take it off. You take it off, and then they say that it's theirs. You are jacked. They punk you for your wedding ring, your gold, your jewelry. "Punk, take off your ring. I like it." You take it off and now it is mine.

A custody staff member described a situation involving extortion.

> Her deal was that she was very masculine. She had one particular girlfriend, a feminine girl. When new inmates came in, they did not know who was coupled with who. The girlfriend would buddy up to the new girl and they would become a couple. She would get commissary from the new girl, you know, trafficking and trading. As soon as the new girl was under her control, she would bring the masculine friend in. They both would extort her for commissary and threaten her with violence.

Inequality within prison provides the context for women to "go for what they know," pressuring and extorting women of means or those who do not "push back." In any world of constrained choice, relative deprivation compromises moral behavior, as a study of middle-class decision making and financial deprivation suggests (Sharma et al. 2013). Prisoners secure in their standing may advise a targeted woman to "handle herself" by meeting any potential exploitation by pushing back with threats or actual physical resistance, or by condemning this behavior in an attempt to stop it, or, in very rare cases, to use force. Reactions are tempered by the depth of prison capital held by all parties, the nature of their relationships, and their standing in this community.

Others are clearly exploiters who target "rich" women for intimidation, coaxing or coercing them to enter into relationships to gain access to their commissary. Sometimes extortion fails, as a staff participant observed.

> One old lady, this was her first time in. They tried it [extortion] with her, but it did not work. They got tired of it not working, so the masculine went into another housing unit, got her in the shower, got a hold of her, and said, "You are giving me commissary, bitch!" And the lady said, "No, I'm not. My money is my money and I don't believe in the gay lifestyle." She had a lot of

guts. They had her pinned up against the wall, but the other offenders came in and surrounded them to protect the older offender.

The combination of pushing back against exploitation and support from other prisoners extinguishes exploitative attempts as women in her social network "school her" in the ways of the prison and the importance of "pushing back" against all threats.

Debt

Debt brings trouble. Those without economic capital can run up debts as a result of nonpayment for goods and services such as braiding hair, cleaning a room, getting ice, doing laundry, or getting commissary items on informal prison credit. Women also borrow from others with more capital. A small number of women act as bankers. Serious debt over contraband such as tobacco and drugs is a highly volatile circumstance and closely connected to violent "get backs." Cyndia illustrated the risk of debt: "It [a fight] was supposed to be over $4. This girl got hurt bad over that much."

Custody and noncustody staff identified debts and theft as one of the most common reasons for violence. One staff member said, "Drug debts and tobacco debts are driving inmates crazy right now. Tobacco is easy to get in here—the availability varies. It is all about getting what they can get when they can get it." Debts quickly become serious because of perceived disrespect and the swift accumulation of interest in the doubling economy of the prison. Sami observed, "If an inmate can't pay when it is due, debt doubles—there is interest or penalties. There is a domino effect. One debt starts another debt." Those who accumulate debt "put themselves in that situation" and, once again, are viewed as responsible for their own troubles. There was little sympathy among women when describing punishments, such as punches or kicks, experienced by some debtors.

Gangs

In men's prisons, gangs are frequently mentioned as a primary source of prison violence. In our study, we received mixed reports about the contribution of gangs to the potential for violence and conflict. Mo saw individual relationships as more important than gang influences.

> I think that women are different than men because men are, like, "We belong to this gang so we are not going to associate with you." But I may belong to

this gang and you may belong to this gang, but if I get angry with you, then I'm angry with *you* [not your gang].

In the NIC survey data, about 30 percent indicated gang-related violence was a problem in their housing units. (See appendix 2, table 3, for more details.) However, the aggressive behavior of youngsters was frequently related to gang activity, with staff more likely to mention gangs as a cause of violence. One correctional officer explained:

> They might not come in with a gang affiliation. Or they might have one and they might not have exercised that here yet. It is not as bad as in the male institution, but now they come in with the swagger, they shave their heads and look and act like men.

Another officer stated:

> Now the younger women have stronger gang ties. They may not be as organized or go under the title of gang, but they are out there. There are some groups that have friction between themselves or with other inmates [from a specific region]. There are all-female gangs now. They have to keep their mouths shut about being in a gang so that they can successfully transport information. If we know, we watch them, so they don't hurt us, but there is a higher percentage than we think.

Women offered similar observations.

> *Jenni:* They [gang members] are a danger to each other. The alcohol, the gangs, if we don't put ourselves into those behaviors, we are pretty safe here from it.

> *Krissy:* There is a new breed of youngster. They are gangbanging. If we [long-termer inmates] get in a fight, we quit because we make our point or we get tired because we are old. With the kids, they will "get them down and keep them down." With us, it was one on one. Now it is a bunch of them.

> *Allison:* A lot of youngsters are gangbangers. They act all bad. There are a lot in gangs on the street and they come in here with the same attitude. Older ones are more laid back. You don't see it as much, not out in the open, not trying to prove a point. Half the time I don't know the older ones who are like that. You can tell the younger ones by the way they carry themselves.

Suzanne, an older lifer, suggests those in gangs were somewhat more vulnerable to violence because of their gang membership:

> One of my roommates was a gang member from the time she was a very young girl. This is the only instance I have observed this. Young gang members are very vulnerable to violence among themselves. I think that gangs are

strikingly similar to cults. I would like to see more education about these groups because these women don't know what the hell they are in. There are women who are sixty years old that are still active gang members and it is one of the most dangerous things in this prison. I didn't understand the danger to her or danger to others till I had this interaction with the younger girl I just mentioned.

Staff and prisoners agreed that gang affiliation was often related to free world male partners or family members, as suggested by one noncustody staff member:

Usually, they are not in gangs themselves, it is their boyfriends or brothers that are in the gang. But as far as gang violence, I don't see the paperwork for it. I don't see the gang violence here. They don't segregate based on prison gangs here.

Other staff members suggested that "territory" and "where they are from" had a greater influence than gang membership on potential conflict. The term "crew" was also said to be more appropriate than "gang" when discussing women's group affiliation. Irwin's (2005) notion of "cliques and tips" captures these loose affiliations.

"Being Messy"

Like Einat and Chen (2012a) and McGuire (2011), we found that gossip and "running your mouth" was a significant source of conflict. Often seen as a form of disrespect, "being messy" involves gossiping, telling stories about others, and generally playing "he said, she said." Being messy can also be a form of violating the "mind your own business" normative construct, creating the potential for violence. As Stephanie said:

Back on that unit, people would say, "You're in my business," and cut her. Or somebody sets you up and someone says you did it. And you end up having a scar behind it [as an injury] but you didn't do it [were not messy]. But you're in the mix and it happens.

Often information exchange leading to violence is based on hearsay or may be intentionally designed to cause trouble. "Being messy" is often a precursor to physical fights, escalating from a verbal to a physical exchange. Yolanda defined messiness as "what normally instigates things in prison is 'he say, she say' things. It's people getting into each other's business." In another prison, Lia elaborated the power of speech in this world:

That is going to get her pissed off and start a big ol' fight. It's not safe at all to tell people's business. They should not go around saying stuff and I know they do it. They do it to get shit started.

Officers and other staff can be messy when they talk or gossip about prisoners with other women, sparking conflict among them. Prisoners claim this staff-instigated messiness is intentional, and is done for the amusement of staff. Violating confidentiality through staff messiness undermines women's safety and trust in the officers' ability to protect them. As Chandra suggested, staff contribute to the "he said, she said" of prison life: "These officers are real messy. If you say something about the other offender they will go to the other offender and say, 'Hey, so-and-so said . . .' That is unprofessional." This "telling" can have violent repercussions, as Dawn observed: "It is not only the prisoners making the violence; it is also the staff. They put us in the crosses. Like, if you go to a staff, and tell them [what happened], someone is going to beat me up and all."

Snitching

Prisons run on information. Providing information about other prisoners to the staff, known variously as "ratting," informing, or "sending a kite," is always considered disreputable, no matter the motivation. Among prisoners, conveying information about another woman, particularly when reporting violations of prison norms, relational behavior, or any other form of "telling," is disrespectful and messy. "Ratting" and informing are serious transgressions in all prisons, particularly when such information results in trouble. The language in the women's prison, however, is slightly less harsh. Women will say, "Don't tell on anyone" or "Don't be a tattletale," in addition to the serious charge of "being a rat." A male staff member from a medium-sized prison remarked on the gendered nature of snitching, "Women come running up and tell you that someone is getting into a fight. The men don't do this. The women tattle on each other and I'm not used to this."

Relative to men's prisons, where snitching can provoke a lethal reaction, the penalties against snitching in women's prisons are generally less severe. Reactions vary from simple disdain to public shaming to a violent "tune-up." Such reactions are conditioned by stocks of prison capital; those with high status and respect, strong reputations, and material prosperity may be able to avoid subcultural sanctions.

Within the dynamics of prison capital, punishments for snitching vary according to one's attachment to the code and how it plays out in different prison neighborhoods. For women who identify as convicts, snitching can result in physical reprisal. Charli described her reaction to snitching: "I fought them because they snitched on me in county jail. I hate snitches—people telling your business. Just the first opportunity I had to get to them, I would." Then, in answer to a question about whether she fought in front of officers, she said, "Sure, why wait? What can they do to me? They [COs] threw me against the wall. It does not matter what I do or don't do. I did not care. I was coming to prison anyway."

This rule against telling decreases the likelihood women would come forward if they saw a fight or knew someone was going to get assaulted. This norm, combined with being "too ashamed to report" (Weiss 2010), can inhibit women from seeking help when threatened by circumstance, other prisoners, or staff. Women are divided in their opinions about the utility of staff intervention in their troubles. Some women said they would never snitch on another under any circumstances. Others took the view that only serious injury would warrant staff intervention. Still others expected staff to protect the women in their charge. Staff members often shared this proscription against snitching. Taneka remarked:

> After you are done [fighting or arguing], they [staff] would pull in the inmate you are complaining about and say, "Oh, so-and-so is snitching on you." Right there now, you are in the crosses and are about to get beat up. This is the violence.

Sandy had endured an abusive relationship with another prisoner and explained her dilemma.

> It is not because you are signing up for the abuse, but you are trapped. I was just in a situation like that [with another prisoner]. I am not going to run to the police [officers]. I do not want a snitch jacket because I don't want to get in trouble. Snitch jackets are not a nice thing to wear here. So you have to endure and accept the abuse until this girl goes home.

Stigmatized Offenses

In any prison, certain crimes are stigmatized, and those who commit them may be targeted for violence. Any crimes against children and, to a lesser extent, older or vulnerable victims are stigmatized. Prisoners in this low caste offense group have little cultural capital. While women generally do not express the same degree of scorn and hatred toward these crimes as men do, they are clear in their antipathy to them. Women doing time for victimizing children are often scorned or shunned. In men's prisons, child molesters ("Chesters") and those who injure children run the risk of being targeted for abuse by other prisoners. In women's prisons, we found gendered reactions. As most are mothers and separated from their children, there are strong feelings against those who had "child cases." Some women mentioned that "child cases" were likely to increase vulnerability for victimization, as suggested by Ink: "Just like the inmate that killed her kid. She is going to get her ass beat." In one of our jail study sites, we were told about a woman whose crime against a child was broadcast on local TV and viewed by others in the jail cell. She was subjected to physical punishment. Owen (1998) found that most women prefer to "not know what she did" and avoid asking about the crime that brought someone to prison. In this community, it was "rude" to ask someone why she was locked up—a cultural convention designed to avoid conflict over stigmatized offenses.

Time and Prison Culture

Time mediates almost all behavior inside. This community is made up of women whose sentences range from very short terms to decades to life. Tensions among women short- and long-termers can lead to trouble. Time is measured by a different metric for those serving long prison terms. These women may have a bigger investment in the prison community and more time to develop their stores of prison capital. Each side of this chronological divide sees the other from their own perspective on "going home." The short-termers define the long-termers and lifers as both more likely to be calm and more likely to be aggressive, another contradiction in this community. Some short-termers cede control to long-termers, considering prison "their house." In this view, women believe long-term prisoners deserve some consideration or have "something coming." Others see lifers and other long-termers as more disadvantaged. The nature of this conflict was recounted by Dona:

> I feel some women have contempt for lifers. It is almost a subculture of short-termers against lifers. I think it is from some of the unfortunate attitudes of some of the lifers, "wanting it my way." The women who are long-termers and lifers [have staff] look out for them [more] than those who are there for a short amount of time. That is my opinion. That is understandable, and they are going to be there for the rest of their lives. They see favoritism with them because they know them for a long amount of time.

While long-termers can accrue significant prison capital, they are disadvantaged in other ways. In some systems, long-termers are ineligible for programming opportunities available to women doing less time. This, too, may create conflict between the two groups. Staff often say, "You are never going home, so why waste resources on you?" Being labeled unworthy is an old refrain for women who have benefited very little from social and educational systems. Among the long-termers, there is some resentment of the short-termers because "they get to go home." Lifers "without a date" to go home may drop out of public prison life (Owen 1998), employing the tactic of the isolate described by Kruttschnitt and Gartner (2005). Women serving longer sentences typically have "more to lose," as they must remain free of disciplinary write-ups to protect their possibility of going home.

Counterintuitively, lifers and other long-termers may be forced to deal with aggression from short-termers, who know when they will walk out the gate. Even when faced with the possibility of a disciplinary report ("write-up," "shot," or incident report), women told us fighting and the "jacket" (reputation) of being willing to fight was critical to surviving and maintaining their sense of self and their safety. In a conversation with a group of long-termers, the women told us they must meet any challenge to their safety by showing a "willingness to fight" when threatened. They must be ready to protect themselves, even if it means new charges, as illustrated in the following exchange between two women serving life sentences.

> TeeTee: You can say anything you want. It will bounce off me and that is it. But if you put your hands on me, I will fight for my life. That is just how I am and is how I have become in here. One act of violence and it is over for us lifers. We will have no chance of getting a date [parole].

> Becks: Sometimes we are tired, but we get to a point that it builds in my mind. It gets kind of dangerous in there [my mind] because of things we have worked for and then it could be over with one little fight. I got into a little thing a few years ago. I lost my lid, but I was lucky it didn't get caught.

> TeeTee: I just don't know what is going to go on. If I have to fight with you, it goes on to the point that it is physical. If I have to fear for my life, I will try to kill you. If I have to die in prison, so will you.

> Becks: I can understand and relate to all of what she is saying. Our life is so vulnerable because we are lifers and we think, Fuck! We have been here too long, watching family members die on the outside. If you are going to fight and hurt me, we are going to get a write-up. I am going to make it worth it for me. It is not that we are violent. If we step out of this prison, we are not coming back. But we have to survive here.

This narrative provides insight into one of the persistent contradictions women must manage to stay safe. TeeTee acknowledged the demands of the prison code to fight "for my life" if touched; at the same time, she is well aware that the ensuing disciplinary action will reduce her chance of parole.

"Short and Shitty"

For women preparing to go home, the last months of their sentence is known as "being short." In some systems, when the countdown to go home reaches ninety-nine days or less, prisoners are said to be "two-digit midgets," indicating the "shortness" of their remaining term. Prisoners may get "short and shitty"— more volatile and short-tempered— as their release dates near. Tania observed:

> If they are getting closer to getting out, the tempers are short. They get short and shitty. They are getting real attitudes and real antsy, and I try to ignore it. When they are getting close to parole, they are scared and don't want to get out there. Maybe have to take care of their kids, answer to a job, pay their bills. They do something in here to get time added [extending their sentence].

At the same time, "being short" made women vulnerable to additional incursions on their well-being. We were told some women who do not have a release date in sight may try to "take your date" out of jealousy or despair. Any investigation or disciplinary action can be cause to rescind a parole decision or add time to a sentence. Engaging a woman soon to go home in a fight, "telling" staff about her illicit behavior, or otherwise putting her in jeopardy can result in the loss of a date. As Sassi said, "There is a lot of fear of going back home." "Keeping your date quiet" is one strategy, as described by Skippy:

> I was in a dorm with a woman doing ninety-nine years. To her, anyone who had little time she was negative to because she had a long time. I kind of feel sorry for them. Lately, they are so overcrowded, so they put short-timers and long-timers together. It's dangerous to me. I have to be quiet [in the room] because there is a long-timer here and she might flip out if she hears me.

Lena, a lifer, advised:

> That's why they tell you not to tell anyone that you made parole. They say, "How's it going to make you feel if you see some woman get parole the first time and you've been sitting here for years?" It makes you miserable and hateful. Even your closest friend doesn't want you to leave. The short-timers

get told, "Don't get hooked up with lifers because they will take your date." If you get hooked up with the wrong group, they will snatch your time and take your out-date and that type of thing.

Embracing Violence as Capital

For some women, violence was a normal part of life; it was not feared or avoided and was even expected in some contexts (Wesely 2006). Although most women avoided situations and people presenting the possibility of violence, others embraced the use of threats and violence in their search for safety. Violence is, again, a form of prison capital. Bunny told us she had become acclimated to the prison environment where violence is an accepted and expected element:

> This is our survival. I have been down so many years that if someone touches me, I am going to go off. There is always violence unless you are going to the convalescent home [medical unit] or the honor dorm.

Some women believe violence to be the only acceptable response for a range of perceived or real wrongs (McGuire 2011). In some interviews, it appeared the prisoners seemed to enjoy telling their violent stories. Perhaps this was a form of grandstanding, or showing off, in the group interviews. In some interviews, questions about violence often triggered laughter, even when women were describing a serious violent incident. Displaying their cultural capital, women in our groups were not shy about discussing their use of violence. Maggie saw it as learned behavior: "Once you hit me, I'll pretty much hit you back. That is how I was raised." Michelle announced her propensity for violence:

> I liked the fists connecting. I would get off on that. If it hurt a little bit, I liked it. It was a part of my addiction to violence. I think that it is part of my maturing or whatever. I am now a different person.

Violence is risky capital in the prison community. In writing about adaptations to racial and other forms of discrimination in many African American communities, Coates (2015) suggests that violence is both born out of fear and scarcity and used as tool to confront it, paralleling our analysis. By wielding violence or its verbal threat, women establish forms of social and cultural capital by being known as willing to fight. Kitty's account of violence was not considered abnormal by her or the group listening to her:

I put two roommates out. One of them was dirty and one of them wanted my cat [sex] so I put him[1] out. I used to participate in homosexuality, but it don't work for me because it makes me violent. I used to have this friend, but she would aggravate me because I am good as gold but I get aggravated. One day she say something real smart and I would turn around and hit her. It got so I needed to leave her alone because I would kill her. Then there was the other roommate. This roommate would eat blades, swallow tweezers, she would bite, throw blood up all over my bed. So I had to whup her up a little bit.

Thus, in the unequal world of women's prison, violence is currency. In describing a "set up" so a cellmate could get off the unit via a medical transfer, Callie talks about using violence as a favor, thus increasing her social and reputational capital: "A person told me to break her finger, so I did it. When I heard it crack, I got sick. But she asked me to do it. Then after I did it, she said, 'You is really my friend!'" Selina described an incident involving retaliation against a woman who would not pay her for braiding her hair. She treated her story of violence as a joke, laughing about the injury she inflicted on the other woman. To Selina, the rational response to nonpayment in this world of scarcity was fighting:

We was in the dayroom eating and I dumped my tray and hit her two times. And she just went down [laughter]. She went to a seizure. The sarge came and talked to me and he said, "You knocked her out?" And I said, "I didn't mean to, but she didn't give me her money." [Laughter] But it went so smooth when it happened. I was already at my door when she went down. So the Sarge asked why, and I said, "Two dollars." But I hurt my hand. [Laughter]

The women well know that violence has consequences. Some women were more worried about "losing their date," their privileges, or other sanctions than experiencing the fight itself. Others resented the fact that officers "wrote them up" for fighting, contradicting their complaints that officers would not protect them from aggressors. Staff, too, have a range of reactions to fights—reactions, we venture, that are based on how they respect the women they are paid to protect. Hilly suggested that staff reaction to women's violence may be worse than the fight itself:

If you fight, seven out of ten times they're going to be OK. They are roommates. They are into drama. If you fight here, staff want to body slam us. They want to take [our classification status]. Sometimes at [another facility], you can have a fight and you go right back to your dorm. On other units, [staff] let you fight. If they can see you're not trying to harm the other woman, they don't even do use of force.

1. The male pronoun is used to designate someone who adopts a male identity inside.

Physical violence rarely involves more than two women. It includes slapping, pushing, hair pulling, punching, kicking, or gouging. Fights are typically brief. Those occurring in public areas or in the view of staff were seen as symbolic. Physical fights involved "making a point" or "taking a stand" so one would not appear "weak" or vulnerable. Also, similar to verbal conflict, instrumental fights were sometimes motivated by a desire to change housing units, get "kicked out" of a program, or, in extreme cases, join a romantic partner in disciplinary housing. Serious fighting was almost always said to occur away from staff members' view, in cells, rooms, showers, or isolated locations.

Most fights did not involve weapons. Unlike men, the use of prison-made weapons, such as "shanks," was uncommon among women; in rare cases, they might use "weapons of convenience," such as a pair of scissors or metal object found in a work setting. Staff members were likely to characterize the majority of fights as "mutual combat" between two equally matched opponents. Women and staff acknowledged fights were most likely to occur between women in troubled relationships, although they could also occur between cellmates or others who had some type of "beef." Although extremely rare, women described serious and extreme physical violence that resulted in injury, disfigurement, and, atypically, death. Across different study sites, we heard accounts of high-profile cases offered as precautionary tales about the violent relationships that may occur among women offenders.

In the NIC survey, we asked women to rate their concerns over inmate-inmate physical violence and conflict. Verbal threats of physical violence were seen as medium to very big problems by almost 60 percent of the survey sample, with 65 percent indicating that fights which escalate from verbal argument to physical conflict were in this high-problem category. In terms of the overall physical violence scale, just under half (46 percent) saw physical violence as medium to very big problems in their unit. The NIC survey data show almost three-fourths of the women said weapon use was not a problem at all (53 percent) or a small problem (16 percent). Gang fights were rated as no problem or a small problem by 70 percent of the survey takers. (See appendix 2, table 3.)

Sexual Violence

Consistent with the BJS prevalence data (Beck et al. 2010; Beck et al. 2013), violent sexual attacks were said to be rare, with abusive sexual

language or abusive sexual contacts more prevalent for both prisoner-prisoner and staff-prisoner victimizations. While women new to incarceration said they were initially worried about sexual assault, most found this worry unfounded over time. Venetta captured this view by saying that while she had seen many incidents of physical violence, it was "nothing like the rapes and stuff in the movies." We did collect multiple reports of mild forms of sexual coercion, or grooming, involving flattery, verbal pressure, and unwanted touching. Verbal threats of sexual violence were also described to us. Most women indicated they eventually learned how to avoid women known to be sexually aggressive as they acquired the smarts of prison capital.

Our focus group participants reported that while sexual violence was rare, it was most likely to occur in the context of an ongoing, troubled relationship. We could not determine the level of "protective pairing" present among women. Protective pairing involves a relationship between one woman with little prison capital with another holding larger stocks of prison capital. Generally, women suggested it was young, naive, or scared offenders who entered into risky relationships with aggressive women, offering commissary and sexual intimacy in return for protection. Yet female prisoners typically saw most relationships as consensual. See appendix 2, table 2, for more specific detail on women's perceptions of sexual violence among prisoners.

The Invisibility of These Troubles

In the PREA legislation, the term "rape" is center stage, obscuring the problems of other, nonpenetrating forms of sexual violence. This term further disadvantages women by focusing on a stereotypically male version of sexual assault and thus deflects attention from the real damage of same-sex assaults by other prisoners and female staff. In our initial NIC interviews with staff around the country (Owen and Moss 2009), a very small number of staff expressed the view that "a woman could not be raped by another woman." Although clearly in the minority, one staff person said that sex between women could not really involve assault "because there was no penetration" (Owen and Moss 2009, 4). Sexual violence between women was said to be more difficult to detect and prove due to the lack of semen and other physical evidence. Staff told us they had difficulty distinguishing between coerced relationships and those that appear to be consensual in the relational context of institutional life. As one staff participant said, "we make the assumption that it [sexual behavior] is consensual, but I am not sure that is always the case" (Owen and Moss 2009, 4).

Women's troubles with sexual violence inside, then, can be invisible to staff, policy makers, and sometimes themselves. We examine elements of staff sexual misconduct and how this invisibility causes further suffering among women in the next chapter. Here we emphasize that many partnerships among women in prison are not violent and destructive and do contribute to their search for safety. There is no doubt that genuine connections, based on mutuality and emotional equality, are possible in this world.

A CONTINUUM OF COERCION

A continuum of sexual coercion describes the range of sexual victimization in women's facilities. In this continuum, no activity is necessarily exclusive of any other.

Sexual Comments and Touching

Sexual and other verbal comments, such as referring to another woman's body or making sexual innuendos, were the least serious form of sexual victimization described to us. Sexual "horseplay" or touching a woman's body in a nonviolent but uninvited and unwanted manner is included here. Note, however, that unwanted hugging and other kinds of touching were described and interpreted as a form of aggression, leading to feelings of vulnerability. A custody staff person described this behavior:

> [The aggressive inmate] will get very close in, very close. Then they will touch their leg and give them an embrace. There are two types of embraces. Here, an open embrace is fine. It is not so much that it is mutual but that it is open. The other is one arm around the neck. Then they bring them down, almost into a headlock. I do martial arts and that is one of the controls. [The aggressor] can smell you, and you are either going to cock back and pound on them or you are going to submit. It is real subtle.

Sexual Pressure or Intimidation

Women can feel pressured by being asked repeatedly to become involved romantically or sexually with someone. Dalinda described such pressure.

> Sometimes I've seen girls who don't like to be touched and [the aggressive one] will touch them in certain ways. They might slap them in the ass, or they grab their titties. The woman feels violated. We might be afraid to take showers [because] we are going to be looked at.

Women expressed fear of being "set up" when pressured into a relationship, suggesting that sometimes it was easier to go along with unwanted behaviors or relationships. At first we were told that sexual intimidation was very rare. But, in further discussions, some women ventured that it was "hard to know" if a woman had been coerced or had entered into a relationship voluntarily. As Dale observed:

> I've basically seen everything from simple physical assault to being cut. I've never seen any type of rape or sexual violence. Well, in some sense, [I have seen] sexual intimidation.

Even bonds that appear consensual may have some element of coercion, as suggested by Terry:

> It can be a consensual relationship, but you really aren't ready to go that far. But they keep pushing it. I was in a situation where several inmates were trying to force me to be in a relationship that was more than friends. Then she said, "Girl, we are going to hit you with a [plastic] cup." She is always trying to come at me real aggressive like, and she is trying to bump and run with me all the time.

Staff also recognized that some women may be coerced or pressured into connecting on overlapping dimensions. One staff member said, "In the female setting, you don't have a lot of direct actions, but there is a lot of coercion. It is implied coercion and not a lot of direct threat."

Stalking and Fatal Attraction

A particular type of sexual pressure or intimidation occurs in "fatal attraction" cases, after the movie of the same name. In stalking cases, a woman enthralled with another seeks a sexual liaison at any cost. Women we spoke with distinguished "fatals" from "hustlers," "bullies," or sexual aggressors who target vulnerable inmates for gain. Sandra offered this observation of the "fatal":

> [The fatal] said first she was going to beat her up and then she said she was going to take her to SHU with her. That is real easy to do. I don't think that this is fair because this lady [being pursued] is trying to break away, and this fatal one is trying to take her to Seg. [The fatal] probably figures that if she

takes her to SHU, she can take time to talk to her and, at the least, she can keep her away from everyone else back there too.

Sexual Aggressors

In very few instances, women described "predators" in the same manner as the "booty bandits" of men's prisons. Such violence was said to be a very rare event. When asked to estimate the percentage of women who took on the role of violent aggressor, figures were fairly consistent at about 5 to 10 percent. Again, "predator," "aggressor," and similar terms referred to all forms of victimization, not just sexual. When Kaylee said, "There is no forced sex here," Miranda remarked, "I am going to disagree with that. There is this lady that forces herself on people. But she knows who to pick. But it is not prominent because it's not like the men." One staff member said that sexual aggression was worse in women's prisons than in men's prisons:

> I locked up an inmate for being a sexually violent predator. One inmate was holding the other down and sexually assaulting her with objects. She was just really bad. But good at getting people to help her. Here, these sexually devious ones seem to get together. I know that sexual deviance here far outweighs the men's facilities. It is bad.

Sexual Violence

Most forced sex was said to take place within an intimate relationship. We received very few accounts of violent or forced sex among nonintimates. Although two women may be involved in an ongoing, seemingly consensual sexual relationship, intimate partner violence is made possible by jealousy, "disobedience," attempts at physical control, social isolation, and other precursors of abuse. Physical violence (as opposed to sexual violence) against partners was much more common. At the most serious end of the coercion continuum, forced sex occurs, reproducing unequal sexual dynamics. Most women had only heard of rapes or assaults in prison; very few had seen a rape personally. Usually descriptions of sexual assault were presented as occurring elsewhere or in the past. Fleischer and Krienert (2006) found that most accounts had the character of stories or prison myths rather than first-person reports. As Tillie told us, "I've heard that women got raped with the toilet brushes. It's not fiction, but it's in the past."

In most situations, women said the motivation for a sexual assault was unclear. We did hear rare reports of retaliatory sexual assault for some personal, social, or economic transgression. In this community of self-blame, sexual assault is, again, interpreted to be the result of the victim's actions. Franny explained, "It is always behind [caused by] something. They stick a plunger in you or whatever. [Because] you stole something; [because] you messed with someone's girlfriend."

Many women also agreed that sexual assaults were about power, control, and humiliation, as Toni told us: "There was one incident two years ago. They humiliated the girl. They made [her] give two or three of them oral sex. But it is about power and humiliation."

Our NIC survey data found sexual violence was generally not perceived as a major problem across the more than four thousand women we asked. A full two-thirds of the survey participants said sexual violence perpetrated by other women was "not at all a problem," inside or outside an intimate relationship. (See appendix 2, table 2, for further details.) Violent sexual attacks were said to be rare; abusive sexual language, mild forms of sexual coercion, and verbal sexual threats were much more common. Most women indicated they eventually learned how to avoid such situations as they developed their stores of capital.

TROUBLED RELATIONSHIPS

As in the free world, couples in prison vary greatly in terms of commitment, intimacy, and emotional, sexual, and material dimensions. Girshick sums up this view in this quote from a woman in her study:

> I mean, [the men] have sex but they don't have relationships. But these women, it is more than sex to them. It's a relationship. You can get a woman who comes in off the street that ain't never been gay and is crazy about men, and she will end up in a relationship. But it's just a substitution, I think for lack of emotional ties, and you know, it's one way to try to have your needs met. (1999, 86)

For women seeking to gain relational capital through connection, prison girlfriends can be a source of both safety and trouble, reflecting the dysfunctional relationships of their pathways. These relationships must be contextualized within their pathway experiences, prior victimization of either or both partners, poor coping skills, the role of economic exploitation in relationships, and the lack of other outlets to occupy women's time or emotions. Jealousy and recycled abusive patterns feed risks in this world of women. Franny described the complexity of connections:

People make these families in here. They show them a bit of love, even though it may be an abusive kind of love, but they can't see it because that's the only love they ever have. So we have moms and stuff, and girlfriends. But some of it isn't a good kind of love. This one girl I knew, this one girl has bruises all over, and she said, "That's just the way it is. She's just physical, but she loves me." And I say, "That's not love." And I ask her why. Why does she stick with her? But it's because she has to have somebody love her and she's willing to take that.

Throughout the country, we listened to accounts of the immediacy and importance of relationships in the lives of incarcerated women. Grounded in powerful emotions and intense attachments, threats to relationships can be the catalyst for desperate, sometimes extreme, reactions. The roots of the relationships and their role in creating the potential for violence were suggested by Emma:

Women are clingy and have too many needs. In prison, we lose our identities and our dignity. We are our [prison ID] numbers. We feel like pieces of shit. We left our kids outside. So in here, if I find someone to focus on and they look at someone else, I'm gonna beat the shit out of them.

Like the dynamics described by Renzetti (1992), Yoshi described the intensity of prison relationships:

Here, there is an overwhelming desire to be "the one" in a relationship. When the relationship does not develop the "oneness," then that is where trouble comes. Friends, family [get ignored]. [The partner says], "Don't go to school because I need you." [They fear their partner] will rise up and [be productive] and leave her here.

This dyadic intensity is arbitrated by other forms of prison capital, particularly the cultural capital of respect.

Disrespect in Relationships

Jealousy is a prime cause of relationship violence. Tessa described her experience:

My biggest downfall was getting into a relationship with a woman. Relationships are not always good and a majority of them end badly. We are women and we are all jealous and jealousy leads to a whole bunch of nonsense and fighting.

In sharing this view, one officer said, "Ninety-nine percent of the violence is due to falling in love, falling out of love, and jealousy." Situations that provoked jealousy ranged from small gestures such as looking at, speaking to, or sitting next to another woman, to one-sided breakups.

Jealously as disrespect can be both internal or external to the relationship. Women told us that when one partner disrespects the other, the dominant woman must make a public claim:

> Your woman might have pissed you off, like not making your breakfast. And then I have to be real loud [in expressing my disapproval] so everyone knows I won't take the disrespect. You want everyone to hear you [dressing her down] because you were disrespected.

External jealousy involves third-party interference. Those believed to be "coming between" the two troubled partners are at risk for violence. The interference could be imagined or unintentional, but it is still perceived as disrespect, with dangerous consequences. Chonny said:

> It goes down to respect with the girlfriend, some girl is messing with your girlfriend behind your back. She is stepping on your toes. She knows me and you are together. Don't come between us! I'm more mad at the other woman because she knows that you are mine. You are gonna get yours after.

Women were adamant about not wanting to "get involved" or intervene in others' troubles as dictated by the convict code prescription to "do your own time." This conversation among long-term and lifer prisoners captures the downside of getting involved.

> *Tian:* Unless it is someone who I know and care about, you really don't get involved. The next day, they make up and then they are both mad at you. And then you are the bad guy for interfering in their relationship.
>
> *Debra:* You don't get involved because the couple has accepted the terms of the relationship. They knew what they were getting involved with. If someone has accepted those terms, there is nothing we can do about it.
>
> *Gloria:* It is just like domestic violence on the streets . . . "Do I have to kill this man so I can sleep at night?" Here we have nowhere to go.

Living with Partners

Living with partners is a point of contention in this prison community. For women with partners, living in the same room or cell can be the focal point of their immediate existence. Most prisons have a formal procedure for requesting a housing change, usually on the basis of compatibility or, more seriously, to escape potential victimization. Perhaps just as often, housing change requests are based on a desire to be housed with a friend or an intimate partner. On the one hand, some women told us intimate partner violence occurred because the partners weren't together, as Jenda stated:

In my life [in prison], there has been less violence when couples are together and not about worrying about who's out there, seeing somebody, being with somebody. Homosexuality is where all the violence is, but that's because, as lovers, we've been locked up away from each other. Yes, they are lovers now who be cutting up each other. Oh my God, they do. But they didn't do that before. Most of the women here have been locked up for twenty years and they didn't do that then.

On the other hand, some women argued that living with an intimate partner did not solve the intense relational conflicts that compromise all forms of safety, as in this extreme case:

Well, look at the girl who just got killed. It was her lover. They will put lovers together. So they put them together to avoid trouble and so look what happened. What's to say that that is not trouble? She slit her throat and hung her because she was with another girl in another cell. And they had put them together so when she went back that night she killed her. Because they were cellies too.

Is that right that you let lovers live together to avoid the traffic and trading? When lovers aren't together, they wanted to avoid the problems of one girlfriend saying to someone, "Give this to my baby in the other dorm." . . . But that's not a good solution. Maybe if they move them off the unit. But you can't keep them separated. In some situations, it pacifies them, but what happens when one of them gets mad if someone else is looking at her and they create these jealousy scripts in their mind and they go off. Putting them together means you can't get away. They are in the cell together. Not like a dorm where there's people around.

Staff members are often skeptical of housing change requests and tend to believe that women who tell them they are in danger are "gaming" or "manipulating" them to be closer to a friend or lover. In some cases, this assumption is correct. We heard stories of women being violent or committing other rule violations to get moved to disciplinary housing if their partners were there. We were also told that some women will falsely claim their cellmate or someone in their dorm is a threat, hoping to get moved to the desired housing unit. One unintended consequence of this belief is staff skepticism when a woman requests a room change and her safety actually is in jeopardy. The problem of "crying wolf" was also acknowledged by the prisoners. Isabella noted:

Here people are abusing the system to get with or away from their girlfriends. They're using it as a ploy to break up. That's the inmates' fault because so many have used and abused the system. [Several others try to interrupt and stop her from talking.] If they follow through with everything [and] look at who has given many complaints, [they could see who was manipulating], but they don't see it.

Economic Exploitation within Relationships

In a study of Israeli prisons, Einat and Chen (2012b, 492) find "economic manipulation" is a strong motive for same-sex relationships, as "the unequal access to money and material goods among inmates directly leads to these relationships." Those who are "well taken care of" can be targets of this exploitation. At the same time, a woman without any prison capital may be "talked into" or coerced to enter into a relationship with a woman who has resources; or the two may be in the relationship freely—one obtaining needed goods, the other obtaining needed intimacy or physical relief. Economic exploitation thus merges with relationship conflict. The extent of coercion and the complexity of such associations, however, make it difficult to determine the nature of such liaisons. Staff members shared this view:

> I knew one inmate that told me she would trick out [trade sex] for commissary. I would have had no idea unless she told me. So you don't always realize what goes on even though you work here.

Almost all women agreed that exploitative and unequal "hookups" are directly tied to limited economic opportunity and inadequate stores of prison capital while in custody. As Latasha said:

> If the system would provide you the appliances like the hot pot, hair dryer, then you wouldn't have to borrow them and make you feel like you owe someone. It would make you feel OK if you had your own and then you wouldn't feel so handicapped and have sex with this girl so I could have shampoo or soap in my box.

KJ provided a realistic view about the practicality of these exploitative and harmful relationships:

> They have a motive, they are feeding me, and buying me tobacco. Why wouldn't I put up with a little arguing? And some is physical.

Intimate Partner Violence

Intimate partner violence among women prisoners parallels classic battering patterns, with attacks against one's sense of self, unequal power and humiliation. As Andie said:

Violent relationships in prison are the same thing as my old man beating me. Or stabbing me or beating me over jealousy or someone looking at me. But you are just trying to get away. I always see that this woman's girlfriend [in here] was always bruised up. It was the same thing as when I was not trying to get away from my old man when I was walking around with bruises.

In the classic pattern, the dominant partner makes demands beyond sexual services, such as housekeeping, laundry, cooking, and economic support. When these demands are not met, violence ensues. Interpersonal violence in prison is domestic violence. Robin said:

I have been beat by my spouse. I have been shot by my spouse. I did not know how, in here, it was as bad [as on the streets] and that it was the same thing. But domestic violence is domestic violence, it is the same thing.

When asked about this connection between past and present violence, Little Bear offered this view:

The violence comes from the person that you are. It comes in from outside in the world with you. If you are an abusive person or have been abused in the world, when you have someone that does love you, you are going to abuse them.

Some women understand the connection between their shared pathways and the intimate partner violence within the prison environment. Lulu observed:

A lot of girls go through domestic violence in the streets. I have been in one with a male. I say it all starts in the home from a young age, a baby. If you always see your dad hitting your mom, if you are a boy, you think it is right to hit on your woman. And then you [as a woman] think that is right for your man to hit on you because he loves you.

But whether you come in here having been beat by a man or what, when you come in here, you look for the same kind of relationship, whether it is a woman or a man. In your subliminal mind, you are looking for the same thing, and before you know it, you are with an aggressor [in here] that is beating on you. Then you have become an aggressor. You find and go for a woman that you can control because you like being over her.

Recycled patterns of prior and present interpersonal violence and abuse are significant barriers to women's search for safety. Lack of capital—economic or emotional—undermines a woman's ability to leave, no matter where she lives. Accounts of the continuing cycle of violence while imprisoned were common in our interviews. In this dynamic, women who had been victims in their past could become victimizers in the present. We saw how a cycle of personal victimization cycle continues in the prison, as Jo Jo recounted:

> This is what they learned. They grew up with this. They seek it out. This is what they are used to. You try to put them in a safe environment; they go back to what is comfortable. If your father has been raping you, hitting you, it is what they know. To me, I always thought that being loved means you have to want to do it [sex] with me. If they don't [want sex] that means they don't love me. I have a big problem with that.

Patrice saw violent partnerships as characterized by arguments:

> You have been together, there is a lot of arguing. One wants to be the man, while the other woman is really aggressive too. But you want to be the man. You want to dominate me and today I may be PMSing and today I do not want you to tell me what to do. So a fight can start if I say hello to [another woman with a girlfriend] and her girlfriend does not like that. That is disrespect and they live together . . . then fighting is going to happen.

In acknowledging the irony of the "because I love you" statement, the following comment by Lorene elicited shared amusement:

> We're incarcerated. We're away from our loved ones. You are the person here that I'm pouring my heart out to and so soon as I feel bad about something, get a bad letter from home, all that [violence] is going out to you *because I love you.*

Lynette told us she has thought a lot about the importance and intensity of relationships and had asked others why they get into relationships in the prison. She recited their answer: "Being lonely, being horny, and needing canteen." She then went on to explain her own experience:

> I was in a relationship for ten years. I was with someone very young who had a life[long] domestic violence history. I was *not* exposed to that and it hurt me [to see] she flinched whenever I moved. I did not understand the background she came from. I never understood.

> I never physically violated her, but I know that I was emotionally abusive. I understand that I emotionally hurt her because I did not understand where she was coming from. I am a control freak and had my agenda.

She continued:

> When I finally understood that broken people get together with broken people, that it is "accepting the terms" [of a bad relationship]. Someone who gets together with me, they consciously or unconsciously accept the terms of how I live. I did not understand what it was to be with someone who had

been constantly violated. [I would say to her when she cowered or seemed to be afraid of me,] "It is me—not him." And I got mad [because she still reacted to me with fear].

Some of the women we spoke with were well aware of the victimization patterns that shape pathways to prison and how they connect to abusive affiliations inside. Some were quite eloquent in their explanations of why bonds are so important ("because it's all we have"). Some identified themselves as the violent partners and struggled to explain why they exploded at partners they loved. A few indicated they had decided to stay single because of their inability to control their own violence. In another example of a story that gave us pause, Eva, a woman who was known to be abusive to her partner, was going to self-help groups for victims of interpersonal violence. Another prisoner asked her why she was attending the program. She replied, "I have to go to this meeting so I can learn how to batter my bitch better." Tracee, a self-identified "masculine" woman, described the complications of her connections:

> Getting involved in a relationship is my downfall. I get violent toward my women. Like this girl that went home in 2004. I was beating her every day. Every day, I would put my hands on her. Busting her mouth. Her eye. By the time she was fixing to go home, I was always hitting her. I was just swinging a tool and it was going to catch her in the head. I went black and then my squad leader yelled when I was swinging it, so I dropped it because I didn't want to kill her, but then I started choking her. So then I knew [the guard and lieutenant] were going to come, so I had to stop because I didn't want them body-slamming me.

Tracee further told us she had been molested by her stepfather and brothers since she was a very young child and began using drugs and alcohol while still in elementary school. She also described a terrifying sexual assault from a larger, stronger cellmate.

In the NIC survey, we asked women to rate the seriousness of physical violence with "intimate partners or girlfriends." This item and "fights that started with arguments" were the two highest rated problem categories in terms of physical violence. About 40 percent of the survey respondents rated these two issues as "big" or "very big" problems. (See appendix 2, table 2 for more details.) The finding that physical violence between same-sex partners is rated so highly points to the volatility of such relationships. Physical violence between partners or girlfriends, we learned in both the interviews and the surveys, was much more likely than sexual violence.

CONCLUSION

In this chapter we focused on the range of vulnerabilities that complicate the search for safety. Gender inequality and coercive power relations take a new form in this world of women, creating troubles and violence between women and with staff. Stratification of prison capital among women creates and reinforces vulnerabilities grounded in inequality. To stay safe, women must find ways to reduce their vulnerabilities by developing prison capital. Some women leverage free world capital to build safe lives inside; other women actively seek out ways to improve themselves and their conditions while locked up; still others develop prison capital by becoming "big ballers" on the yard, claiming their place in the prison world by means of aggression. We turn next to the issue of inequality as expressed through interaction between women and correctional staff.

6

Intersections of Inequality
with Correctional Staff

The power differential between "the keeper and the kept" (Crouch 1980) structures the starkest forms of inequality in the prison community. All prisoners—women and men—are confined to an inferior social caste, regardless of their free world capital. In their search for safety, women must develop strategies to manage this power differential from their disadvantaged position. The overwhelming formal power of the State, embodied in the authority of the correctional officers, reinforces this chasm. Few forms of capital exist to counter this fundamental inequality that women must negotiate daily.

Kruttschnitt and Gartner (2005) assert that women's strategies for doing time inform their interactions with staff: those using the adaptive strategy tend to have constructive and reciprocal interactions with staff, whereas those adopting the isolate and convict strategies avoid involvement with staff except to seek help for formal tasks. Resisting or undermining the authority of individual staff members is one way to push back. "Gaming," or compromising staff through blackmail or other leverage, is also possible. Collaborating with staff for economic gain or engaging in emotional or sexual relationships is yet another way for women to mitigate their subordinate position. While attention to interactional inequalities provides insight into women's pathways and deleterious prison conditions, the expression of racial, gender, and class inequalities between women and staff requires more interrogation. Prison staff comprise people of color, women, and individuals who come from class backgrounds similar to those of many of the women in prison. Many staff have experienced violence and abuse in their own lives. Despite overlapping racial, gender, class, or cultural identities, the stigma of the "convict" identity overwhelms most other claims to dignity and respect. Women are thus further propelled into powerlessness, leaving them to accommodate staff power at every level as they do their time.

THE ROLE OF CORRECTIONAL STAFF

Staff attitudes and behavior determine almost every aspect of daily life in prison. Staff interact with women everywhere: in housing units, offices, work, school, programming spaces, recreation yards, kitchens, and chow (dining) halls. Women are dependent on staff for almost everything in the total institution, as they control all movement and distribute almost every resource. Women often have to ask staff to open doors and gates, for permission to move from one area of the prison to another, and for sanitary products and other material items. Such interactions can be helpful to hostile.

In jobs from clerical staff to warden, both women and men work in the modern prison. Most staff are employed in custodial roles as line officers and supervisors. As women's prisons evolved from the Reformatory Era of the late 1800s to the current era of the modern warehouse prison (Irwin 2005), the gender composition of the staff also changed. Initially, female matrons staffed women's facilities to provide "good role models" for the women in their care, emphasizing nurturing and, sometimes, dependence (Pollock 2014, 239). Until the early 1980s, employment in prisons was quite segregated by gender: women worked in women's prisons, and men worked in men's prisons. In the 1960s, several legal challenges based on equal opportunity were brought by female officers to gain the right to work in men's prisons (Owen 1988; Pollock 2014). As women won this right, men too gained the right to work in women's facilities. In many states, men now make up the majority of custody staff. Some U.S. prison systems limit male presence in some areas, such as housing units, or at certain times, typically at night. International standards, such as the Bangkok Rules and other human rights instruments, limit the role of men working in women's facilities. These human rights standards are ignored in the American prison.

Correctional staff have the legitimate authority to direct and control women's behaviors and bodies. They are guided, in principle, by training, policy, post orders, and operational practice. The majority of staff want to do their job through professional and respectful interaction, assisting women with their problems and monitoring all forms of safety. However, some number of staff abuse their power, abuse made possible by the contradictions of the contemporary prison. Staff are paid to protect women in their care but have unbridled authority to harm the women in their custody. This extreme advantage feeds the potential for abusive interactions, ranging from an asymmetry of respect in language and actions to serious physical and sexual harm. Women told us that disrespectful staff words, tone, and volume contribute to anxiety and tension in their daily lives. Such disrespect stokes conflict, violence, and victimization among prisoners and with staff.

Since women have little capital to confront this absolute power and control, managing this asymmetry is essential to the search for safety. Accommodating this political differential by cooperating with rules and regulations, treating staff politely and deferentially, and deflecting staff attention are common safety strategies. Like all subordinate persons, women develop ways to manage or resist control of the more powerful (Bosworth 1999). Some women avoid officers and other staff whenever possible. Other women work in the subcultural shadows to counter staff power through hustles and other forms of resistance. Women with the prison capital of connection may go "over the head" of the line officer and present their case to a supervisor, manager, or staff person with whom they have social capital. This is a risky strategy, as such expression of disrespect of the line officer can bring retaliatory violence. Women prisoners can appropriate staff power by recruiting staff in illicit activities such as smuggling, conspiring to exploit other women prisoners, or initiating sexual activities. Another tactic is to openly challenge authority verbally or, more rarely, with physical resistance or attack.

Women prisoners are particularly vulnerable to inequities of power and status. Tripp, a woman serving time in one of the remaining cottage-style facilities, offered her view on the relationship between staff and women.

> There is a vulnerability on the side of the inmates, and there is a power with the staff. There is an attitude of contempt for inmates among the staff, especially the ones that want to have sex with us. It is like she is "deliciously below us." There is that taboo that draws people. A sick perversion. The inmates gain more power by association with someone more powerful than us. It was seen with the Nazi concentration camps. The bald Jewish women were so provocative to a Nazi man.

As we know from national data collected by the Bureau of Justice Statistics (Beck, Harrison, and Guerino 2010; Beck et al. 2013) and our NIC survey, overt staff violence is not a dominant feature of this community, but the very real potential serves as a destabilizing undercurrent in women's day-to-day lives. In this gendered world, most staff do not feel the pervasive physical challenge found in men's prisons. We suspect this gendered difference in staff expectations of prisoner violence against them further contributes to the asymmetry of power, creating the potential for mistreatment. Although women have the real potential to cause serious harm to staff, random attacks on staff appear to be rare. However, staff's absolute privilege over women in everyday interaction results in actions and attitudes that create or compromise safety for imprisoned women.

Interactions and Interests

Interactions between women and staff vary. Interests can intersect, as most prisoners and staff share a common interest in running the unit smoothly by minimizing chaos (Owen 1988). Just as most women want to avoid trouble, most staff want to perform their duties professionally and go home safely at the end of the day. But this is not always the case. Staff and prisoners can also share illegitimate interests in sex, money, and other forms of prison capital, and staff may act outside the scope of their authority for personal satisfaction and gain. Shared interests can contribute to safety or form the context for abuse, exploitation, conflict, and violence.

Women offered a wide range of definitions of "good" and "bad" officers. A good officer might be one who helps you with "your issue" or "writes a ducat" to facilitate movement within the prison. To a woman doing time as an isolate or convict (Kruttschnitt and Gartner 2005), a good officer is one she can avoid. Officers who can "be played," or recruited to conspire in hustles and other illegitimate activities, might be considered "good officers" by women embedded in the mix. Staff members who are caring and helpful to the women under their supervision are also seen as good, as are staff members who "just leave us alone." In the middle of the spectrum, we heard descriptions of staff who were indifferent to women's problems and concerns, often "too busy," "too lazy," "can't be bothered," or otherwise disinterested to help or provide information or issue material goods. Staff actions can make a unit run smoothly or be "off the hook." As Paula commented, "Not all officers are bad, but you do have officers that do what they can to make life a living hell." The small number of staff who were said to participate in a campaign of dehumanization by word and action were at the negative end of the spectrum. At the extreme, we heard reports of staff who actively and overtly harmed incarcerated women. Staff can "switch up" and behave inconsistently across shifts or with certain individuals or groups. This lack of consistency is yet another challenge to women's safety.

Women have their individualized perspectives on "good staff" and "bad staff" and can look forward to, or dread, when these staff members come on shift. The importance of staff attitudes and subsequent interaction was described by Anya:

> The thing is, they are in charge of care, custody, and control. When they fail to control the environment we are in, it becomes a problem. It's so intense. It is a hostile environment. The officers don't control their dorm, they say, "Go away! Don't bother me!" Maybe they don't feel well or have a problem at home, so then when someone does ask them [and they do not respond], then I'm pissed off. Then I piss someone else off.

We heard many examples of positive and professional interactions among these diverse members of the community. In one time-bounded example, workers and women serving long (or repeated) sentences were said to "grow up" in the system together. Perhaps the asymmetry of power is dampened somewhat by long-term interactions that produce reciprocal respect between staff and prisoner. Staff "old-timers" and prisoner "OGs" (Original Gangsters) develop a common perspective, particularly shared disapproval and dismissal of the "youngsters" in both staff and prisoner uniforms. Some, especially lifers who had entered prison as young women, felt real warmth for some officers, as Ariana illustrated:

> Some of the laws [officers] have raised us. I look up to some of these laws. I call them mom, dad, grandpa. [Brief laughter] They don't care. They'll just say, "Ah those kids." I mean, they've known us for ten to twelve years. We've gone through family deaths, and they have helped us. They've guided us. They have not crossed the line. We have an inmate that just had her mother die. And one officer [showed sympathy] because she had been at visitation and seen the mother and talked to the mother. So it's kind of hard. So you get close to some of these officers emotionally. But every shift is different.

Other confined women argued that the closeness between the lifers and some officers creates problems when staff privilege is used to disadvantage women. Della observed:

What it is, see, is older people, that been here for a while, become a family. When one gets into it [trouble with staff], they all go down. The way that the guards are, the majority of them have been working with them [older inmates] for so long, they become buddies. The officers will tell them what you said. They are going to go back to the inmates and tell them what's happening with you.

Challenging Staff

Women are upfront about their role in antagonizing staff and acknowledge that such "in their face" opposition makes doing their time harder. Andrea detailed her journey to recognizing the cost of resisting staff authority:

> I came in when I was twenty-five years old, a wisecrack with an attitude. [I thought], "He [the judge] sentenced me to do life, not to work." But through the years, I have changed. And some women are more vulnerable and some hit the wrong note with the wrong staff. And I talk to others and say, "You can't talk to the staff like that, you have to bite your lip and either defuse or come back and defuse with us." Some of the older women, even being assertive is difficult. In our unit on the weekends, one CO is very hard to deal with. If you don't have to see her, it is a good day. There is some staff and some inmates we just need to avoid. When I see youngsters coming in, [I tell them,] "Don't get foul with the bosses because you are going to get your ass crossed out." But they don't listen. [I say,] "Don't get fly. Just say 'Yes ma'am,' 'No sir.'" But, like you [points to another focus group participant], some of these youngsters don't listen and get into trouble anyway. Then you wake up to the reality of staff power afterwards.

We also heard from women who explained that staff members could be "handled" and "manipulated," as Valentina's comment illustrated:

> I think you could put manipulation under it. Not just inmates but staff too. Just like, I don't know, getting over. You can make a lot of the COs bend to your way so you won't get the little write-ups. My experience is that it works better with the men than with the women, but you can do this with the women too. You follow them for a few days and know them. You sort of manipulate them.

"Getting over," or taking advantage, is one of the few ways that women can assert any form of power, no matter how small. Sometimes women clearly flatter male staff by complimenting their masculinity in this mixed-gender world. However, in this community of multiple sexuality, female staff are also subjected to and sometimes influenced by such attention.

Staff as Protectors

Women using the adaptive strategy are most likely to seek help from officers and other staff (Kruttschnitt and Gartner 2005). Some women were able to identify individual staff members who they felt confident would help or protect them. Sometimes this was a high-ranking officer, and sometimes it was a person whose position involved receiving requests for assistance. Nicole explained:

> Some of the older officers, they are just trying to do their job. Like Miss _____. She's got her ways, but if you got a problem, she's on top of it and she'll solve it. Don't traffic and trade in front of her, but if you are being threatened, you can go to her and she will nip it in the bud. Then you go to others and they would do nothing.

In the NIC survey, women were quite mixed in their perspectives on staff. In answering our questions about the levels of staff and managers' concern about their sexual safety, women were divided: about 40 percent felt staff were concerned about their sexual safety; 25 percent were neutral ("neither agree or disagree"); and the remaining women did not feel that staff were concerned at all. Administrative staff were seen to be somewhat more concerned about sexual safety than line staff—although the differences were not great. (See appendix 2, table 12.)

Some staff members are said to "look the other way" when women are in jeopardy. According to Olivia, staff apathy supports intraprisoner exploitation:

> The staff turn their head when women are getting into trouble. They just turn their head. There are some [prisoners] that have to pay [a prisoner shot caller] to stay in the room because staff won't help us.

Others, as Joie suggested, "let things happen" for their own amusement:

> If it's a good fight, they [COs] let it happen before they call a code. They find it interesting if Pit Bulls [two aggressive women] are fighting. They want to see what happens.

The Asymmetry of Respect

The complete authority of prison staff that creates structured inequality in prison capital leads to an asymmetry of respect. Quoting Michael Ignatieff, Rhodes (2004, 57) suggests that prisoners "feel the silent contempt of authority at a glance, gesture or procedure." In the gendered community, however, contempt is not always silent. Treating women disrespectfully is a pervasive theme throughout the country. In the 2013 NIC study, we asked women about their experiences with verbal harassment by the staff. A significant majority of women identified "cursing" and "yelling and screaming" as "big" and "very big" problems in their housing units in every prison and jail we surveyed (see appendix 2, table 4). One woman wrote on the NIC survey form:

> The staff cuss out the women inmates and dog us out, downgrade us any way they can. They make fun of us, and yet we are supposed to try and better our self-esteem. Our low self-esteem is part of why we're here. It's just wrong.

General "disrespectful comments" were rated as problematic as well (see appendix 2, table 4). The following written comment on the survey described the asymmetry of respect that shapes their world:

> I feel as though staff here are very rude and disrespectful to inmates but expect us to treat them with respect. They talk down to us and yell at us. I don't think it's fair because if we talk to them a certain way, they don't agree, and we get wrote up. And it's not right when the mission statement says "We care about inmates."

Ashley described this asymmetry in terms of women's inability to respond in kind when called names:

> They can call you everything—ho, bitch, black bitch. They aren't supposed to say that stuff, but let us say that to them and we get written up.

Staff name calling is not exclusive to male officers. Female officers also engage in this form of disrespect, as this survey comment illustrated:

> Female officers are rude, use their tone of voice offensively, have a demeaning lower character & will raise their voice & make one feel threatened & afraid of them. Then laugh with each other under their breath.

For women whose pathways were paved by abuse, such talk reinforces their feelings of inadequacy. Noa said:

> The staff has no respect for us women; they call us bitches, hos, whores, cunts every day, all day! They yell at us like trash. [I think] they would hit us if they could! After hearing how dumb, how worthless you are, you start to believe it too!

Screaming at confined women was said to be an everyday occurrence. Olivia gave one example:

The new COs must know how to scream because that is all they do. They should learn not to be screaming. It [screaming] does not mean that the inmates are out of control. It could be something else—problems with his kids, his wife is cheating on him. He comes in here and can control 140 women who will do whatever he wants. I have seen staff out of control—screaming, spittle, neck cords [bulging], and you see the women shrink back.

Melly said, to her, the verbal abuse was worse than other forms of staff misconduct:

You can talk about the beatings and the rapes. But for women here, it is the subliminal messages that we are worthless. When an officer looks at you like something he scraped off his shoes. When you wait patiently [when requesting something] and see them joking, passing magazines. They don't want to be bothered with us. That [disrespectful speech] is a rape of my spirit. You come into my cell and terrorize me. You rape me every single day [with the demeaning attitude]. I can take the physical violence. You can wash that away, but it is the emotional violence that is so hard here.

Women reported that some staff routinely tell women they are "worthless," "not good moms," and "retarded" or "stupid." Remarks about body shape and size and degree of attractiveness and other gendered observations are routine. The women we spoke with and surveyed made it clear that not all staff members used degrading language, but they were troubled that other staff members did not intervene. Some felt that this lack of response by a "good officer" was as troubling as the name calling and verbal harassment of others. Laura suggested this explanation for the verbal abuse: "This is my take, especially for the men [COs]. They were all disrespected or abused by their mommas and they come in here and take it out on us." Although insults continually undermine women's feelings of safety, more extreme language can be found in interactions between prisoners and staff. The following disturbing example was reported to have occurred on a transportation bus:

I heard him tell this Mexican girl that, "I am not your old man or your husband. I will pull over this bus and fuck you and fuck you hard." And I am like, "He cannot say that. That is wrong."

When prisoners are moved from prison to prison, to and from jails and courts, and to outside services such as hospitals, women are particularly vulnerable to staff abuse. Tangie described a time when a private transport officer assaulted her in a bathroom after threatening her with "taking me into the desert, shooting me, and leaving me for dead" if she reported his abuse.

Staff too are deeply invested in the concept of respect. Some staff members claimed that women in jails and prison had to earn their respect. For example, one female custody staff member noted:

> I was walking on the yard, and there was a woman [inmate who] said, "Hey, what time is it?" I said I didn't know. Then she screamed out, "Thanks, bitch!" So I turned around, like, "Come here, now it is time to counsel you." She needed to keep her mouth shut. They can come in and spit at us and hit us and all of that. How do they expect our respect? Oh, no. Not me.

Some staff members recognized that staff culture can contribute to their problems, as this longtime officer told us:

> Here you still have officers not teaching correctly, teaching bad attitudes [to new staff]. If an officer has a bad attitude and passes it on [to other officers], like, "You run this place; that inmate can't tell you nothing. You are never wrong." They are teaching the wrong attitude.

The idea that there was not much difference between officers and the women in custody is a standard refrain among those we interviewed, as shown by Julianne's statement:

> The officers that come to work here, they just pick them off the streets. If you don't have a felony you can work here. It does not matter if you do drugs or have a misdemeanor, you can work here. I filled out an application to work here and I caught a felony right after that. I came in, instead of working here!

Teresa described staff coming to work under the influence of some substance:

> They [officers] come in high. Third shift is real good and toasty [high]. Some of the guards come in smelling like drugs or alcohol. I know what crack smells like. One officer here tries to cover up the [crack] smell with perfume.

Focus groups with staff echoed concern about the problematic quality of employees. A supervisor said:

> Lowering standards for employment is the biggest problem. We have officers that are illiterate. Some of the reports we have seen can't spell "when" or "are." Half the time you can't read it. I got hired through law enforcement. There were ninety people in the room to get that job. We had to write an essay. I was one out of seven hired. I thought "Damn, I'm good. I'm the best." It made me feel good about myself. I don't feel special anymore when you're hiring people who just got their GED and are eighteen years old. Every word starts with "F," and that is the only word they know how to spell. And these are my peers.

Another staff person echoed the feeling that others were ill prepared:

> My opinion is to raise pay and education level and age level requirements and hire people that truly believe that their position is a role model and to conduct themselves that way. I have officers say, "It's weak to say 'Thank you' and 'Please' to inmates." That's the stupidest thing I've ever heard.

Lack of consistency in running a unit is another contradiction of prison life that contributes to chaos and tension. Differences in staff behaviors (across different staff and sometimes by one who "blows hot and cold") force women to shift safety strategies to accommodate personal procedures or unpredictable actions, as Janis observed:

> Each CO has a different way of doing things, and we are supposed to do it one way one day and another way another day. One CO puts the lights on at 6 A.M., and if you turn off the lights, she gets mad. We tell her that the flies are attracted to the lights. The inmates ask if they can turn the lights off, and she says no. And yet this other CO will keep the lights off and it is not a problem. It is different each day and you never know.

Officers also recognize this inconsistency. The following quote is from the officer who described the "Bessie Bad Ass" female officer:

> It makes it hard when you come in, and your unit is off the hook [disrupted]. You can look at the unit and know exactly who you are relieving. You are cleaning up their mess. The Bessie Bad Ass and the Inmate-Friendly do not realize that their shift is horrible, and what you have to do to clean it up. I was a preschool teacher and when I first got this job, I was scared [of inmates]. I learned in the first two weeks I was here that it was the other officers you had to worry about, not the inmates.

Staff inconsistency creates risk to women and staff. In our conversations, women were incensed about situations in which housing unit officers put them "in the crosses" with other women and staff. We heard many examples of one staff member giving women permission to do something out of the normal routine or the typical schedule, such as using the restroom, being outside a room or cell, or making a phone call. When such "out of bounds" behavior came to the attention of another officer, the staff who had given permission typically did not cover for the prisoner, putting her "in the crosses" for breaking a rule. In some cases, women were given disciplinary reports for this behavior, even though they had received permission from another officer. Women knew that whatever the circumstances, it was unlikely that staff would "back them up," by taking their side against another staff member. This perception of unfairness further undermines faith in staff, underscoring the asymmetry of power.

Gendered Staff Relations

Gender complicates prisoners' perspectives on staff. We found no consensus among prisoners about the relative merits of female and male officers. Again, the definition of a "good" officer shifts according to a woman's stocks of capital and her strategies for seeking safety. Some women thought female officers were more likely to use force; others said the male officers were. Some did not like the fact that the males were more distant, but at the same time female officers were described as nosy or "too involved" with their lives. This remark from Sweets captured a common attitude about male staff:

> The male staff are very confrontational with women. They like to get into your face and talk crazy to you. They want to lock you up. They want you to go off. When the male officers work, they come in here with an attitude. They say, "If you don't do what I say, you're going to the hole."

However, just as many women indicated they would rather be guarded by men. One woman, Bobbie, said, "I would rather have men in general. They are less petty and invasive."

Some prisoners preferred female officers. Trixi, for example, suggested, "The CO women are more concerned and more sympathetic than the men who come in." Some women are more comfortable around female officers and prefer to interact with them. Toni expressed concern that female officers could be harmed by women prisoners:

> I have to give female officers their props because I've been in a jail and I saw a woman grab a female officer and slam her head into the bars. For the males, the guy cops, there is no aspect that this woman is going to beat the crap out of me [because they are generally stronger]. The women [COs] have to have this in the back of their mind. There are some big women [prisoners] out there, and they are bigger than me. That would be a constant thought for me.

Some women felt female staff are "way worse," as Suki said:

> All of the problems I have had with staff were with females. When they are stripping us out, just derogatory comments, or just being rude. They grab your boobs, and it was just not OK to me. The women COs are more violent and aggressive than the men, especially if you're sure of yourself. They want you to bow down to them, they seek you out to see how far they are going to push you.

Staff members too have opinions about the differences between male and female officers, although there was no consensus as to which was more likely to be more effective. One male staff member said:

> It is mainly male staff members [that are verbally abusive] with female inmates. Females [inmates] are more emotional. They [male staff] say, "I can't say anything to them without them snapping about it. I need to quit."

Another male officer was succinct: "Men are more strong of character. It's more effective to have men." Still another offered this typology:

> There are three kinds of female officers: (1) Inmate-friendly officer, (2) Professional, and (3) a Bessie Bad Ass. The second one has an easy time. One and three have problems. Three will write reports all night long. Having to relieve them [3s] is a mess.

Staff Perceptions of Women Prisoners

As the history of women's prisons demonstrates, attitudes and interpretations of imprisoned women shift according to political winds and public will. Treated as correctional afterthoughts in the contemporary era (Ross and Fabiano 1986), women are further disadvantaged by policies and procedures designed for male prisoners (Bloom, Owen, and Covington 2003). The lack of gender-informed policies plays out in staff attitudes toward women. Previous research has examined staff interaction with women prisoners, focusing on their "emotionality" (Pollock 1984), the impact of staff gender on supervision (Pollock 1986; Zupan 1986, 1992), and the "dislike" of women in their care (Rasche 2000). Luna offered her view on gendered prison management: "They need training, gender-responsive, because they do not know how to talk to us." In another group, Hope suggested that staff should have training on how to "stand, talk, and walk in the presence of women." A male staff member noted that women prisoners should not be treated the same as their male counterparts:

> With these women, they come up to us from this roundabout way. From the male perspective, we are like, "Get to the damn point." If people were trying to address that in training and trying to get people to know that women and men communicate in different ways, that would help.

Another staff person concurred:

> The gender-responsive training doesn't cover that as much as it should, and that was one letdown. Many custody staff have the old mentality dealing

with women as men. And it doesn't work. I don't think that they can deal well with the gender-responsive stuff.

Martina summed up a prisoner perspective on gendered attitudes:

> We are not men, and they need to not talk with me like a man. The new staff have little attitudes that they have from working in a men's prison and they need to change up. I think there is an attempt by the COs and the administration that they need to become more like the big guys' prison, and there is no need for it, but they do it and it is very intimidating.

Intrastaff Conflict

Like any work setting, staff do not always get along with their coworkers. Women are well aware of the conflict among staff members. Prisoners watch staff "24/7," day in and day out, for years, developing specific and sometimes quite personal knowledge of staff lives. Although it is prohibited, staff routinely talk about their personal lives when on duty, often within earshot of prisoners. Women know who is sleeping with whom, who is having personal and financial trouble, which marriage is in difficulty, and which staff are "mad with each other." In addition to interpersonal conflicts, racial and other political conflicts among officers are well known. Anne offered an example of intrastaff conflict: "I've seen shirts come off between officers [in preparing to fight] on a lot of racial issues. We laugh, but it's not really funny." Getting caught up in "staff games" places prisoners in vulnerable positions. Jas felt she was caught in the middle when a staff conflict was "played out" on her, resulting in her placement in administrative segregation while under investigation for intrastaff troubles outside her control.

Prisoners may be put in jeopardy when they are in a position to observe arguments between staff members. Women will attempt to leave the area when they can, but often they have nowhere to go. Romina offered a complicated example:

> Two COs had a fight. It was a husband and wife. They had a fight right here in the parking lot. The [female] CO had an inmate girlfriend in another unit. One day, she was talking to her [inmate girlfriend], but the CO husband was listening in on the phone when she was talking to her.
>
> The girl [prisoner] also has a [prisoner] girlfriend, but she is saying [to the girlfriend], "Let me just use her. Let me get what I can get from her." But the girl's [prisoner] girlfriend got jealous and went to the warden. The CO husband was so pissed that he and the wife went at it in the parking lot.

Like coworkers anywhere, staff members develop personal relationships. Prisoners are attuned to the nature of these relationships, particularly if they turn serious or sexual. Tasia flatly stated, "Staff are so busy sleeping with each other that they don't know what is happening." Some women may "keep their mouths shut" about their knowledge of staff unprofessionalism, but everyone must stay vigilant in the event that staff conflict threatens their search for safety. Some women may file this information away to be used to compromise staff in the future.

Staff Contributions to Violence

While we agree that all staff members have the right and responsibility to use appropriate force to subdue a problem prisoner or gain compliance to a lawful order, excessive force is always outside the law. In certain situations, some officers are more likely to resort to violence, just as some women were more likely to engage in physical altercations with officers. These two groups, together, create an escalating dynamic. Given a more submissive, less argumentative, and nonaggressive woman, officers may not respond with physical force. Given a more professional, calmer officer, who does not react in kind, the situation may not escalate. Regardless of the context, women always lose in any contest between staff and prisoner. This is especially true when the use of force involves male officers. Vanessa described this gender effect when she tried to stop a fight:

> I wasn't fearful of what the ladies [inmates] could do. I was more fearful of what the officers would do if we were fighting. They come in and slam everyone around. I was more fearful of that. I could deal with the two women.

While male violence against women is an easy stereotype, such an explanation ignores the violence potential between women prisoners and female staff. Beck (2015, 9) points out that female staff involvement with prisoners has typically been understood as a boundary violation but should be reframed instead as "predatory in nature, initiated by the staff, and involving explicit force or threat of force." This is true, regardless of gender. Melissa gave us an extreme example of staff-prisoner conflict that escalated into violence:

> She [the CO] kept harassing me over a period of months. She was provoking me. She harassed me all day long and I just snapped. I was in the [officer's dining room]. I've stabbed sergeants [before]. When I went into [there] and said I'm going to beat her, they had to stop me.

Some women claimed that correctional officers goaded them into being violent so that they could, in turn, deploy violence. As Josie recounted:

> I was going through some issues and [a female CO] was always nitpicking. I could be acting perfect and she would pull me out of line and make me wait for nothing. Just stuff like that. That day I was having a real bad day and the officer was working. She and I did not get along at all. She would talk crazy, real, real crazy and real, real flying off the handle. We got into it. She started pushing the door open, and I started putting on my socks and shoes. I was ready to fight. I told her I got just enough time [left in my sentence] to cover [serve the disciplinary time for] what I was going to do to her.

Staff "setups" to provoke women to react with violence were described by Patrice:

> Now staff will set you up. They go out of their way to provoke you. The kids [younger women] bite [at the provocation and then get into trouble]. We [older prisoners] know that we can walk away. When I walk away, I cry, but I will not let them see my tears. But the youngsters have not learned that.

Casey recalled overhearing an officer who stated, "I wish there was more violence here so I can have more to do."

In their search for safety, women become very aware of the violent officers and learn to avoid interacting with them whenever possible. As Tally described, "He's just got a reputation for slamming females. Everyone just knows that." Women also told us that staff violence against any individual woman had a ripple effect, often triggering women who have been traumatized by violence in their pathways to prison. When one woman is mistreated violently by officers, the incident raises the tension level, and all are affected. Alicia described an event that took place in a jail:

> And she [inmate] told the lady [officer], "If you touch me again, I'll kick you." And so she kicked the lady. And, oh God! The male guard, he slammed her head against the wall, and they were literally punching her like that [demonstrated fist blows to the stomach]. She was shackled and she fell to the ground and they pulled her up by the arms. And I was sure her arms were broken. They were punching and kicking her. And we were all crying.

The women in our study had complex attitudes toward violence among themselves and with staff. While some women were not strangers to violence, deploying it as prison capital, they also described limits on what they view as acceptable. Fights among women seemed to be perceived as normal, but violence delivered by staff was not. Bethanie said:

There was this lieutenant. He was so violent toward the inmates. He broke their arms, broke their teeth. There was this little girl, one hundred pounds. He got her on the ground, beating her. We were all afraid of the lieutenant. You didn't want to do nothing. You wait till he's not there if you want to fight 'cuz he'll kill you.

In contrast, some custody staff believe coworkers who are afraid to use force against women place themselves and other staff members in harm's way, as this veteran custody staff member suggested:

The inmates know the new officer will try to go by policy, but, with us, we will be spontaneous right along with you [prisoners who fight]. [It] causes violence because they hesitate. We just jump in.

Not all staff feel violence against women is appropriate. A noncustody staff member said:

I have seen and heard a number of things about physical violence. It's what I consider abuse. I felt like the officers were excessive a number of times. I saw them body slam an inmate against the wall. A number of things happen more to mentally ill inmates. I was told by one officer that a mentally ill inmate who was very psychotic and unable to control her actions was pulled by the hair and dragged from one unit to another.

It is also true that officers can be hurt, sometimes seriously, by women prisoners. We heard stories of extreme violence perpetrated against staff members by women, such as sticking a pencil in an officer's neck, cutting an officer's face, and hitting an officer with a "lock in the sock." There has been group violence against officers as well, although these incidents are rare. One officer described one such incident:

I had three officers taken down. The inmates planned on killing them. An offender escaped the cellblock and came and told us they were going to kill them [the officers]. We ran in there. One officer was down and unconscious. I could see her laying down at the end of the run. I figured she was dead already. The other two were practically unconscious. They were being held up and pummeled in the face. They could not stand on their own. Two of the officers were tough officers. One officer was not tough but was in the wrong place at the wrong time and she was weak. The other two were by the book, very tough but consistent. Excellent cellblock officers, but they messed up that day. Assaults on officers were not a felony then, they were a misdemeanor. Now they are back to a felony. I would love to tell you we were appropriate when we went in there, but we weren't. If there was ever an excessive use of force, that was it, and I would do it again.

Although we heard many stories about conflict and violence perpetrated by staff in the interviews, the findings from our survey seem to contradict them. Even with these intense descriptions of staff violence against women in their charge, our NIC survey data did not indicate that staff physical violence was a major problem among the majority of prisoners surveyed. While the expected variation occurred across the housing units and the facility types, about three-fourths of the survey participants rated their perception of staff physical violence while being searched as a minimal problem. About one-fourth of the women indicated staff "have used too much force when physically controlling women." (See appendix 2, table 6.)

We conclude that physical violence is not an essential feature of interactions between staff and women but, like violence among women prisoners, "could happen anywhere, at any time." We can surmise that for most women this is not the first experience with disrespect and conflict, and perhaps they accept it as unexceptional. While the majority of women did not see staff violence as a big problem, it is a real possibility in the ever-changing dynamics of prison life. For women who feel vulnerable, who have little prison capital, or who live in the 'thunder domes" of violent prison neighborhoods, this concern may be more immediate. But for all members of this community, the potential for staff violence lurks as a threat to their safety.

STAFF SEXUAL MISCONDUCT

We learned more about staff sexual misconduct by examining letters written by imprisoned women to the prisoner advocacy organization Just Detention International (formerly known as Stop Prison Rape). We reviewed fifty-seven letters from women describing serious assaults by staff. (See appendix 1 for our methodology.) These letters expressed women's anguish and despair that the abuse of their pathway experiences was "happening to me again." Excerpts from the letters are presented throughout this chapter.

The vast majority of staff members come to work every day for the right reasons. But for some small number, staff sexual misconduct represents another potential for state-sponsored harm (Baro 1997; Amnesty International 1999; Flesher 2007; Henriques and Gilbert 2000; Human Rights Watch 1996, 1998; Just Detention International 2009; UNODC 2015; Labelle 2013). As Beck (2015, 9) articulates, all "sexual relations between staff and inmates are considered abuse, even if the sexual activity would have been considered consensual had it occurred outside of a prison or jail." Due to the "inherently unequal positions" between staff and prisoners, prisoners "do not have the same ability as staff members to consent to a sexual relationship" (Beck 2015, 9). He concludes:

> It is the power and authority that the staff member holds over the inmate, even when the inmate may have initiated the sexual contact, which defines the contact as abuse. Most forms of staff sexual misconduct are illegal, while sexual harassment is typically a violation of professional codes of conduct. In every case, such activity alters the boundary between professional roles and personal relationships. Moreover, such activity compromises the safety and security of the correctional facility in which it occurs. (2015, 9)

Under international law, staff sexual assault is torture (Just Detention International 2009); it violates the basic protections of human rights.

All members of the prison community are well aware of this misconduct. Most staff and managers express disgust and puzzlement about their colleagues who betray their professional duties. As a custody staff person said in our initial exploration of staff perspectives on sexual safety, "Staff sexual misconduct involves using power to get what the staff member wants. We are supposed to be taking care of the offenders, not hurting them" (Owen and Moss 2009, 9).

Some staff are obvious in their appreciation of attractive prisoners. Several women described how staff members have told them they were "too pretty to be in prison." We also heard stories of officers competing for attentions of an attractive prisoner or of those who became jealous because their desired woman was in a relationship with another prisoner. Such emotions may cause staff members to perform in an unprofessional manner, as Bettina related:

> When I was nineteen years old, I was in a relationship with a male officer. He would come to my cell, but I was scared to get sexual with him. It wasn't physical. But in the process, I started messing with [another prisoner], and he didn't like that. When he found out that I was messing with women, he got mad about it. He would cross her [girlfriend] out all the time so that I would intervene. He kept messing with her and messing with her.

> One time, we were in line waiting to get our food and I'm talking to her. He started giving her a hard time, so I said something to him, and he said he wasn't talking to me. But I said, "If you're talking to her, you're talking to me." He said to go to my house [cell]. I walked away and he wouldn't get off my back. Then he took me by the back of my neck and slammed me into the floor. I hit the floor so hard everyone in the dayroom heard it. I was thin

then, no more than 110 pounds, and he was over 6 feet tall. This side of my face was twice as big and my eye was swollen. A lot of inmates told [the investigators] about our relationship. I denied it. I ended up getting a major case because he lied.

In this world of constrained choice, "consensual" relationships between prisoners and staff occur, but the degrees of willingness are difficult to determine. Women prisoners are not a homogeneous group of passive victims and can exercise agency within these constrained choices of sexual behavior. Some fall in love with staff, some actively exploit male or female officers who fall in love with them, and some willingly participate in sexual banter. When female prisoners actively seek out sexual relationships with male and female staff members, it may be the case that such relationships are truly consensual, or it may be that such relationships can be understood as the tactics of the oppressed, a result of sexualized identity with few other sources of prison capital. Regardless of motivation, sexual relationships with prisoners are unprofessional, against policy, and illegal, regardless of consent.

Women have wide-ranging perspectives on prisoner and staff sexual relationships. Caren dismissed any possibility of a sexual relationships with staff: "I would not get involved with a man. I have free will and do not get myself in that situation." Perhaps Caren felt protected by both her resolve to "not get involved with a man" and her stocks of prison capital. Her view may also reflect a sense that so many women were available for these illegal liaisons that she could fully opt out and leave this messy behavior to others.

Prisoners do initiate relationships with staff as an expression of agency or resistance or for romance or sex. Such relationships can also be a form of prison capital as "being the girlfriend" can provide goods, services, and privilege. As Brandi said, "Inmates try to bring themselves out like that to [attract] the men. Try to seduce them. Trying to show off a little bit or try to come at them a bit." Some women "flirt in an obvious way" and "get away with everything" when their "boy toy" is on duty. Tommi provided a detailed account of her relationship with an officer during a previous term in another facility. Esther, who did time with Tommi in the past, listening to her recount these events, exclaimed, "I knew you were sleeping with him. I knew it." Whether public or private, relations with staff can provide some capital to those involved but also create risk. When caught, women are almost always the losers. But, sometimes it is the staff member who loses, as in Hillary's example: "They had a five-year relationship. He would key her out at night and then he started dating a girl from the free world and she got mad. He got walked off and now she is filing a lawsuit." (See appendix 2, tables 4, 5 and 6.)

Some staff members may respond openly to these overtures. Bernie observed:

> We have one guy who came in with a hard-on walking around in our pod, and he is teasing the girls and looking at them in their bras and he was dancing for the girls. And, you might think it is funny, but I think it is very unprofessional. They [inmates] make sexual comments toward the guys [COs]. I don't think the staff should fall for this. He should not flirt with them. It goes both ways. The women can be rather blunt, obvious, even with the visitors, and making comments. It goes both ways.

Certain types of male staff members were said to be particularly open to attention from women, as suggested by Kerry:

> When men come to work in a place like this, we call them "prison superstars" 'cuz they are a legend in their own mind. They can't get women to pay attention to them on the streets so they come in here and they get attention because we don't see a lot of men. Some of the women act certain ways to get a man to pay attention to them and the officers get them [the prisoners] to depend on them.

These intersections of power and gender play out in interactions between male staff and the prisoners. But how should we frame trouble and violence between female officers and female prisoners? Like the same-gender violence among the women, physical and sexual violence perpetrated by female staff also may occur. Most women who reported sexual assaults in surveys conducted by the Bureau of Justice Statistics indicated their perpetrator was male (Beck, Harrison, and Guerino 2010, 5). About one-fifth of those reporting misconduct, however, reported victimization by both female and male staff.

Staff acknowledge these problems with misconduct, but their view is complicated by the contradictions of "consensual" sexual relationships. A custody staff person observed:

> It's a problem or people wouldn't get walked off. There is a problem with staff being overfamiliar or inappropriate with the inmates. Sometimes it can be sexual. It has been consensual, and although by law it is not, but you never know. We have a lot of staff that get in trouble here for inappropriate behavior with inmates and two or three times a year someone gets walked off. I wouldn't classify it as victimization because the inmate is doing it consensually.

With the advent of the PREA legislation, and subsequent state and local laws developed in response, prison and jail systems are now required to take this problem seriously.

A CONTINUUM OF STAFF SEXUAL MISCONDUCT

Our data allowed us to construct a continuum of staff sexual misconduct. The low end is anchored by claims of love, seduction, and inappropriate comments and conversation. Risk and victimization can escalate across this continuum, with violent, forced sex at the most extreme end.

Love and Seduction

In any setting where humans are in close proximity, there is the possibility for mutual attraction, even in the unequal world of the prison. We heard stories about officers falling in love with prisoners, women falling in love with staff, and mutual attraction. Exploitation of all sorts is embedded in these unequal equations. In another example of a woman losing out in her relationship with an officer, one JDI letter writer reported that she had "not had sex yet but planned to do so" and had discussed "sexual positions" with this officer. She described the relationship as a "flirtation." It appears the relationship was interrupted by an investigation, resulting in sanctions against the prisoner but not the staff member. The woman wrote to ask JDI "where to turn for help" as she felt she "took the blame" because she did not want the CO to lose his job. Relationships "gone bad" are very likely to have serious negative repercussions for women prisoners.

Inappropriate Comments and Conversation

Verbal harassment was both the least serious type of victimization and the most common. Sexual banter between officers and prisoners is routine. Sometimes it is mutual (although unprofessional); other times it is more threatening. It is not clear to us whether staff members did not understand the inappropriateness of these comments, whether they were unconcerned with the consequences, or whether these comments were intended to explore sexual possibilities. This is a typical story: "I was in the front row [of the shower] and someone [a staff member] came in and said, 'Damn, that should be illegal' [referring to her body]. I felt very uncomfortable." Nia added:

> There was this officer who called me out. He gave me a note one time about how I was sexy. I did not know what to do, who to tell. I had just got to prison. I felt like he just could do that because I was a prisoner. When he

would come in to do a cell check, he would come over to my bunk and stand there over me. He would make little comments . . . sexual comments . . . stuff he should not be saying. I threatened to tell the lieutenant.

Women prisoners participate in sexual banter because they enjoy it, think they may get something from it, or do not know any other way to interact. They may also be afraid to not participate. Given their common backgrounds of inappropriate sexualization, sexual interaction with authority figures is a way to survive.

Sexual Requests

Sexual banter can escalate into direct requests. Kala recalled this experience:

> This man last month said, "Oh, I wish I could take you in the room and you know what." I said, "What?" He says, "You know, so you could give me some head and then I could do you." I was, like, "What?" I couldn't believe he said that and I was, like, "You nasty bastard, you mf-er." I got embarrassed.

When staff members are confronted about these indecent requests, they are often reframed as "jokes" or, when reported, dismissed by supervisors as insincere and "just kidding." Women's reports of such harassment are often minimized. Florrie said:

> If you tell an officer that you are being sexually harassed, they will tell you that the officers are just joking. They say just because the other officers asked to see your titties, doesn't mean they really wanted to.

Sexual requests sometimes escalate into sexual assault. In another letter to JDI, a woman wrote, "Other women have said that this officer had asked them to show him their breasts and watched them while they showered," but "I did not expect him to be a rapist." However, when the assault occurred, "The guttural tone of the voice he used and the glazed, scary look in his eyes made it clear to me that he was not kidding and that I had better not question what he told me to do." For women with extensive experience with sexual violence, these experiences with those in authority reinforce gendered pains of imprisonment.

"Flashing," Voyeurism, and Touching

More assertive sexualized behavior included looking at women in inappropriate ways, asking a woman to expose herself, and inappropriate touching. Being encouraged to display a body part is not uncommon, as Miranda noted: "He likes for you to bend down [to show your breasts], and then he rubs his hands on his pants and says, 'Look! Look!' to show you that you are turning him on." "Peeping" on women while sleeping, showering, or going to the bathroom is common in this world of women. Sometimes women would cooperate in the peeping by not wearing underwear or otherwise giving the officer a "show," usually for some compensation, as described by Molly:

> The male officers watch the girls. They prey on those girls that are in their area. They go around at night. They peep. [Laughter] They [prisoners] give them a peep show. They lay there naked. [The prisoners] give them their eyes full so they give her a trinket.

As always, women are attuned to their vulnerabilities to staff power. One woman told us:

> The officers go around and they single in on the weak woman and they boost her up. Then when they get caught, the female says [staff] promised me this or that, and then they write up the woman.

Officers and other staff members may touch women outside the scope of their duties. Izzy shared her experience with staff sexual assault at an outside hospital, describing her passive acceptance of the abuse.

> I had to go to hospital for surgery. So I was prepped for surgery. They had me in a room with empty beds. They left me in there with a man for four hours. I had no clothes on. So he was there when they were doing my blood work. He was listening [to make sure] that I didn't have AIDS, that I was clean. I was drifting off to sleep, and I felt his hand was feeling my tits. I could see the nurses' station, and here he is by me, watching for them too, but with his hand on me. He was running his hands under my gown, on my breast. I said, "No. No." I ended up not having the surgery, but I couldn't believe it. He like said, "You're OK with this, right?" I said, "Whatever. Whatever."

Abuse of Search Authority

When male officers are permitted to physically search women, re-traumatization is a possible outcome (Covington 2013). For women with trauma histories, the experience of being under the control of and touched by a man in this situation is frightening and may trigger feelings of anxiety and seemingly irrational reactionary violence. Tamara observed this incident: "One girl has this white T-shirt that she has had forever and it is getting thin and she wears a black bra. The officer had his hands all over her tits when he patted her down."

However, "maleness" is not a necessary cause of such misconduct. Women were just as likely to feel victimized by female officers who abused their power to conduct body searches. Tonya provided this illustration: "The female staff searches me so thoroughly that I think they owe me dinner. I am glad that the men do not search, but the women have become very bad."

Also speaking about female staff, Beatrice added, "They will touch your private parts and she will grab you up all up in here [as she demonstrates by grabbing herself]." In some locales, male officers are prohibited from patting down female prisoners unless it is an emergency. In other prisons, there are no such restrictions.

Just as women differ on their preference for female or male officers in general, there was no consensus as to gender and search preferences. Some women prefer to be searched by male officers. Others object to searches by female officers they perceive as gay, as Faye remarked:

> It's a couple or few who are gay. One girl told me one of the guards said, "I feel like I'm going to strip someone. I ain't seen no such and such [genitals] lately." Then there's this one lady. Lord help me! Please don't let this lady pat me down. This lady goes up in your crotch and goes up and grips your stuff [demonstrates grabbing the genital area]. And then [she] goes up and lifts up your breasts [demonstrates by squeezing breasts]. And you can't say anything to them. Then you'll get in trouble.

On the other hand, Beanie suggested that lesbian officers might be afraid of accusations of inappropriate searching and do not perform thorough searches:

> I know two gay officers in my dorm. And in all the years I had known them, they would not pat search us. Anyone that is openly gay would not pat search us and a lot [of prisoners] would be glad [because they could sneak things into the dorm]. When you get the straight ones, they most likely are going to touch you.

Sexual Exchange

Sexual exchange may be a reasonable solution to lack of capital. With histories of past sexual victimization, inappropriate sexualization, and sex work, women can offer their bodies to obtain material goods or privileges from staff. Such exchanges are another expression of the constrained choice that shapes women's behaviors under conditions of inequality. Loni explained, "One cup of coffee can get you whatever you want in here. The men and female officers know that and they use that to manipulate and degrade us." Women scoff at those who receive very little in exchange, as Junie recounted:

> She did [sex acts] for him and all she gets is a pen. He gets to watch her take a shower. I want more than a pen and a phone call. You better bring me some Coca-Cola. I have a list. [Laughter from other women participating in the interview.]

Lack of prison capital can lead to naive and unrealistic estimations of staff members' ability to deliver on their promises. Kristi said:

> You have those where an officer promises you something, like to call your family, put something under your mattress, or write you a recommendation to parole. The young ones, they don't know any better. They will do oral or whatever, because they don't know [staff can't deliver] when the officer says, "I'm going to get you out of here." It wasn't forced, but it was manipulated. We are vulnerable.

The unevenness of such a sexual exchange was described by Graciela:

> I think that young women would do this [have sex with staff] because they think that they can get gratuities from it. Whatever the reason, it is their business, but these men can take advantage of us because they have power over us.

In a letter written to JDI from jail, Aman described a practice whereby a staff member who brought both female and male prisoners into his office to "make phone calls, play cards, drink coffee and eat food." She said that the officer told her he would help her stay out of prison, but this help "came at a price." Aman further reported, "[He] scared and harassed me until I performed oral sex on him."

Exchange relationships, even when women actively participate, are clearly outside the realm of legal and ethical conduct. Although unfair, this exchange of sexual favors, Holly told us, is good for everything "from a double cheeseburger to a couple of dollar bills to a pack of gum." She exhorted us to "be real" about the economic status of women in prison and the practicality of leveraging staff sexual interests for material gain. After all, in this community of scarcity, "You can get a couple of cigs for a peek-a-boo, a side show [flashing genitals or breasts], hand jobs, lap dance."

In another letter to JDI, Daniella described serial victimization by many staff members that began with an exchange relationship.

The officer made comments about my breasts and gave me cigarettes and food. He kissed me, had his fingers inside of me, and asked me to show him my breasts. I did do this and allowed him to touch me. Did I want him to? NO. Did I like him? NO. Did I want to smoke, eat good food? Yes.

Daniella went on to write that both she and the officer were reported. "I was called snitch even though I did not want to cooperate," she wrote.

While in the hole, another officer also gave me cigarettes and food, and I gave him oral sex. He then pulled out a condom and I said no because I was on my period. I have never told anybody about that. I was in the hole and staff were giving me hell already. Sometimes I feel guilty about what happened.

For women who seek to improve their prison capital through sexual exchange with staff, the situation may be defined as a business transaction. Prisoners often use the language of sex work, describing officers who engage in these sexual exchanges as "tricks."

Intimidation

In the unequal power relations of prisons and jails, there is a fine line between economic exchange and intimidation. If a woman says no to sexual entreaties made by an officer, the officer may turn to threats. Women express the view that they would do whatever they needed to not get moved to less desirable prisons or to avoid a disciplinary "ticket," or write-up. Letty said:

We put up with the abuse because we don't want to move to [another facility]. If the price of staying here is to get down on my knees, then I will get my knee pads.

Acknowledging that formal attention to staff misconduct has increased, Jada observed:

Back in the day, they would come in your cell and forcibly take it [have sex]. But now, I don't know, they have a little more finesse. But they will threaten you to do stuff with your room. The cops are known to set women up with drugs and let them get caught. Let the woman go down for the count.

Janell related this story of staff threats of disciplinary action:

He'd say, "You don't want to mess around? I'm going to cross you out [write a disciplinary report]." He got caught with his dick in her mouth. He was walked off. Fired. Some girls said, "It's about time he got caught; he's been doing it for about twenty years."

Sex without Physical Violence

As women have little power to object, differentiating between consensual and nonconsensual sex in the prison environment has little utility. All too often, women recognize that they have little recourse and must submit to these threats and intimidation. After all, women who report staff misconduct run the risk of not being believed and facing retaliation from several fronts. Many women understand the cost of refusing sexual advances. Others actively seek sex with staff and are willing participants in a sexual relationship. They may not "love" an officer, but they do not feel they are intimidated into a sexual relationship either.

Officers may be involved with several women at the same time. Ruthie talked about the power of officers to groom women for sexual activity:

> When you are vulnerable, when someone says he loves you, and cares about you, you let things happen to you. He said he was going to help me restore my relationship with the family. That was the open door that let down my walls and that led to the other things—rubbing my breast, touching me, kissing me. And there were other girls too.

> They were already suspicious of him 'cuz there were two other girls that said, "He sucked my finger," and "He kissed me."

> Everybody thought he was so wonderful. They thought he was caring for them. He did things for them that he shouldn't have, so they had a secret. Like my friend. He was making a phone call for her [as a favor] and she had a piece of candy. But then when she put the candy in his mouth, he sucked her finger. She instantly went crazy over him and she was so in love with him. She would get jealous whenever anybody was talking to him.

> But, see, he instigated that. Then he turned the tables on her and said she was stalking him and stuff. And he told them [the authorities] they needed to get her away from him, and so she was transferred off the unit. That's one of the girls that they didn't believe.

Another complication arises when staff involved with prisoners are married to another staff member in the same facility. Carly related:

> There was a guy that would invade my space in the kitchen. He would follow me back to the supply closet while I was doing inventory. I got fussed at [by his wife who was a lieutenant in the prison]. I got called into the count room with the lady from Internal Affairs, the Warden, and the lady from classification. They told me to go pack [to be transferred] and that they could protect me from him but not from her.

Our NIC survey data show that, unlike harassment, two-thirds of the women we asked rated overall staff sexual misconduct at the lowest end ("not a problem at all") on the scale. Some questions, however, received higher problem ratings: "staring at women's bodies" and "invading privacy" were seen to be some kind of problem by the majority of women participating in the survey. (See appendix 2, tables 4, 5 and 6, for our findings.)

Sex with Physical Violence

We heard very few stories of officers or other staff members physically forcing a woman to have sex. We could not determine whether this was due to the relative rarity of the event or the focus group method we used to collect the accounts. Through optional private interviews and the analysis of letters sent by women to Just Detention International, we have some insight into the severest staff sexual violence. These sources portray the worst staff sexual behavior, and while this behavior is perhaps infrequent, it demonstrates the potential for sexual harm delivered by those expected to protect women in their custody. One woman wrote to JDI, saying her assaulter "acted as if [sexual assault] was a natural part of the job."

Samantha told us about a friend who was in a consensual relationship she thought was romantic until she discovered the officer thought of her as a prostitute rather than a girlfriend.

> She consented to have sex with one of them, but then the other [staff member] came in and said, "You're going to take care of me, too." And she was liking the [first] officer, and she thought he loved her and stuff, but this was the way he treated her. Basically saying that he could get the same thing from anyone else. So the other officer did it in her anus and she was bleeding and she was mad and she reported it.

In a letter to JDI, Taylor described a violent assault, followed by threats of retaliation. She wrote that an officer "forced my pants down and opened his zipper as he pushed me down." Another prisoner who knocked on the door interrupted the assault. Taylor continued, "[The officer] told me that he would crush my skull if I said a word." Despite this threat, Taylor reported the assault. An investigator asked her if "it [the penis] was in there long enough" to count as a rape. She was very nervous about reporting the assault, explaining, "I had heard of the horrific retaliation the victims had suffered at the hands of the guards."

When she reported the assault to a female staff person, Taylor continued, "she told me to put everything in writing, but she said I would regret reporting the event." A lieutenant asked Taylor to recant, because "he would not have this in his prison." "I refused and was told I would be in disciplinary housing for a year." In addition, she wrote, an investigative officer "told me that I did just not get it. Prisoners never win." She was also told that the investigation would be done by his friends. Finally, Taylor was denied visits because the staff person said "she does not deserve" them. "That is what you get for reporting rape," she was told. Retaliation is a very real consequence for women in these untenable situations.

COLLATERAL CONSEQUENCES OF STAFF SEXUAL MISCONDUCT

Women who do report staff sexual misconduct run risks. In addition to the suffering inflicted by the same people being paid to protect them, women's safety and well-being are threatened by the collateral consequences of such misconduct. The JDI letters contain specific details about the serious consequences of sexual assault. Many women wrote about "not being believed" and other official reactions that discouraged the women from reporting. One woman who tried to report an assault was told that "there is no such thing as assault in this place" and that if she continued to pursue reporting the incident she would be punished by being put in protective custody. She persisted in making the report and was placed in disciplinary housing, losing her privileges, and her job.

Another woman wrote that when she told her prison counselor about a staff assault, he responded that she "had too many problems" and that "he did not know how to deal with" her. Another letter writer reported being told by a correctional officer that a certain woman "deserved being raped by other prisoners because she was a snitch" and "that no matter how many times she reported it, she would not be protected." This writer concluded her letter, "The Warden is the only one who cares about what happens to prisoners here." In yet another letter, a woman reported an assault to the PREA officer of the facility but felt that this official was "stand-offish" and did not take her claim seriously.

Many women said that retaliation by other officers was a form of continuing the abuse. One woman wrote, "All the guards know what has happened to me and with each passing day it gets worse." Others told of being forced to recant during the process of investigation because no one was going to believe them. Another woman wrote that she was continually asked, "What do you hope to gain by your claims?"

In yet another expression of the asymmetry of power, some women will protect an officer at the expense of other prisoners. In reporting on staff sexual misconduct, women who have been victims run the risk of displeasing other women who are "in the car" with staff and serve as instruments of staff retaliation, as Marla illustrated:

> The others [women] were ready to fight the two girls [who reported] because they thought they had a good staff person and they didn't want to lose him. He had everyone swooning over him, everyone in administration, the officers, because he was good-looking. So anyone that was talking against him was sent away. They moved her off in the middle of the night [and transferred her to another facility].

In her letter, Kala claimed the officer "hired a girl to sexually assault me" after the prisoner-officer relationship ended. The "girl" said she did it because she was told Kala was a "snitch." Concern that "friends of the officer" or "predatory women" would retaliate as a favor to the officer was a common collateral consequence.

In the letters to JDI, women also wrote about the emotional consequences of violent assaults. The majority reported their inability to feel safe after the incident and other feelings of helplessness. One woman wrote, "I thought I could deal with this by myself, but I can't." Among the most poignant reactions we found in the letters were statements about hopelessness and despair. These letters convey reflections on shared histories of violence and victimization. As one woman wrote, "I've been done worse as a child, even raped, but right is right and wrong is wrong." Not "mattering" was another painful theme. After describing her violent assault, this woman concluded, "That is what happened to me. It may mean nothing to them—but it means something to me. I didn't invite what happened. But the fact is, it did happen." Another letter echoes this theme: "There is nothing I can do about it. It's just something that happened to an already abused woman. Done. I didn't/don't matter." More simply, one letter writer said, "I can bear no more pain in my life."

LITIGATION AND INVESTIGATIONS
REGARDING STAFF SEXUAL VICTIMIZATION

About half of all verified staff sexual misconduct is perpetrated by female staff members guarding male prisoners (Beck 2015; Beck, Harrison, and

Guerino 2010; Beck et al. 2013). This is not surprising given that the vast majority of correctional staff are employed in men's facilities. However, most of the litigation and civil rights investigations focus on sexual assault of women. Here we discuss litigation in Michigan that highlights the extent of sexual violence committed by staff against imprisoned women.

Women in Michigan prisons have been engaged in litigation against the Michigan Department of Corrections since the 1990s, articulating criminal levels of sexual misconduct and assault. Evidence for this and subsequent lawsuits was collected by Human Rights Watch (1996, 1998), local journalists, and the legal team filing the lawsuit. The report *All Too Familiar* details the nature of this abuse.

> Male corrections employees vaginally, anally, and orally raped female prisoners and sexually assaulted and abused them. In the course of committing such gross abuses, male officers not only used actual or threatened physical force but also abused their near-total authority to provide or deny goods and privileges to female prisoners to compel them to have sex or to reward them for having submitted to sexual acts. In other cases, male officers violated their most basic professional duty and engaged in sexual contact with female prisoners absent the use or threat of force or any material exchange. In addition to engaging in sexual relations with prisoners, male officers used mandatory pat-frisks or room searches to grope women's breasts, buttocks, and vaginal areas and to view them inappropriately while in a state of undress in the housing or bathroom areas. Male corrections officers and staff also engaged in regular verbal degradation and harassment of female prisoners, thereby contributing to a custodial environment that was, and as this report documents, continues to be highly sexualized and excessively hostile. (Human Rights Watch 1996, 3)

The report shows both a pattern of unrelenting abuse by staff in the Michigan system and a systematic disregard for women's safety by ignoring their claims. Human Rights Watch confirms that such sexual assaults are clear human rights violations.

> Under both international and national law, states are clearly required to prevent and punish custodial sexual misconduct. The International Covenant on Civil and Political Rights (ICCPR) and the International Convention Against Torture and Other Cruel, Inhuman and Degrading Treatment or Punishment (Torture Convention), both of which the United States has ratified, require state parties to prohibit torture and other cruel, inhuman, or degrading treatment or punishment and to ensure that such abuse is investigated and punished. The ICCPR further guarantees prisoners a basic right to privacy, which has been interpreted to preclude strip searches by officers of the opposite sex. These rights are further enumerated in the Standard Minimum Rules, which call on governments to prohibit custodial sexual abuse, provide prisoners with an effective right to complain of such misconduct, ensure appropriate

punishment, and guarantee that these obligations are met in part through the proper training of correctional officers. In addition, the United States Constitution expressly protects prisoners from cruel and inhuman punishments and has been interpreted to accord prisoners' limited privacy rights as well as to guarantee them access to the courts. (Human Rights Watch 1996, 1)

Kubiak, Hanna, and Balton (2005) describe reactions of women who were assaulted in Michigan. Just as we found, one woman in their study had a fatalistic response to a male officer telling her he was going to have sex with her, responding to him by saying, "Yeah, right. Whatever" (164). Such fatalistic acceptance of sexual assault reflects the women's assumption that the correctional officers—like male adults when they were children—were omnipotent and would punish resistance. And in the prison world of profound inequity, officers do appear omnipotent and fully capable of punishing any resistance to their demands. In the women's eyes, acceptance of sexual assault is survival.

Many women believed that if they reported the incidents the officers and other staff members would retaliate. Their concerns about retaliation were borne out by subsequent research by Human Rights Watch (1996), which documented extreme levels of retaliation after the set of lawsuits the organization brought were settled. Officials and politicians did not cooperate and in fact interfered with investigations by the U.S. Department of Justice and the United Nations. The first case, involving thirty-two women, was settled in 2000 for $3.8 million. The second case, a class action suit involving around four hundred women, was settled for almost $100 million (Rigby 2006).

Rigby (2006) asserts that the problem of sexual violence in Michigan's women's prisons is "entrenched and unchecked" despite this litigation. He writes, "Prosecutors and prison officials are typically quick to dismiss prisoner complaints of sexual abuse, assuming that because they're in prison they must also be liars (10)." Commenting on the lawsuits, he notes Michigan's "failure to protect the state's 2,000 female prisoners from abuse by guards and other employees. Sexual misconduct complaints are routinely dismissed on dubious grounds. Investigations are often superficial and incomplete. And guards who sexually assault prisoners are rarely punished" (12).

CONCLUSION

The daily interactions among women prisoners and staff are fundamental to the search for safety. Staff have almost unlimited control over those in their custody. While many staff was seen as responsible and professional, others were not. Women described the latter as "just not caring," "playing favorites," "enjoying their fears," "refusing to take their fears seriously," "covering up for their buddies," and telling them, "This is prison—deal with it."

The most common problem reported by the women in our interviews and in the survey was "down talk"—disrespectful and derogatory verbal interactions, often in the form of racial and gender slurs. Most of the misconduct described occurred at the lower end of a coercion continuum. By far the most prevalent form of officer sexual misconduct was inappropriate touching, sexual comments and suggestions, or other nonphysical assaults. In most locations, women said that policies and sanctions regarding staff sexual misconduct had curtailed the most extreme forms of this victimization. More extreme staff sexual misconduct appears to be rare, as described in our studies and the national data collected by the Bureau of Justice Statistics. While numerically rare, the damage done by such sexual exploitation of women remains an ongoing challenge to their safety. Again, sexual victimization, in childhood or adulthood, seems to be correlated with revictimization. Women and girls who are raped are more likely than nonvictims to experience subsequent sexual victimization (Breitenbecher 1999; Messman-Moore and Long 2000; Tjaden and Thoennes 2006). This certainly seems to be true for incarcerated women, although exactly why such women are vulnerable to revictimization is unclear. Messman-Moore and Long (2000) identified a greater vulnerability to sexual harassment and coercion from authority figures for those women who had experienced prior sexual victimization. In the final chapter, we show how the fundamental inequalities embedded in the prison community violate human rights by creating systematic and unnecessary harm to women in custody.

7

Gendered Human Rights and the Search for Safety

I can bear no more pain in my life.

—From a letter sent to Just Detention International

In a November 6, 2014, editorial in the *Washington Post,* the women's prison scholar Patricia O'Brien asks, "What purpose is served by subjecting the most disempowered, abused and nonviolent women to the perpetually negative environment of prisons?" We join O'Brien in this challenge and pose further questions: Why has the United States and much of the world subscribed to a policy of overincarceration of women (and men)? When did prison become the only response to crime and justice? As Coyle (1998) suggests, we have forgotten the purpose of prisons in the rush to imprison more and more people. As for women, he makes a particular point:

> Locking up human beings, depriving them of their liberty is a grave punishment. It is particularly traumatic when applied to women. The consequences of deprivation of liberty, the removal of many fundamental aspects of human integrity, of individuality and of personal responsibility have a particular resonance when the person being so treated is a woman. (Coyle 1998, 52)

We have made the case that prisons harm women in unnecessary ways, exposing them to risks endemic to the prison environment. Prison can be toxic to staff as well; there is evidence that working in prisons undercuts staff well-being and health (Wells et al. 2008; Lambert et al. 2015). Mass incarceration also harms the community, as the collateral consequences of disproportionate sentencing policies seep into society in unintended ways (Clear 2007; Danner 1998). Mass imprisonment has created an entire class of people—women and men—whose struggles continue when released. We argue that this struggle is based on the absence of the essential capital necessary to live safely in prison and the free world. Without this capital, the formerly incarcerated are likely to become further marginalized from, rather than reintegrated into, families and work in the free world. As imprisonment erodes capital, so it erodes life chances at release. When so many resources are invested in law enforcement, drug interdiction, community surveillance, and prisons, other forms of community investment funding declines—for social services, adequate housing, livable wages, and local education. In the present system, upon their release imprisoned persons are "freed" into deteriorated communities that have been deeply harmed by this community disinvestment.

Women and men often leave prison with a worldview of unfairness and a distrust of authority, undermining participation in the conventional world. We suspect also that there is an inverse relationship between large stocks of prison cultural capital—particularly those grounded in respect and hustles—and healthy functionality in the free world.

We believe that the human rights approach offers a way forward. Thus far, this approach, based on the inherent dignity and worth of incarcerated persons, has gained little traction in U.S. prison policy, practice, and research. To make our case, we quote at length from international human rights documents, which highlight the great disparity between the standards they lay out and the current U.S. policies.

GENDERED HARM IN THE CONTEMPORARY PRISON

By framing the harm of imprisonment as human rights violations, we argue that prisons in the U.S. sustain gendered and other intersectional inequalities, producing a system of State-sponsored suffering. We have documented harm in three general areas: prison conditions, conflict and violence among imprisoned women, and staff actions.

Prison Conditions

Gender inequality is embedded in the operational practice and security procedures designed originally to control the behavior of male prisoners. Prison conditions, particularly relating to unsafe housing, crowding, aging and inadequate physical plants, and unconstitutional health care, undermine women's abilities to do their time safely. Such conditions violate the human rights of incarcerated women set forth in U.N. minimum standards and norms for criminal justice (United Nations 2015, 2010; UNODC 2012, 2015; Coyle 2009; Labelle 2013).

Health care is a prime example of this unnecessary suffering. Persons who are incarcerated have the human right to community-level health care, a requirement established by international agreements and U.S. Supreme Court decisions (Simon 2014). The United Nations finds medical care for imprisoned women to be a gendered issue:

> Therefore female prisoners often have greater primary healthcare needs in comparison to men. Their condition may become worse in prisons due to the absence of adequate medical care, lack of hygiene, inadequate nutrition and overcrowding. In addition, all women have gender-specific medical requirements and need to have regular access to specialists in women's healthcare. (UNODC 2015, 10)

The Handbook for Prison Managers and Policy-Makers further argues:

> Prisoners' right to health is a fundamental human right recognized by numerous international instruments. The right to health encompasses the right to proper healthcare, equivalent to that in the community, as well as the underlying right to live in an environment which does not generate disease and mental disabilities. In all cases, prison health policies should ensure that prison conditions and services are designed to protect the health of all prisoners. They should recognize that providing the underlying determinants of health, such as adequate space, nutrition, clean drinking water, sanitation, heating, fresh air, natural and artificial light, is key to the protection of the physical and mental well-being of all prisoners. The provision of purposeful activities and mental stimulation, as well as contact with the outside world, is also vital in this context. (UNODC 2015, 48)

Unsanitary conditions, which women see as a primary challenge to safety, are also addressed in the *Handbook:*

> The maintenance of sanitary conditions in prisons is important in preventing illness and disease while maintaining human dignity. In this context, female prisoners have special hygiene requirements which prison authorities are obliged to provide for. Dormitories and rooms used for accommodation of female prisoners must have facilities and materials required to meet women's special hygiene needs.
>
> Ready access to sanitary and washing facilities, safe disposal arrangements for bloodstained articles, as well as provision of hygiene items are of particular importance. These should be available to women under conditions in which they do not need to be embarrassed asking for them (for example, either dispensed by other women or, better yet, accessible whenever needed).

> The European Committee for the Prevention of Torture and Inhuman or Degrading Treatment or Punishment (CPT) considers that the failure to provide such basic necessities can amount to degrading treatment. (UNODC 2015, 217)

The Supreme Court's long-term hands-off policy assumed that prison officials knew best how to manage their prisons without judicial intervention. Over time, however, the lower courts have selectively taken on the egregious treatment of prisoners, such as in recent decisions on medical and mental health care in California (Simon 2014). Other court interventions, such as decisions on staff sexual misconduct in Michigan, and U.S. Department of Justice settlements on the conditions of confinement in Alabama bear witness to the harm of imprisonment. In some cases, prison systems are required to remediate these unconstitutional conditions by improving conditions for confinement. Labelle, however, has a more pessimistic view of the impact of U.S. court intervention:

> The conditions in U.S. prisons and jails have been consistently degrading over the last decade with courts retreating from interventions in operations and legislatures imposing steep barriers to incarcerated individuals attempts to raise challenges to their treatment and their punishment. Edging back to the days of civil death statutes, during which a person convicted of a crime was divested of civil and political rights on the notion that they ceased to exist as a legal person after conviction, federal and state statutes have erected stiff barriers to challenging mistreatment which international human rights bodies have deemed equivalent to torture. (2013, 1)

By focusing on the neglect of prisoners and the unwillingness to address conditions of confinement, Labelle demonstrates the limits of the civil rights approach to prison reform in the United States. We join Labelle, Fellner (2012), and others who see a human rights approach to prison reform as the way forward.

The Context of Conflict and Violence among Women

As women learn to do time, they must negotiate potential conflicts and tensions among themselves. Conflict and violence are fed by inequalities of human, social, and prison capital. Verbal conflicts, economic exploitation and much of the physical violence among women are rooted in these inequalities. Intimate partner violence also finds expression in troubled relationships, grounded in material, emotional, and relational inequalities. Violence and other forms of exploitation of other women are used as a strategy to obtain economic or reputational capital. For women with extensive histories of violent victimization, troubled relationships in prison mirror the "harmed and harming" women identified in Daly's (1992, 1994) pioneering work on pathways. Although we argue that most women's pathways to prison are paved by structural and cumulative disadvantage, we also recognize some women make an active, if constrained, choice to commit acts of violence.

The search for safety is undermined by the lack of gender-sensitive programs and services inside prison. While we of course agree that educational and vocational programs do prepare women to reenter the free world, we argue that these activities and services are equally vital to their safety inside. Economic and material instability contributes to women's diminished choices in prison and conditions interpersonal jeopardy in their relations with other prisoners and staff.

International standards point to the need to provide constructive ways for women to do their time:

> The type and quality of prisoner activities and programmes, and the level of prisoners' access to them, underpin the success of social reintegration efforts in prisons. Activities provided for prisoners should enable them to live law-abiding lives after release, by increasing their job skills and improving their education, especially. Research indicates that steady employment following release is one of the most important factors that prevent recidivism, together with strong family ties and support.

> Female prisoners, typically from marginalized and disadvantaged sectors of society, are likely to have suffered particularly from discrimination prior to imprisonment. They are less likely to have been employed than men at the time of imprisonment. In a majority of cases they commit an offence due to poverty. Many are unable to end violent relationships due to the lack of economic freedom. By providing women with adequate and equal opportunities for vocational training in prisons, and thereby assisting them to gain employment after release, prison authorities can make an immense contribution to the social reintegration of women prisoners. (UNODC 2015, 48)

The lack of programs and services—particularly mental health services—to treat trauma and related substance abuse and mental health problems reinforce women's symptoms inside prison and destabilize life chances upon release. The UNODC supports our finding:

> Women's mental health is likely to deteriorate in prisons which are overcrowded, where differentiation of prisoners based on a proper assessment is not made and prisoner programmes are either non-existent or inadequate to address the specific needs of women. The harmful effects on mental health are exacerbated when women do not feel safe, if they are supervised by male staff and feel at risk of further abuse. (2015, 10)

Harm by Staff

Unnecessary suffering is also created by the actions of the few staff that violate women's rights through disrespect, harassment, violence, and sexual misconduct. We repeat that very few staff are involved in these harmful activities. We also acknowledge the efforts of prison managers to identify aspects of operational practice, including staffing, that harm women and removing staff involved in this misconduct. Throughout the country, however, women told us about the ongoing threat of staff verbal disrespect, including name calling, shouting, and other acts that undermine women's dignity. All forms of staff misconduct, including sexual misconduct, reproduce the harm women experienced in their lives outside. Staff sexual and physical assault, while somewhat rare, damages women in both its actuality and potential.

The vast inequality between the keeper and the kept (Crouch 1980) leaves women with few ways to resist staff power (Bosworth 1999). As the UNODC states, imprisoned women are particularly vulnerable to this inequity of power:

> Another fundamental requirement is to take account of women's special protection needs in prisons, as a safe environment is what women in prison need above all else. Under international law, the rape of a woman in custody by an agent of the State may constitute torture for which the State is held directly responsible. Other forms of sexual abuse or serious physical abuse committed against women, such as the deliberate use of intimate searching, groping and threats, also amount to torture or ill treatment if carried out by an agent of the State. States are responsible for protecting women from all forms of sexual abuse and violence in prisons, and ensuring that perpetrators of such acts are brought to justice.

> It should also be noted that female staff might also be responsible for the abuse, including sexual abuse, of women prisoners, and measures taken for the protection of female prisoners should take account of this risk. (UNODC 2015, 34)

The UNODC continues:

> There should be clear policies and guidelines in place relating to use of force, violence and sexual misconduct by staff in prisons, aiming to provide maximum protection to women prisoners. All forms of violence, sexual intercourse with prisoners and sexual touching should be criminalized to prevent rape and other forms of abuse. Prison officers should be obliged to report instances of abuse or sexual misconduct perpetrated by other staff.

> Female prisoners are at particular risk of abuse by staff during prison transfers and transfers between pre-trial detention facilities and courts. Adequate

safeguards should be in place to protect women during this time and they should be escorted by a female staff member, or more than one, depending on the number of women being transferred. (34–35)

Finally, privacy is a necessary component of safety, as stated by the UNODC:

> The deprivation of privacy that is inherent in incarceration becomes much more of a deprivation than is necessary to accomplish the proper goals of incarceration. Previously traumatized women who might choose to avoid the gaze of males in order to create a safe place are forced to live in a situation where male officers are constantly present and might intrude on their most personal and private activities at any moment. The woman can develop a generalized fear, and this situation is quite likely to make her symptoms and disability worse and more long-lasting. (28)

Our data and research on imprisoned women around the world clearly demonstrates the urgent need to reform prisons through the human rights model, emphasizing gender-responsive practice to create conditions in which women can truly find safety.

HUMAN RIGHTS AND STATE-SPONSORED SUFFERING

We characterize the contemporary women's prison as State-sponsored suffering that violates universal human rights. We agree with Simon (2007), who says the contemporary prison—confining women or men— is a political reaction to social problems grounded in inequality and disadvantage. The self-perpetuating cycle of punishment and degradation in both prison and free world communities holds women responsible for their situations but provides few tools to address the roots of their behavior and suffering. Suffering has become one of the personalized collateral consequences of imprisonment (Haney 2006; de Alemida and Paes-Machado 2015). Accelerating punitive sanctions has pushed thousands and thousands of Americans into prisons, stripping away the capital needed to survive in any community through spiraling marginality. The spoiled identity "former prisoner" further undermines chances of community reintegration. This suffering is maintained by the billions of dollars that funds U.S. prisons and their warehousing policies.

The challenges to safety and well-being of women prisoners are not only problems in America's prisons. Globally, women in prison face many forms of discrimination and other consequences of gender inequality, reproducing the harms identical to those we find in U.S. prisons

(Barberet 2013; Baker and Rytter 2014; Ataby and Owen 2014; UNODC 2015; Bastick and Townhead 2008). The United Nations supports our contention that many women are incarcerated unnecessarily:

> It is evident . . . that the profile of female prisoners is quite different to that of men. Their backgrounds, offences they commit, their caring responsibilities and the particularly harmful effects of imprisonment on women need to be taken into account in devising criminal justice policies, in order to ensure that women are not imprisoned unnecessarily and unjustifiably, putting pressure on the scarce resources of prison systems worldwide.
>
> It cannot be adequately emphasized that a large majority of female offenders do not pose a risk to society and their imprisonment does not help, but hinders their social reintegration. Many are in prison as a direct or indirect result of the multiple layers of discrimination and deprivation experienced at the hands of their husbands, family and the community. What most female offenders need is to be treated fairly in the criminal justice system, taking into account their backgrounds and reasons that have led to the offence committed, as well as care, assistance and treatment in the community, to help them overcome the underlying factors leading to criminal behaviour. By keeping women out of prison, where imprisonment is not strictly necessary or justified, their children may be saved from the enduring adverse effects of their mothers' imprisonment, including their possible institutionalization and own future incarceration. (UNODC 2015, 82)

REDUCING HARM THROUGH REFORM

Our recommendations for reducing harm in America's prisons has two dimensions: reducing the number of people in prison and decreasing State-sponsored suffering by bringing human rights into American prisons. *Unlocking America* (Austin et al. 2007) calls for policy and legislation changes to reverse the punitive trends of increased arrests, higher conviction rates, and longer periods of incarceration.[1] Reducing the length of stay of sentenced prisoners, diverting technical parole and probation violators from prison, and decreasing the length of time individuals spend under community supervision are practical and achievable measures to reducing the U.S. prison population (Austin et al. 2007, 26).

While we enthusiastically endorse all of these recommendations, we must also acknowledge the role of all forms of social inequality and inequity in producing crime and thus punishment. Realistically, prison

---

1. Barbara Owen had the pleasure of working with the Austin et al. (2007) workgroup.

managers cannot possibly be charged with solving the complex dispari-ties in free world society. But, they can be held accountable for the gendered degradation and harm of the contemporary women's prison.

Reducing suffering in prisons for women also involves confronting the inequalities *within* prison, decreasing the iatrogenic damage of prison conditions, and addressing the sources of conflict and violence among women and with staff. Women's prisons can provide opportuni-ties to remediate pathways by increasing all forms of capital. Prisons should protect women from, rather than expose them to, violence, harm, and suffering. The suffering of women in prison has been aggra-vated by the prison population boom. This problem must be addressed by sentencing policy reform in tandem with internal prison reform.

We advocate sound operational approaches that diminish suffering inside prisons and prepare women for reentry by increasing their stocks of capital through vocational training, education, trauma and mental health treatment, medical care, and staff commitment to maintaining gendered respect and dignity. Incorporating the principle of sanctuary, as suggested by S. Bloom (1997), and expanding the definition of safety to include physical, psychological, moral, and sexual safety are other worthwhile goals. In addition to the human rights model, we find utility in noncustodial measures, as expressed in the community justice model, and in implementing gender-responsive and trauma-informed practice inside women's prisons.

A Community Justice Model

A moral, ethical, safe, and productive prison for women is only possible when administered within a human rights framework. But prisons should always be the last resort. Alternatives to imprisonment, by pro-viding community-based resources to improve women's free world cap-ital, avoid much of the unnecessary harm and costs of incarceration. The community justice model is one example of the noncustodial meas-ures advocated by the human rights model and encoded in the Bangkok Rules. Bloom and Owen describe the application of the community jus-tice model for justice-involved women:

> The Women's Community Justice Blueprint offers a gender-responsive approach to integrating criminal and community justice systems in San Fran-cisco, California. Building on the growing body of evidence that demon-strates that the majority of female offenders can be more effectively managed in community settings that provide women-centered and gender-responsive

services and programs, this Blueprint outlines multiple strategies to reduce recidivism and break the intergenerational cycle of crime and incarceration. Given the nonviolent nature of most women's crimes and their low-level of risk to public safety, this approach is consistent with the values of public safety, community investment, restorative justice and rehabilitation. (2013, 1)

Gender-Responsive Practice

The prison environment further creates unnecessary suffering for women because it is predicated on male-based penal philosophy and policies that reinforce gender inequality (Bloom, Owen, and Covington 2003). Research on gender-responsive services and advances in theoretical understandings about women's pathways into and away from crime provide new insights for improving outcomes for women offenders (Wright et al. 2012). Gender-responsive practice is based on the pathways approach, which we have expanded throughout this book to include cumulative disadvantage and other intersectional inequalities. Knowledge of these gender-based life experiences and subsequent consequences can shape appropriate policy and operational and programmatic responses to women offenders. Echoing the call for a human rights approach, the gender-responsive principles emphasize the importance of respect and dignity.

Programs and services that increase women's social and human capital; treat trauma, substance abuse, and health problems; and prompt resilience through agency are key features of gender-responsive practice (Gobeil, Blanchette, and Stewart 2016; Van Voorhis 2012; Holtfreter, Reisig, and Morash 2004). The NIC report *Gender-Responsive Strategies: Research, Practice and Guiding Principles for Women Offenders* defines this approach:

> Gender-responsive means creating an environment through site selection, staff selection, program development, content, and material that reflects an understanding of the realities of women's lives and addresses the issues of the participants. Gender-responsive approaches are multidimensional and are based on theoretical perspectives that acknowledge women's pathways into the criminal justice system. These approaches address social (e.g., poverty, race, class and gender inequality) and cultural factors, as well as therapeutic interventions. These interventions address issues such as abuse, violence, family relationships, substance abuse and co-occurring disorders. They provide a strength-based approach to treatment and skill building. The emphasis is on self-efficacy. (Bloom, Owen, and Covington 2003, 75)

The gender-responsive approach is directly compatible with human rights, as the United Nations Office of Drugs and Crime asserts:

> In addition to ensuring that women prisoners are not discriminated against in practice—e.g. in maintaining links with their families, having access to prison activities etc.—there also needs to be an understanding that women prisoners have requirements that are very different to those of men. What is still lacking in most systems is the recognition that these different needs must be reflected in the management ethos of women's prisons, with changes being made to management style, assessment and classification, programmes offered, healthcare and the treatment of women with children. (UNODC 2015, 27)

Further, the components of gender-sensitive prison management include taking direct action to counterbalance discrimination encountered by women prisoners that results from their small numbers; adopting a gender-sensitive management style; and recognizing the different needs of female prisoners, including those from different cultural backgrounds, and providing programs and services that address these needs (UNODC 2015, 28).

Gobell, Blanchette, and Stewart (2016) and Messina (2011) have documented the success of gender-responsive programming through interventions that increased all forms of capital, resiliency, and agency. Case management has also been shown to improve outcomes for women in correctional facilities and in the community (Millson, Robinson, and Van Dieten 2010b). Morash (2010) has found that effective community services must focus on the individual goals of women and their families by providing coordinated services over time that address women's pathways away from crime.

Trauma-Informed Practice

Trauma-informed practice improves safety for women and for staff (Benedict 2014; NRCJIW 2014a; Messina, Calhoun, and Braithwaite 2014). Covington (2003, 2008, 2012, 2016a, 2016b), a pioneer in trauma-informed practice, tells us that correctional facilities can increase safety and improve rehabilitative options by becoming trauma informed. Being trauma informed is a necessary foundation of a safe correctional environment for staff and women prisoners. She provides some basic principles of this practice:

- Creating an environment that is both physically and emotionally safe. This means that female offenders are safe from abuse by other women, visitors, and staff.

- Treating female offenders with respect and dignity.
- Addressing women's concerns about safety and treatment.
- Providing a predictable and consistent correctional environment and operational practice.

Interactions with staff are pivotal to a woman's sense of well-being and perceptions of safety. Aggressive and harmful speech and action undermine women's safety at every turn. Beyond the obvious need to train staff and monitor all issues surrounding sexual safety,[2] policies and training emphasizing respect for and dignity of women prisoners in all interactions are cost-free, obtainable, and worthwhile goals for all prison systems. Becoming gender-responsive and trauma-informed is essential to creating an environment based on respect and dignity. Quite simply, as one woman remarked in our conversations, staff should "stop yelling at us and calling us names."

WOMEN'S PRISONS AND HUMAN RIGHTS

But there is more to do. The human rights approach provides clear direction. Reducing suffering in women's prisons requires a system reform that goes beyond staff training and the provision of treatment programs for women. As the UNODC (2015, 26) argues, "Prisons need to be managed within an ethical framework, guided by international standards developed to protect the human rights of prisoners and to ensure that prisoners' treatment aims to facilitate their social reintegration, as a priority."

Principle 5(2) of the Body of Principles for the Protection of All Persons under Any Form of Detention or Imprisonment states that special measures to address the particular needs of women prisoners are not in themselves discriminatory (UNODC 2015, 27). The U.N. (2015) notes these rights and principles are set forth in other international instruments, including the International Covenant on Civil and Political Rights; International Covenant on Economic, Social and Cultural Rights; Convention on the Elimination of All Forms of Discrimination

---

2. Our research is used as the basis for an NIC-sponsored training program addressing sexual safety in women's prisons and jails.

against Women (CEDAW); Declaration on the Elimination of Violence against Women; and Convention on the Rights of the Child.[3]

The Sentencing Project (Mauer and Epstein 2012) outlines a vision for a more humane response to crime and punishment derived from lessons learned from public health, social science research, and international human rights. In this call for reform, Fellner (2012) asserts that respect for human rights is the only way to improve the U.S. incarceration system. She, too, sees that affirming the dignity of all people will counter the human rights violations of the U.S. criminal justice system that include racial discrimination, excessive sentences, and wretched prison conditions.

The human rights approach, in principle, is consistent with U.S. constitutional protections. However, as Labelle (2013, 3) notes, the international human rights approach provides broader protections than American constitutional laws, which are increasingly narrowly interpreted in the courts. The call for human rights for prisoners is found in the International Covenant on Civil and Political Rights (ICCPR), ratified by the United States in 1992. Article 10 of the ICCPR states, "All persons deprived of their liberty shall be treated with humanity and respect for the inherent dignity of the human person" (cited in Labelle 2013, 3).

Labelle (2013, 16) points out that the U.N. standards insist, "except for those limitations that are demonstrably necessitated by the fact of incarceration, all prisoners shall retain the human rights and fundamental freedoms" set forth in U.N. protocols. Labelle (2013) summarizes the key components of the ICCPR:

- The penitentiary system shall comprise treatment of prisoners, the essential aim of which shall be their reformation and social rehabilitation.

- The treatment of prisoners should emphasize not their exclusion from the community, but their continuing part in it.

- The treatment of persons sentenced to imprisonment or a similar measure shall have as its purpose, so far as the length of the sentence permits, to establish in them the will to lead law abiding

---

3. See the websites of the United Nations and the Office of the High Commissioner of Human Rights, www.un.org and www.ohchr.org, respectively, for these instruments. See also Prison Reform International's website, penalreform.org, for contextual discussion.

and self-supporting lives after their release and to fit them to do so. The treatment shall be such as will encourage their self-respect and develop their sense of responsibility.

- No one shall be subjected to torture or to cruel, inhuman or degrading treatment or punishment.

While multiple instruments expand on these fundamental issues, two documents target the human rights of prisoners: *Standard Minimum Rules for the Treatment of Prisoners* (Mandela Rules) (United Nations 2015) and *The United Nations Rules for the Treatment of Women Prisoners and Non-Custodial Measures for Women Offenders* (Bangkok Rules) (United Nations 2010). The updated UNODC publication *Women and Imprisonment: The Handbook for Prison Managers and Policy-Makers* (2015) is also a significant contribution to efforts to translate human rights principles into concrete operational practice.

The Mandela Rules

Originally developed in the 1950s, the Standard Minimum Rules for the Treatment of Prisoners (SMR) has been updated and named the Mandela Rules, in honor of Nelson Mandela (United Nations 2015). The Rules of General Application are based on the human rights to dignity, respect, protection from torture, and safety. Rule 1 states:

> All prisoners shall be treated with the respect due to their inherent dignity and value as human beings. No prisoner shall be subjected to, and all prisoners shall be protected from, torture and other cruel, inhuman or degrading treatment or punishment, for which no circumstances whatsoever may be invoked as a justification. The safety and security of prisoners, staff, service providers and visitors shall be ensured at all times.

Other Rules address living conditions and specifically parse the state's responsibility to provide adequate health care (including reproductive care for women prisoners). Although the Bangkok Rules (described below) address women's policy and practice in much more detail, the Mandela Rules addresses the problem of cross-gender supervision, specifically prohibiting men from working in direct contact with women prisoners.

The Bangkok Rules

The United Nations Rules for the Treatment of Women Prisoners and Non-Custodial Measures for Women Offenders (United Nations 2010) is known as the Bangkok Rules, following the U.N.'s practice of naming human rights instruments after the city or country that sponsors their development. The Rules have been adopted by the United Nations as the basis for a universal human rights approach to improving the lives and situations of incarcerated women as well as those under all other forms of criminal justice supervision. The Bangkok Rules are intended to supplement existing international standards for the treatment of prisoners and those under other forms of confinement by providing a gender-appropriate blueprint for female offenders, both adult and juvenile.

The Rules are based on several dominant themes relevant to women offenders: providing for their safety, rehabilitation, and social reintegration while in custody or under any form of noncustodial measure; requiring that the programs and services address their gender-based needs in terms of health care (including pregnancy), mental health, and other therapeutic needs; and recognizing their histories as survivors of interpersonal violence and their caring responsibilities for children. Training staff on these specific issues is a fundamental aspect of the Bangkok Rules.

The Bangkok Rules in addition emphasize the role of noncustodial measures and community corrections alternatives for women offenders. Supplementing the Tokyo Rules in the development and implementation of appropriate noncustodial responses for women offenders, the Bangkok Rules outline such community corrections practices as gender-appropriate probation, fines, and community treatment and training. The noncustodial approach includes requirements for diversion from incarceration wherever possible and other pretrial measures, considerations of parental caring responsibilities of women, and the role of nongovernmental organizations in providing protective measures and services for women in these forms of supervision.

The Bangkok Rules describes the type of programs that should be made available to women in noncustodial care, including gender and culturally relevant interventions and therapies. In our view, they discuss the need to improve all forms of capital through community programming.[4]

---

4. The Bangkok Rules, the implementation index, and corresponding multinational research on characteristics of women in prison are available from Penal Reform International (www.penalreform.org/) and the Thailand Institute of Justice (www.tijthailand.org /main/en/topic-focuss/the-bangkok-rules).

The Handbook for Prison Managers and Policy-Makers:
Women and Imprisonment

Published by the UNODC, *The Handbook for Prison Managers and Policy-Makers: Women and Imprisonment* (2015) provides practical guidance on implementing the human rights approach in women's prisons. The *Handbook* supports our assertion that prisons are unnecessary for most sentenced women:

> The majority of these women do not need to be in prison at all. Most are charged with minor and non-violent offences and do not pose a risk to the public. Many are imprisoned due to their poverty and inability to pay fines. A large proportion is in need of treatment for mental disabilities or substance addiction, rather than isolation from society. Many are victims themselves but are imprisoned due to discriminatory legislation and practices. Community sanctions and measures would serve the social reintegration requirements of a vast majority much more effectively than imprisonment. (UNODC 2015, 3)

In introducing the concept of dynamic security, the *Handbook* stresses the importance of "developing positive relationships with prisoners, diverting prisoners' energy into constructive work and activity, and providing a decent and balanced regime with individualized programs for prisoners" (37). Further:

> An emphasis on dynamic security in women's prisons is especially suitable to the needs of female prisoners, due to the particularly harmful effects high security measures can have on women to the detriment of their mental well-being and social reintegration prospects. Creating a positive climate in prisons and using disciplinary measures only when strictly necessary should comprise essential components of a gender-sensitive approach to prison management. (37)

REDUCING HARM IN WOMEN'S PRISONS: THE WAY FORWARD

Reducing the unnecessary suffering in women's prisons is an obligation according to international human rights agreements. The human rights model of imprisonment, with its strong emphasis on gendered dignity, is the way forward. We further propose a policy debate about the purpose of the contemporary prison. John Irwin, pioneer in prison sociology, prisoner advocate, and mentor to many of us, raised the issue decades ago: "My position is that we must understand exactly what we intend to accomplish by imprisonment and what happens in prison, and we must stop doing all the unnecessary things that degrade, embitter, cripple and dehumanize prisoners" (1980, xxiii). Like Irwin, we are forced to conclude that contemporary American prisons are damaging institutions. With prisons as the policy of first resort, many Americans have unquestioningly come to consider imprisonment as the only possible response to crime. In part driven by the war on drugs, itself an exercise in futility and inequality, incarceration has become "the new Jim Crow" (Alexander 2010) in reproducing racial and class inequality. Prisoners are demonized and, given the ethos of personal responsibility, blamed for their economic and social situation. Women, with greater vulnerability to interpersonal physical and sexual violence, are further disadvantaged in an economic and social system based on income and class disparities. For women of color, such intersectionalities can compound the strain of racial oppression. These issues should be part of the public conversation about the purpose of imprisonment.

Prison policy makers have the principal obligation for reducing the harm and pains of imprisonment. Again, as John Irwin suggests, we must stop doing things that harm prisoners unnecessarily. Many of these unnecessary things are gendered harms, grounded in the intersection of inequalities and limited capital that propel women into the justice system. But the solution is not in the hands of the prison managers alone. Charging, prosecution, sentencing, and sanctioning polices that drive imprisonment rates must be addressed (Austin et al. 2007). An easy first step is to remove penalties for low-level drug crimes as a class of offenses, as some states have done in recognizing that misguided drug policy causes enormous collateral damage to individuals, families, and communities. Decriminalizing other low-level criminal offenses, such as minor property crimes, will deflect many women from the toxic environment of the prison and avoid the collateral damage of incarceration.

But diverting low-level offenders from prison is not enough. Reducing prison populations cannot be accomplished only by decriminalizing these low-level offenses. Sentencing policy must develop more rational responses to violent crime. Reducing disproportionately long sentences and improving reentry support are promising initiatives, with community reinvestment equally necessary. Dialogue on reducing the use of prison for women and men must coincide with debates on reducing the social inequality and absence of capital that are at the root of most crimes. Public policy initiatives must acknowledge the role of class, race, and gender discrimination in women's pathways to prison.

While we join the calls for reducing the prison population, we have our eyes on a more immediate prize: reducing the unnecessary suffering of imprisoned women. Combined with gender-responsive and trauma-informed practice, the human rights approach demonstrates that safety inside prison and improved outcomes at release can be designed and implemented in women's prisons. It is more than possible to develop a prison system that ensures women are safe by protecting them from the iatrogenic harms of prison conditions, keeping women safe inside by increasing all forms of capital, monitoring staff for appropriate interactions with women, and providing opportunities to address the gender inequalities that pave women's pathways into prison. As Nelson Mandela stated, "It is said that no one truly knows a nation until one has been inside its jails. A nation should not be judged by how it treats its highest citizens, but its lowest ones."[5] We should all be judged by the unnecessary suffering created and sustained by our nation's prisons. Reducing this suffering through a clear commitment to the inherent dignity and respect of all prisoners—both women and men—is essential to the search for safety.

5. www.amnesty.org/en/press-releases/2015/05/mandela-rules-on-prisoner-treatment-adopted-in-landmark-revision-of-un-standards-1/.

Methodology

GENDERED VIOLENCE AND SAFETY: A CONTEXTUAL APPROACH
TO IMPROVING SECURITY IN WOMEN'S FACILITIES
Owen et al. 2008

Methodology

Initial Instrument Development

Using a unique focus group methodology developed specifically for this study, a total of forty focus groups, with 161 prisoner and 30 staff participants, were completed by the research team during the course of the project. The processes associated with focus group site selection, sampling, methodology, data collection, coding and analysis are described below.

Study Sites. Prison and jail facilities selected for study were in four geographically dispersed regions of the country. Each of the prison facilities housed multiple custody levels of female prisoners, from minimum to maximum, and ranged in size from a few hundred to several thousand. All three jail facilities held both female and male offenders, housing women in a separate area, and included sentenced and unsentenced women. The jails were representative of most small to mid-size jails in the United States.

Prisoner Groups. Our sampling strategy was purposive in nature. For the prison participants, groups were constructed according to security level, time served, housing designation, age, and program participation. For the jail participants, focus groups were constructed based on housing designation, sentencing status, and security level. All sampled prisoner groups included five to ten women who met the focus group criteria.

Of the total 40 groups completed, 27 were various types of prisoner focus groups, and the remaining 13 were staff focus groups. Of the 27 prisoner focus groups, 21 were drawn from prison populations and included general population low security (4), general population high security (4), reception center groups (5), long-termer groups (5), an older prisoner group (1), and substance abuse programs (2). The remaining 6 prisoner focus groups were drawn from jail populations and included sentenced (2), unsentenced (2), violent (1), and nonviolent (1).

Staff Groups. To capture the perspectives of staff in all job classifications, staff focus groups were selected based on set group criteria as well. These group criteria were specific to the employee's job classification and types of contact with prisoners. Each of the sampled staff focus groups contained five to seven staff members, including both male and female staff together. The 13 focus groups completed with staff members consisted of 7 custody and 6 noncustody groups.

Measures. The focus groups' questions were developed through a multistage process. Drawing from the literature, the intent of the PREA mandates, previous work conducted by the project team, and one meeting with subject matter experts, we developed basic questions about women's experiences with violence and safety. These initial questions were pretested in four preliminary prisoner groups and revised and modified in team discussion.

The questions pretested in focus groups were identical to the final questions used in the study. The pretest found that these questions elicited the range and depth of the responses sought in the study. The pretest, however, resulted in two changes to our protocol: (1) we added more details to the prompts; and (2) we determined that one focus group session was inadequate to capture the rich and "thick description" (Geertz 1983) surrounding these issues of safety and violence. The one-session approach also wasted the opportunity to capitalize on the rapport that developed in Day 1. As a consequence, we retained the original questions and supplemented them with more detailed prompts and expanded the focus group meetings to two sessions, as described below.

In focusing on the context and correlates of violence and safety and not addressing questions of prevalence or specific individual experience, the questions were designed to elicit prisoner and staff perceptions and to capture prisoner and staff perspectives on broader issues. In addition to yielding complex and detailed narrative descriptions, the focus group findings were used as the basis for constructing the survey instrument.

Four questions structured the core of the interview for the female prisoner and detainee groups: What do you know about violence or danger in this facility? How do women currently protect themselves from violence in this facility? What are some things that can be done here to protect women from danger and violence? What else should we know about violence and danger here?

There were five questions for the staff participants: What do you know about violence or danger among women in this facility? What problems are associated with preventing and responding to female sexual and physical violence in this facility? How do women currently protect themselves from the violence in this facility? What are some things that can be done here to protect women from danger and violence? What else should we know about violence and danger here?

Procedures. A detailed protocol was developed to ensure that the focus groups were conducted in a consistent manner across all sites. In addition to outlining the steps for arranging the interviews, the protocol contained a comprehensive interview script used to structure the focus group process.

The focus group method for both staff and prisoner groups follows the traditional size of five to ten, guided by a facilitator, and a note taker. In some sites, two facilitators were used. We introduced an additional dimension to the focus group approach by conducting two sessions with the same group. The richness and complexity of the narratives developed in the pretest focus groups led us to develop a two-session approach. In the final form, each prisoner group met with the research team for two hours each for two consecutive days, totaling four hours of focus group data collection with each prisoner group. In addition to collecting more data, the two-session approach built on the rapport established in the first session, allowed for revisiting any topic or thread, and gave the prisoner participants time to reflect on the issues overnight. We found the two-session approach enormously productive.

In the initial two-hour meeting with prisoner focus groups, the research team introduced the project, obtained informed consent, and asked participants to complete a demographic card. The team also addressed any questions raised by the participants. After these items were completed, all questions were reviewed with a focus on obtaining the participants' views on all forms of violence and safety. On the second day, the group resumed the discussion where it left off. Participants gave every indication that they were increasingly comfortable with the discussion and were willing to share openly and freely.

Given the constraints of the correctional environment, including varying staff schedules and coverage issues, conducting a staff focus group on consecutive days was not possible. Staff interviews typically took between 60 and 90 minutes and were conducted in a single session.

Analysis. Each of the completed focus groups was documented by the note taker and then promptly reviewed and cleaned for accuracy. The reviewed transcriptions were given to the facilitator for a second review. The transcripts were then formatted for uploading to a qualitative data analysis program called The Ethnograph©. The Ethnograph© software was chosen for this project because of its capacity to code by segments. Once coded, searches can be done by one or more code words.

The Ethnograph© format assigns a number to each of the lines of the transcript for easy reference and assigned code words. The focus group transcripts were printed out in hard copy for the coding process. To improve the inter-rater reliability of the coding process, the hard copy of focus group transcripts was coded by the primary coder and then reviewed by the secondary coder. Almost two hundred codes were used to capture the complexity of the focus group narratives.

When the coding was finished on the hard copy transcripts, a third research team member was solely responsible for entering these codes into The Ethnograph© program. After all transcripts were coded, program output files were converted to hard copy and distributed to the research team members responsible for the analysis.

Beta Survey Development

It is important to note that from the focus groups we learned that living units shaped the context of violence and safety; hence we decided to focus our measurement activities on living units rather than sampling from the facility at large. In addition, while consulting with facility managers, we determined that some living units were known to be "high problem" for potential violence and others were defined as "low problem." We suspected that any measures pertaining to violence and conflict would discern differences in this prison neighborhoods. After team members reviewed existing surveys and discussed the focus group data and the results of content analysis, they agreed on several themes or constructs worthy of survey measurement.

After team members reviewed existing surveys and discussed focus group data and results of content analysis, they agreed on several themes or constructs that should be measured using surveys.

Additional quantitative data were collected from focus group participants on simple measures or ratings of violence and safety in women's prisons. After these qualitative data were collected and analyzed, several existing surveys that measure prison social climates and related constructs were reviewed. Potentially relevant items from these surveys were transferred to one document for review by team members.

These constructs examine the context of vulnerability and include individual, living unit, and facility factors, as well as staff factors, in conjunction with the ecological model. Although we originally proposed development of survey items modeled after existing instruments, analysis of focus group data and the resulting constructs convinced us that this approach was not feasible. Most of the constructs we developed had not been investigated and measured by prior researchers. For both substantive and operational reasons, we concluded that the complexity of conflict, violence, and safety in women's facilities warranted construction of original instrumentation. New potential survey items were developed by the research team over a series of several meetings and discussions. Particular attention was devoted to ensuring that items had both face and content validity and that the items tapped the breadth and depth of identified constructs. To further assist with assessing convergent validity, a few items in instruments developed by other researchers were adopted and embedded in our instrument. Once an initial survey battery of approximately 200 items was drafted, it was reviewed and revised through several independent processes within the research team.

Second, following a carefully planned and prepared protocol, the survey was reviewed and revised six separate times based on the pretest feedback with

34 prisoners from 6 different correctional facilities. In addition, the survey was reviewed and revised three separate times based on the feedback of 10 staff members from 3 different correctional facilities. After these revisions, the instrument contained a total of 184 items.

Third, a rigorous face and content validity assessment procedure was designed utilizing a validation assessment tool. The Professional Validation Assessment Tool was pilot tested with eight team members and later completed by six outside subject matter experts with expertise in instrument validation as well as research and practitioner experience in corrections and criminal justice. The Professional Validation Assessment Tool was used to assess the 184 items for face validity of each individual item, content validity of groups of items, and degree of consensus or inter-rater agreement on the above-mentioned face and content validity assessments.

After further item refinement based on feedback from the subject matter expert validation process, 20 new items were added. Also, to assess convergent validity, 19 items from previously validated instruments were added. A revised survey containing these 223 items was again pretested with two different groups of prisoners (one from a state prison and one from a jail facility). Results of this pretest resulted in further revision of some demographic items (e.g., items were revised to accommodate greater variation in sentence type). In addition, results of this pretest confirmed our suspicions that the number and type of items on the survey made it difficult for respondents to complete such a long instrument or to maintain focus throughout the survey. Consequently, we split the survey into two versions. Version A contained 169 of these 223 items, and Version B contained 112 of the items. Note that 58 of these items appeared on both versions; these items facilitated various comparisons of data collected on the two survey versions and, if justified, combination of the data. Together with 15 items that measure several demographic characteristics of the women offenders, there were a total of 238 survey items generating data on 561 variables.

To test our survey administration protocol, a large-scale pilot of the instrument was administered to two different housing units in a large women's state prison. Of the prisoners available, the pilot yielded 316 usable surveys and an overall 83 percent response rate. Results from the pilot test suggested that revisions were needed to the survey format (e.g., completed examples needed to be on a separate page from the items that followed), the administration protocol (e.g., administering the survey to smaller groups resulted in a better completion rate), and the wording of certain demographic items (e.g., to better accommodate prisoners awaiting trial or sentence).

The psychometric properties of the final version of the beta survey instrument were assessed through a confirmation process with surveys collected from four state prisons and three jails in three different states. Given that the survey instrument was designed for housing units rather than entire facilities, purposive censuses of housing units from the seven facilities were used. Most of the staff ratings (over 73 percent) coincided with the identification of high- and low-problem units from the structured interview.

Surveys were then administered to prisoners and detainees in low- and high-problem units at six different facilities. The average response rate across all survey administrations was 83.20 percent. Response rates from the low-problem units averaged almost 92 percent (544/592). Response rates from the high-problem units averaged almost 74 percent (402/545).

Response rates were calculated based on the number of prisoners or detainees available for survey participation rather than the number housed. Some prisoners were not available to participate in the survey because of court hearings, visits, sick calls, work details, community service, or involvement in other programs.

After all of the survey instruments were collected in each administration, the survey administrator reviewed each one that same day and noted on the front cover those that might be invalid or ineligible and why. Observations made during the survey administration aided this decision. Once all of the surveys were collected at the data entry site, they were again reviewed for eligibility for analysis. Surveys were declared ineligible if the respondent was illiterate in English or if the respondent was from a housing unit not included in the survey administration. They were declared invalid if the respondent left large portions of the survey blank or if the respondent checked the same item throughout the survey (including those that were negatively worded). Of the 947 surveys that were collected, 917 (96.8 percent) were determined to be valid and eligible. Twenty-three (2.4 percent) were determined to be invalid and seven (0.7 percent) were determined to be ineligible.

A series of quality control checks were then performed to assess the accuracy of data entry and merging. Based on individual accuracy results for each data entry person combined with the number of cases entered by each, and corrections made during quality control activities, the research team estimated the final master database of 947 cases is 99.74 percent error-free. Although a 0.26 percent error rate suggests approximately 700 errors remain in the final database, this number of unpatterned errors can have no significant impact on the analysis of the 292,000 data points involved.

Once the number of valid cases was confirmed, the psychometric properties of the different constructs and respective dimensions of the overall instrument were explored and later confirmed via several different methods and statistical analyses.

Eleven different instruments containing 518 variables or items had to be factor analyzed; the intended product at some point in the future is a much shorter, more manageable and easily administered instrument or battery of instruments, the data from which facility administrators can use to make informed decisions about safety and violence in women's correctional facilities. As such, our analytic approach was to attempt to develop much shorter instruments that contained items with the highest loadings (also known as pure measures because they are most highly correlated with one factor) and yet held up to be most valid and reliable using the validation and reliability techniques available to us.

Prisoner Letters Sent to Just Detention International (formerly Stop Prison Rape)

Part of our methodology in the NIJ study involved a content analysis of letters received by Just Detention International (JDI). These letters described serious and violent sexual assault committed by staff. JDI is an advocacy organization that "seeks to end sexual violence committed against men, women, and youth in all forms of detention." We examined all the letters from women contained in the archives of letters from prisoners across the country. These letters were written by prisoners who have been sexually assaulted or from prisoners and free world individuals who are seeking help for an imprisoned person. While most of the letters concerned male prisoners, we were able to review fifty-seven letters either from female prisoners or others connected to them. There were many letters written by a third party—typically a husband or significant other—who was seeking help for a prisoner.

We examined these letters to obtain an additional level of detail about women's experience with sexual assault from another data source. JDI staff explained that these letters were in no way representative of the prevalence of sexual assault in prisons and jails. The difficulty of writing about a traumatic event and obtaining the necessary materials needed to write a letter, in addition to concerns that staff will prevent it from being sent, combine to make writing a letter to JDI a rare event.

The letters were coded, omitting any identifying details such as names, states, or facilities to protect the confidentiality of the writers. The letters ranged in length from a few lines to several pages. Like the focus group interviews, these descriptive data often reflected the anguish and pain of sexual assault victimization. Few of the fifty-seven letters we reviewed described incidents of sexual assault involving other prisoners. Of those few that did, some mentioned assault by female prisoners in same-sex facilities and some mentioned assault by male prisoners in mixed-sex faculties, typically jails.

DEVELOPMENT AND VALIDATION OF THE WOMEN'S CORRECTIONAL SAFETY SCALES (WCSS): TOOLS FOR IMPROVING SAFETY IN WOMEN'S FACILITIES
Wells, Owen, and Parson 2013

Methodology

Instrument Development and Testing

Building on the initial survey constructed at the end of the Phase I NIJ-funded study (i.e., the NIJ beta survey), instrument development in Phase II proceeded on two fronts. First, current PREA-related research and policy documents were reviewed to update our understanding of sexual safety issues in correctional settings. This review included several types of data and sources to determine the saliency of the items in relation to the PREA standards; findings from the focus group narratives; and theoretical concepts derived from the ecological and escalation models used in the NIJ study. Most important, the preliminary statistical findings were examined in the context of operational practices, including staffing, training, prisoner programs, and assessment. Particular attention was paid to the draft PREA standards and their applicability to women.

Second, the data and findings from the NIJ beta survey were reviewed to establish an analysis plan to begin the survey revision process. Extensive statistical analyses including descriptive statistics, exploratory factor analyses and regression analyses were undertaken to begin to assess the validity of the Phase 1 (NIJ beta) instrument. These reviews included the results of three detailed sets of factor analyses that were conducted on each of the four instruments contained in the WCSS. A total of 48 factor analyses were conducted to assess the validity of the Phase 1 (NIJ beta) instrument. Once the above-mentioned sources were assembled, a survey item revision protocol was drafted. It included the following steps:

1. Examine statistical output from the NIJ PREA study. Here we reviewed the descriptive statistics (frequency distributions, means, rankings, percent agreement), factor analyses, regression analyses, and other relevant results from the initial NIJ survey.

2. Prepare draft listing of high-scoring items based on statistical output above. Once these items were sequenced in terms of relevance (e.g., high frequencies, rankings and agreement across sites), the research team discussed their fit with the goals and purpose of the validation project.

3. Review the substantive findings of NIJ PREA study: After steps 1 and 2, a revised WCSS instrument was compared to the results from the focus group narratives. Items in the revised WCSS were then reviewed in relation to the primary findings in the NIJ work; this was done to ensure that safety and violence concerns identified in the focus groups were represented in the new instrument.

4. Consult theoretical models for salient concepts. We carefully examined the theoretical models that emerged from the NIJ work, where the Escalation and Ecological models best explained our findings. The Escalation model posits that relatively small conflicts among prisoners and with staff can escalate into more serious physical and sexual violence. The Ecological model conceptualizes conflict as a function of the interaction of individual, relationship, prison cultural, facility, and societal factors. The draft WCSS was examined to ensure salient concepts were measured.

5. Review external documents. The research team examined several other sources. Specifically, the PREA Commission Draft Standards and NIC documents describing operational practice in women's facilities were reviewed to explore issues and concerns related to safety and violence.

6. Examine the revised WCSS. In this step, we determined which items from the above five steps were supported or otherwise salient.

7. Compare this review to the revised WCSS with particular attention to the underlying constructs. In this final review, we revisited the initial constructs underlying the original survey instrument and considered how they were represented in the revised instrument. Survey items were simplified, condensed, or deleted based on this process.

8. Develop the WCSS survey. A file was developed to document this process in a matrix.

9. Finalize items and order of the WCSS. The final step was to discuss the written justification and rationale for modifying items and reach consensus on changes.

Survey Administration Documents

In addition to revising the WCSS survey instrument, multiple documents that accompany the administration of the survey were also reviewed and revised throughout the project. Instructions and definitions were added to improve prisoners' understanding of the survey and its purpose. The Unit Staff Interview Questions and Rating Form was reviewed and revised so that several of its items were identical to those the prisoners would complete on the survey. An Informed Consent Form for Staff was used in conjunction with the Unit Staff Interview Questions and Rating Form. The survey administration protocol, survey talking points, and Informed Consent Form for Prisoners were also reviewed and revised.

Staff Focus Groups

In addition to the WCSS survey, the study called for focus groups with staff and the completion of rating forms on the sampled housing units and the facility. A focus group interview script was utilized to increase consistency between groups and enhance reliability. The focus groups were composed of staff very familiar with the housing units surveyed. To diversify the focus groups, both newer staff and very experienced staff were included in each group. During the focus groups, we asked staff to identify the most problematic and least problematic housing units. At the close of each focus group, we asked participants to complete rating forms for the housing units they were most familiar with. The rating form asked participants to rate housing units on physical violence in the unit, sexual violence in the unit, likelihood of being physically victimized in the unit, and likelihood of being sexually victimized in the unit. Thus we collected both qualitative data (from comments made by focus group participants) and quantitative data (from the staff unit ratings).

Readability and Grade Level Assessments

Readability and grade level assessments were performed on all survey-related documents to ensure that they were written at a level appropriate for prisoner and detainee populations. All survey documents were subjected to the Flesch Reading Ease and the Flesch-Kincaid Grade Level assessments. After several rounds of revision during the NIJ phase of the project and during the NIC phase of the project, readability scores have improved dramatically: (1) the current version of the survey (v2.0) is written at the eighth- to ninth-grade level (8.5) and has a Flesch Reading Ease score of 58; (2) the current version of the prisoner consent form is written at the eighth- to ninth-grade level (8.6), with a reading ease score of 56; (3) the survey definition sheet is written at the ninth- to tenth-grade level (9.7), with a reading ease score of 48; and (4) the staff information sheet and consent form is written at the tenth-grade level (10.1), with a reading ease score of 48.

Pretest

In July 2010, survey administration documents were again revised and prepared for pretesting with female prisoners from both jail and prison settings. One pretest was conducted with four female prisoners who had previously served time in a large western prison but were now enrolled in a less restrictive community program. Another pretest was conducted with six female prisoners at a second western facility. In addition, two pretests were conducted with two different groups of detainees at a small county jail. One pretest was conducted with seven female detainees from the high-violence/problems cell, and the other was conducted with five female detainees from the low-violence/problems cell of the jail.

After pretest revisions were incorporated, the survey administration documents were submitted for subject matter expert validation and prepared for a pilot test at a large southern prison.

Subject Matter Expert Validation

A Subject Matter Expert Validation Tool was prepared and administered with the August 2010 version of the survey to two different subject matter experts. This version of the survey contained 79 items (not including demographic items, which were not validated); these included 71 "single" items and 8 "multipart" items that were split into 27 "single" items for validation purposes. Thu, the validation assessment tool contained a total of 98 items.

Pilot Test and Post-Pilot Review

In August 2010, the survey administration documents were piloted with women from four different housing units in a prison located in a southern state. Of 425 women who were available to take the pretest, 386 agreed to participate in the survey, resulting in a 90.82 percent response rate. The Unit Staff Interview Questions and Rating Form was completed by two correctional staff from each unit. The staff from each unit consisted of a veteran correctional officer and a fairly new correctional officer.

After the data from the pilot test were cleaned, coded, and partially analyzed, exploratory factor analyses were conducted to assess whether the intended constructs and their respective dimensions were being measured with the current survey. Although the factor structure of the survey was better than anticipated with the constructs "issues involving women prisoners," "likelihood of violence," and "reporting climate," it became apparent that the four intended dimensions in the construct, "issues involving staff" (i.e., staff verbal harassment, staff sexual harassment, staff sexual misconduct, staff physical violence) had merged into two dimensions: (1) staff sexual harassment/misconduct and (2) staff verbal harassment/physical violence. This merging was in part due to some of the survey items cross-loading in the factor analyses. Although these preliminary factor analysis results based on the responses from one facility were most likely being influenced by a smaller n (i.e., prisoners from only one facility) and reduced variability, results were nonetheless closely examined, and suggestions for better distinguishing these dimensions were incorporated into the next version of the instrument.

After the survey and all of its related administration documents underwent a through internal review, the next version was prepared for translation into Spanish.

Spanish Translation of Survey

The survey and related survey administration documents were translated into Spanish. Four different survey-related documents were delivered to a qualified Spanish interpreter/ translator with extensive experience in providing interpreting /translation services. All the documents underwent the following procedures during the translation phase of this study: (1) translated by court-certified Spanish translator, (2) reviewed and edited by a second translator, (3) reverse translated by a third translator, (4) reviewed by a fourth translator (a member of the research team), (5) pretested by a Spanish-speaking prisoner (a federal prisoner temporarily held at a local county jail), and (6) final revisions.

Site Selection and Access

The initial plan called for six data collection trips. At each locality, we anticipated that at least two facilities would be surveyed (e.g., one jail and one prison) and that at each facility at least two housing units (i.e., one high-problem and one low-problem) would be surveyed. We originally estimated that a minimum of 24 housing units in 12 facilities would be surveyed. The facilities would vary in type (i.e., county, regional, state, federal, private), size (i.e., small, medium, large), and geographic diversity according to the following designated census regions: West, Midwest, South, and Northeast. However, as discussed below, the project was able to expand the number of sites (and the number of cases collected at each site), resulting in data collection at 15 distinct facilities.

Planning Activities

We began by drafting a site plan of potential facilities to be surveyed. The project team was sensitive to travel costs and designed a site visit plan that included multiple facilities in each geographic area. The detailed site plan grid incorporated specific facility information from the latest American Correctional Association (ACA) directories of adult correctional and detention facilities. A written narrative was conveyed to NIC describing the rationale for sites chosen for the study. Follow-up discussion of the site plan with our NIC partners was well received.

Contacting the Sites

A protocol for contacting sites was developed. Initial contact was made by the principal investigator personally (e.g., at the ACA conference or other meetings) or via telephone and email to assess cooperation, availability, and application requirements. While some sites had very specific and lengthy requirements for submitting research requests, in general the following documents were sent to potential sites: proposal (designed to meet the requirements of the particular correctional system), the survey instrument, survey definitions insert, consent forms, survey administration protocol, and multiple site-specific forms and applications. In each case, the research proposal was revised and modified to reflect the specifics of the facility and agency. Materials conveyed included research team vitas and biographies.

Project staff collaborated in part with NIC partners in contacting agency directors, facility wardens or superintendents and facility PREA coordinators. Arranging site visits was often complex and time consuming. Multiple and unique steps were required across the various sites and time zones, including phone calls, emails, conference calls, completing proposals and forms, undergoing human subjects review by multiple layers of institutional review boards, and customizing proposals, surveys, and consent forms to meet the requirements of specific sites. These arrangements involved considerable project time and resources.

We received permission from 15 sites to conduct the study, although several of these expressed concern about the staff time required to assist the project team. One site initially declined to participate, indicating that although the research proposal had strong merits, budget cuts prohibited their participation. Later in the project, however, this site reconsidered and agreed to participate. Ultimately, only one site declined to participate due to stated staff shortages.

Once a site indicated a willingness to cooperate, a site liaison was designated to coordinate with the research team and facilitate access. Facility-specific information collected at each site included descriptive details such as name, type of facility (jail or prison, public or private, etc.), population size, mission, and information about housing unit classification/size.

Facilities were informed that we wished to (1) survey women on their perceptions of violence and safety in their housing unit; (2) conduct focus groups and individual interviews with staff knowledgeable about these issues in the housing units; (3) ask staff to complete unit rating forms; and (4) provide the facility with a report based on our preliminary analyses.

This initial contact also covered the process for conducting the survey, meeting space, privacy requirements, equipment and materials, and clearance procedures. The procedure for selecting women to participate in the study was also explained in some detail. Originally, we intended to conduct a census of women who lived in two discrete living units. The first category was designated as a "high-problem unit," as subjectively defined by local staff persons very familiar with the facility in terms of levels of violence, disciplinary action, and/ or higher security classifications. Similarly, the second category, "low-problem housing units," was subjectively defined by facility staff as those housing units with low levels of these incidents or classifications. Over the course of the study, these judgments were made both at the initial contact, during the introductory meeting with the staff upon arrival, and during the staff focus group.

We reiterate that a significant amount of project staff time and resources was devoted to the process of contacting potential sites, complying with divergent requirements or processes specific to each site, and operational arrangements for the data collection visit once approval was obtained. Although ultimately we were successful in gaining access to most sites, it was a time-consuming and resource-heavy process.

Human Subjects Review

Some systems had additional human subjects protection requirements that led to the creation of the independent Institutional Review Board (IRB). After consulting with human subject protection experts at the U.S. Department of Justice (DOJ), U.S. Department of Health and Human Services (HHS), and elsewhere, we embarked on the lengthy process of creating a federally registered independent institutional review board. Note that while IRBs are hosted by institutions (e.g., private research companies, hospitals, universities), they are largely independent bodies empowered by federal law to exercise broad oversight in order to ensure the protection of research participants. Although a host institution can require additional protections for research participants, they cannot approve or proceed with research that an IRB has disapproved.

While recruiting appropriately credentialed IRB members, ensuring adequate training, filing the required federal-wide assurances, adapting standard operating procedures, and pursuing the various other steps as required by federal regulations, we moved forward with an independent and external human subjects review. In order to conduct an external human subject review, a document titled "Protecting Human Subjects: A Review of the Proposal Improving Safety in Women's Facilities 2010" was developed. This document requires qualified human subjects reviewers to answer and comment on several questions about all of our project's survey administration documents.

Several experts in correctional research, women's facilities, and sexual violence were recruited to serve as external reviewers. This review found that our approach met all of the requirements, and resulted in an overall recommendation that this human subject plan be approved. Some comments and recommendations from reviewers were incorporated into our survey administration materials. An example was working with each facility to incorporate into our information sheet and consent form a listing of their local resources and contacts should a prisoner respondent have concerns about sexual or physical violence.

We also had the proposal reviewed by the IRB once the board was fully constituted and registered with the Federal Office of Human Research Protection. The IRB approved the research proposal pending several minor modifications to consent forms, survey orientation, and administration protocol.

Survey Administration Protocol

A formal survey protocol was developed to guide on-site data collection activities. This section summarizes these steps.

Preparation Activities. In addition to contacting the site and making the logistical arrangements for the site visit, multiple tasks were necessary prior to the visit. All documents (e.g., the survey and consent forms) were customized to reflect site-specific language. For example, we included facility-specific terminology (e.g., whether housing units were called pods, quads, dorms, cells, etc.; whether line custody staff were referred to as deputies, correctional officers, detention officers, etc.), name, title, and contact information of PREA officers or counseling staff, as directed by the site liaison. We also developed a consent form that fit both human subjects protection requirements and local regulations (e.g., whether duplicate or triplicate copies were required). Once all materials were prepared, the next step entailed copying and packing the survey and related materials (pencils that met security requirements, information and consent documents, definition sheets, envelopes for filing completed surveys, erasers, sign-in sheets, and the like). Conveying these bulky materials to the site, particularly when traveling by air, was another logistical task. The multiple survey sites planned in each geographic area necessitated careful trip planning and coordinating.

Arrival at the Site. Typically, the study team (usually consisting of both principal investigators and two research assistants, one Spanish speaking) met with the executive staff of the facility prior to survey administration. At this meeting, Research staff introduced themselves and the survey purpose and process, answering questions and finalizing the survey arrangements. More detail on the staff focus groups and rating forms, as well as on the housing units to be surveyed, was also provided at this time. Arrangements were made to provide the research team with an up-to-date roster of each housing unit to be surveyed. Inspection of the survey location and facility tours were often part of this first meeting.

The Survey Day. Research staff arrived early to begin setting up the survey room (see below for changes in this approach). Surveys, definition sheets, information sheets/consent forms, and pencils were readied for prisoner arrival. Up-to-date housing unit rosters were provided to the research team. Specific processes for checking prisoners into the survey location using housing unit rosters evolved at each location. Arrangements for Spanish-speaking prisoners, those with reading limitations, and other considerations were also reviewed.

Upon arrival, prisoners were welcomed and asked to sit at individual tables. The fact that women were called away from their regular program was also acknowledged. Although most women were cooperative and patient as they waited, the survey team was prepared to answer questions, particularly from those who indicated an unwillingness to participate. Research survey staff responded to the question, "Do I have to do this?," with a polite request to listen to the orientation once everyone was settled. At all times prisoners were assured that their participation was voluntary. The protocol specified that facility staff would not be physically present during the survey administration.

Prisoner Survey Orientation. A written orientation was developed that outlined the survey purpose and process. After thanking women for attending, the survey team individually introduced themselves. The availability of information in Spanish, help with reading, or other assistance (e.g., the site team brought extra pairs of reading glasses) was also explained here. The commitment to confidentiality at every stage of the survey process was emphasized. Women who indicated an unwillingness or disinterest in participating were given more information by individual team members; they were reassured that they had the right to decline to participate without any repercussions. The content of the survey, the definitions and instructions for completing the survey, and procedures for handing in the survey to members of the research team were also described. Prisoners were told that the survey provided opportunities for open-ended comments.

Those women who chose to complete the survey were then asked to sign the informed consent form, which a member of the research team also signed. Each participant retained a copy of the information sheet and informed consent document.

Collecting the Surveys. Upon completion, prisoners handed in their survey to research team members who reviewed the instrument quickly. When missing data, double answers, or illegible items were discovered, prisoners were given an opportunity to correct the item. In rare cases, this conversation revealed that an individual was unwilling to complete the survey. Again, prisoners were assured that their participation was voluntary and were permitted to decline to futher participate. Initial calculations regarding the number of eligible prisoners, number present for the survey administration, number agreeing or declining, and other issues related to accountability and response rate analysis were made here. Surveys were then filed in envelopes indicating housing unit name and type. Surveys were always under the control of the Research team, and facility staff members were never given access to completed surveys; the completed surveys were removed from the facility daily, sometimes twice daily.

Cleaning the Surveys. At the end of every survey day, the Research team met to review the collected surveys, cleaning stray remarks and clarifying written comments. Although every effort was made to identify problems with the surveys upon collection, this second review process identified some ineligible and invalid submissions. Completed documents were then packed and conveyed to project office.

Revised Survey Administration Protocol

We at first planned to conduct a census of two housing units fitting the subjective definitions of "high" or "low" problems in each facility. Over the course of the study, however, this approach was modified. At many of the facilities, the survey team was encouraged to administer the instrument to more than the two units initially planned. In some smaller facilities, we were able to survey the entire female population. In larger facilities, we surveyed two or more of the "high-problem" and "low-problem" units, and in some cases, units that were "not rated." Primarily due to the generosity of our sites, this enabled us to collect many more cases than we originally intended.

Another change from the original protocol involved the survey location. During the pretest and pilot test, we intended to "call out" survey participants, anticipating that visiting room, dining halls, and common spaces would provide the necessary privacy and setting (tables, chairs, and restrooms) most conducive to survey activities. The time involved in this process was often excessive. The time needed to make the call-outs, arrange for escorts, and assembly sometimes became unwieldy, limiting the number of cases we could collect during a survey day. This movement, along with the need to dedicate facility staff to our survey, contributed to the burden on the facility. Over the course of the study, again at the suggestion of facility managers, we began to administer the survey in the housing units. This change enabled the participation of many more women in the survey process and allowed the survey team to cover many more housing units in less time than we had originally planned.

Courtesy Local Facility Report

Although not included in the original proposal, each of the facilities that participated in our study received a facility-specific, preliminary courtesy report titled "Validation Project for Improving Safety in Women's Facilities." Given the urgency of getting feedback from participating facilities, the report was based on a preliminary database containing all of the survey data (some data were later dropped as a result of additional quality control procedures or certain analyses).

All of the agencies were very eager to receive the courtesy report and expressed their gratitude once they received it. In fact, one agency scheduled a conference call and discussed the results with the Research team and their executive staff.

Data Collection Activities and Descriptive Results

Housing Unit Rating Procedures

As mentioned above, we conducted a staff focus group at each site we visited. During the focus groups, staff discussed which housing units they considered most and least problematic. In addition, staff were asked to complete rating forms for the housing units they were most familiar with. The rating form asked focus group participants to rate housing units on: physical violence in the unit, sexual violence in the unit, likelihood of being physically victimized in the unit, and likelihood of being sexually victimized in the unit. Thus we collected both qualitative data (from comments made by staff focus group participants) and quantitative data (from the staff unit ratings).

The quantitative staff ratings generally agreed with the high- and low-problem units identified in focus group discussions. Of 200 possible comparisons between units (within facilities) where we had both individual staff unit rating forms and focus group ratings, 157 (78.5 percent) were in agreement, 32 (16 percent) produced ties, and 11 (5.5 percent) were not in agreement.

Survey Administration and Response Rates

A total of 4,040 surveys were collected from 15 diverse facilities, including county jails and state prisons, as well as a federal prison and a privately managed state prison.

Response rates for each facility and housing unit surveyed were calculated in two ways: first, based on the number of prisoners or detainees housed (assigned) to the living unit at the time of the survey; and second, based on the number actually available for survey participation. Some prisoners were not available to participate in the survey because they were out for court hearings, visits, sick call, work details, community service, or involvement in other programs. Likewise, in some cases prisoners were asleep and unavailable for the survey because their work detail took place the previous night. Since these prisoners were not available to participate, we felt it appropriate to calculate two response rates, one of which takes prisoners' availability into consideration and one that does not.

Response rates were quite good overall: 89.0 percent of available prisoners completed the WCSS Survey. Response rates for individual facilities ranged from 71..2 to 100 percent for available prisoners and from 63.7 to 96.7 percent of all assigned prisoners. Overall, 89.9 percent of available prisoners and 85.1 percent of available jail detainees completed the WCSS Survey. Similarly, 89.4 percent of available prisoners in low-problem units, 89.0 percent of available prisoners in high-problem units, and 88.4 percent of available prisoners in "not rated" units completed the WCSS survey.

Data Entry

Prior to beginning data entry activities, training sessions were conducted for all data entry personnel. A senior research associate developed and conducted the training based on (1) emerging patterns identified during quality control checks (e.g., common errors to avoid), (2) issues specific to upcoming data entry runs (e.g., familiarization with instruments and databases to be used, procedures for addressing potential gray areas), and (3) tips for using the data entry software (SPSS) more accurately and efficiently. Data processing trainings were revised and expanded several times to address issues identified by the research team and issues revealed by quality control procedures. In each case, support staff received additional training as necessary.

Quality Control

The research team developed and employed a variety of quality assurance and quality control (QC) procedures to prevent, reduce, and identify errors during data collection, data entry, data management, data analysis, and other stages of the project. All quality testing results were well within established tolerances and unremarkable, with one exception: QC testing of data entry accuracy for the pilot data collected in State Prison #1 (the first major data collection site of the current project) revealed unacceptably high levels of errors. A 17 percent random sample (N = 66) of the 382 usable surveys collected at the facility were completely reentered by a second research assistant. Moreover, given identified patterns among the errors, the research team revised and expanded relevant training for all research assistants who entered or managed data. Subsequently all data collected at this facility were reentered and retested for accuracy.

Other QC measures included (1) determining whether data could be considered as missing at random, (2) checking points of inconsistency among the data, and (3) checking for discrepancies in data entry. A variety of statistical, visual, and pattern recognition analyses revealed no discernible pattern in the missing data.

The final database consisted of 3,499 usable cases, or 85.5 percent of the collected surveys.

Tables of Findings

Derived from Wells, Owen, and Parson 2013

For tables 1 through 12, some results will not sum to exactly 100% due to small rounding errors in calculating the scales.

TABLE I INMATE ECONOMIC CONFLICT

Survey Items	Distribution of responses (%)					Number of Cases	Standard Deviation	Mean (Average)
	0 = Not at All a Problem	1 = Small Problem	2 = Medium Problem	3 = Big Problem	4 = Very Big Problem			
Q1: Women here have gotten into verbal arguments over debts.	20.1	20.7	22.6	15.9	20.7	3,496	1.41	1.96
Q2: Women here have used pressure or threats to collect on debts.	29.1	20.8	19.3	14.6	16.2	3,489	1.44	1.68
Q3: Women here have gotten into physical fights with other women inmates over debts.	32.9	18.1	17.7	13.8	17.5	3,489	1.49	1.65
Q4: Women here have used pressure or threats to steal from others.	35.5	21.5	18.8	13.5	10.7	3,493	1.37	1.42
Q5: Women here have gotten into physical fights over theft.	26.8	18.7	18.6	18.7	17.1	3,490	1.45	1.81
Q6: Women here have used physical force to steal from others.	45.1	21.4	16.1	9.0	8.4	3,491	1.31	1.14
Inmate Economic Conflict Scale (Overall):	31.6	20.2	18.9	14.3	15.1	3,458	1.25	1.61
Inmate Economic Conflict Scale (by Facility Type):								
Prisons	30.4	20.0	18.7	14.7	16.3	2,807	1.27	1.67
Jails	37.0	21.2	19.5	12.2	10.1	651	1.13	1.37
Inmate Economic Conflict Scale (by Housing Unit Rating):								
High-Problem Units	19.7	18.2	21.4	17.7	23.0	1,284	1.23	2.06
Low-Problem Units	36.3	19.9	17.7	13.8	12.2	1,439	1.22	1.45
Unrated Units	43.2	24.2	16.4	9.1	7.1	735	1.08	1.13

TABLE 2   INMATE SEXUAL VIOLENCE

Survey Items	Distribution of responses (%)					Number of Cases	Standard Deviation	Mean (Average)
	0 = Not at All a Problem	1 = Small Problem	2 = Medium Problem	3 = Big Problem	4 = Very Big Problem			
Q7: Women here have used physical force to touch, feel, or grab other women in a sexually threatening or uncomfortable way.	57.2	20.9	11.5	5.6	4.8	3,489	1.14	0.80
Q8: Without using physical force, women here have touched, felt, or grabbed other women in a sexually threatening or uncomfortable way.	46.0	21.8	13.8	8.9	9.4	3,496	1.34	1.14
Q9: Women here had to pay "protection" to other women in order to keep themselves safe from sexual assault.	73.3	13.9	6.6	3.5	2.7	3,475	0.96	0.48
Q10: Women here have offered to protect other women to get them to perform UNWANTED sexual activity.	74.6	13.0	6.2	3.8	2.4	3,488	0.94	0.46
Q11: Women here have asked other women to perform UNWANTED sexual activity.	64.5	16.8	8.8	5.3	4.6	3493	1.12	0.69
Q12: Women here have paid (with money, goods or services) other women to perform UNWANTED sexual activity.	68.0	15.9	8.3	4.2	3.7	3,495	1.05	0.60
Q13: Women here have threatened other women inmates with sexual violence.	71.3	14.7	7.2	3.7	3.0	3,493	0.99	0.52
Q14: Weaker women have been sexually assaulted here by other women inmates.	67.9	15.9	7.4	5.0	3.9	3,488	1.07	0.61
Q15: Women here have used physical violence to force other women to perform UNWANTED sexual activity.	73.9	14.0	6.1	3.6	2.4	3,489	0.93	0.46

(continued)

TABLE 2 (Continued)

Survey Items	Distribution of responses (%)					Number of Cases	Standard Deviation	Mean (Average)
	0 = Not at All a Problem	1 = Small Problem	2 = Medium Problem	3 = Big Problem	4 = Very Big Problem			
Q16: Women here involved in intimate relationships have used physical violence to force their partners or girlfriends to perform UNWANTED sexual activity.	66.9	16.7	7.9	5.0	3.5	3,483	1.06	0.62
Q17: Women here have been sexually assaulted by other women inmates.	62.5	19.2	8.4	5.2	4.7	3,492	1.12	0.70
Q18: Women here have been sexually assaulted by another woman inmate acting alone.	65.1	18.9	7.5	4.7	3.8	3,493	1.06	0.63
Q19: Women here have been sexually assaulted by a group of women inmates.	77.1	12.4	5.4	2.8	2.2	3,492	0.89	0.41
Q20: Women here have to defend themselves from sexual assaults by other women inmates.	69.6	16.7	6.4	3.9	3.3	3,491	1.00	0.55
Inmate Sexual Violence Scale (Overall):	67.0	16.5	8.0	4.7	3.9	3,385	0.88	0.61
Inmate Sexual Violence Scale (by Facility Type):								
Prisons	65.7	16.9	8.4	5.0	4.0	2,760	0.90	0.64
Jails	72.7	14.6	6.2	3.3	3.2	625	0.78	0.48
Inmate Sexual Violence Scale (by Housing Unit Rating):								
High-Problem Units	56.8	20.4	10.7	6.4	5.7	1,239	0.98	0.83
Low-Problem Units	70.1	15.2	7.1	4.3	3.3	1,423	0.84	0.54
Unrated Units	78.6	12.3	4.9	2.3	1.8	723	0.66	0.35

TABLE 3   INMATE PHYSICAL VIOLENCE

	Distribution of responses (%)								
Survey Items	0 = Not at All a Problem	1 = Small Problem	2 = Medium Problem	3 = Big Problem	4 = Very Big Problem	Number of Cases	Standard Deviation	Mean (Average)
Q21: Women here have verbally threatened other women inmates with physical violence.	23.8	19.7	16.5	16.4	23.6	3,490	1.50	1.96
Q22: Women here have gotten into physical fights that started with arguments.	17.5	18.0	18.3	17.1	29.1	3,497	1.47	2.22
Q23: Women here have had to pay "protection" to other women in order to keep themselves safe from physical assault.	62.2	15.7	10.4	6.3	5.6	3,476	1.19	0.77
Q24: Women here have gotten into physical fights with other women inmates they did not know.	30.3	18.2	16.7	15.5	19.3	3,480	1.50	1.75
Q25: Women here have gotten into physical fights with their roommates/cellmates.	20.2	21.4	18.7	17.0	22.8	3,493	1.45	2.01
Q26: Women here have gotten into physical fights with their friends/others they know.	22.9	22.5	19.7	17.0	18.0	3,483	1.42	1.85
Q27: Women here have gotten into physical fights with their intimate partners or girlfriends.	24.1	18.2	15.4	15.7	26.6	3,489	1.54	2.03
Q28: Women involved with gangs have gotten into physical fights here.	54.8	15.3	11.7	8.4	9.8	3,491	1.37	1.03
Q29: Women here have hit, slapped, kicked, or bitten other women inmates.	23.0	21.6	16.2	15.3	23.8	3,493	1.50	1.95

(continued)

TABLE 3 (Continued)

Survey Items	Distribution of responses (%)					Number of Cases	Standard Deviation	Mean (Average)
	0 = Not at All a Problem	1 = Small Problem	2 = Medium Problem	3 = Big Problem	4 = Very Big Problem			
Q30: Women here have used a weapon to physically assault another woman inmate.	53.0	16.1	11.8	8.9	10.2	3,487	1.38	1.07
Q31: Women here have to defend themselves from physical assaults by other women inmates.	36.5	20.4	14.5	12.3	16.3	3,492	1.48	1.52
Inmate Physical Violence Scale (Overall):	33.5	18.8	15.4	13.6	18.6	3,395	1.22	1.65
Inmate Physical Violence Scale (by Facility Type):								
Prisons	31.6	18.8	15.6	14.0	20.0	2,758	1.23	1.71
Jails	41.6	19.2	14.6	12.0	12.7	637	1.15	1.35
Inmate Physical Violence Scale (by Housing Unit Rating):								
High-Problem Units	21.1	16.2	17.1	18.4	27.2	1,253	1.13	2.14
Low-Problem Units	38.7	19.3	14.9	11.4	15.8	1,418	1.22	1.46
Unrated Units	44.8	22.7	13.7	9.6	9.3	724	1.06	1.16

TABLE 4   STAFF VERBAL AND SEXUAL HARASSMENT

Survey Items	Distribution of responses (%)						Number of Cases	Standard Deviation	Mean (Average)
	0 = Not at All a Problem	1 = Small Problem	2 = Medium Problem	3 = Big Problem	4 = Very Big Problem				
Q32: Staff here have made disrespectful comments about women inmates when talking with other staff.	18.7	14.4	14.7	18.1	34.1		3,494	1.52	2.35
Q33: Staff here have made disrespectful comments to women inmates.	13.6	15.3	14.5	19.0	37.5		3,497	1.46	2.52
Q34: Staff here have cursed when speaking to women inmates.	13.8	12.6	13.3	16.9	43.3		3,495	1.48	2.63
Q35: Staff here have yelled or screamed at women inmates.	10.2	12.1	12.7	17.1	47.9		3,493	1.40	2.80
Q36: Staff here have made sexual comments to women inmates.	54.0	16.7	11.3	6.6	11.4		3,489	1.39	1.05
Q37: Staff here have made sexual gestures or noises in front of women inmates.	59.2	14.8	9.5	6.7	9.8		3,494	1.35	0.93
Staff Verbal and Sexual Harassment Scale (Overall):	28.3	14.3	12.7	14.1	30.7		3,470	1.20	2.04
Staff Verbal and Sexual Harassment Scale (by Facility Type):									
Prisons	27.3	14.5	12.8	13.9	31.5		2,819	1.22	2.07
Jails	32.4	13.4	12.1	14.9	27.2		651	1.12	1.91
Staff Verbal and Sexual Harassment Scale (by Housing Unit Rating):									
High-Problem Units	21.0	11.9	12.5	15.5	39.0		1,283	1.12	2.39
Low-Problem Units	28.8	15.3	13.0	13.8	29.2		1,449	1.20	1.99
Unrated Units	39.9	16.5	12.2	12.2	19.2		738	1.16	1.54

TABLE 5 STAFF SEXUAL MISCONDUCT

Survey Items	Distribution of responses (%)					Number of Cases	Standard Deviation	Mean (Average)
	0 = Not at All a Problem	1 = Small Problem	2 = Medium Problem	3 = Big Problem	4 = Very Big Problem			
Q38: Staff here have stared at women inmates' bodies.	43.7	17.9	11.9	9.6	16.8	3,493	1.52	1.38
Q39: Staff here have invaded the privacy of women inmates more than what was necessary for them to do their jobs.	37.5	17.9	13.4	11.4	19.8	3,495	1.55	1.58
Q40: Staff here have touched women inmates in a sexual way.	66.8	13.5	8.5	4.6	6.6	3,489	1.20	0.71
Q41: Staff here have touched women inmates in a sexual way while searching them.	62.0	13.8	9.9	6.0	8.4	3,496	1.30	0.85
Q42: Staff here have exposed their genitals and/or breasts (if female staff) to women inmates.	82.1	7.8	4.6	2.1	3.4	3,487	0.93	0.37
Q43: Staff here have engaged in sexual activity with women inmates.	63.9	14.0	8.7	5.8	7.7	3,490	1.27	0.79
Q44: Staff here have pressured or threatened women inmates to engage in sexual activity.	78.3	9.4	5.7	2.8	3.8	3,487	0.99	0.44
Q45: Staff here have forced women inmates through physical violence to perform sexual activity.	83.7	7.2	4.3	2.1	2.7	3,488	0.87	0.33

Q46: Staff here have pressured or threatened women inmates with physical violence to keep quiet about staff-inmate sexual relationships.	78.7	8.5	4.8	3.6	4.4	3,486	1.04	0.47
Staff Sexual Misconduct Scale (Overall):	66.3	12.2	8.0	5.3	8.2	3,443	0.98	0.76
Staff Sexual Misconduct Scale (by Facility Type):								
Prisons	64.6	12.6	8.5	5.7	8.5	2,797	1.00	0.80
Jails	73.5	10.5	5.6	3.6	6.7	646	0.85	0.58
Staff Sexual Misconduct Scale (by Housing Unit Rating):								
High-Problem Units	58.4	14.4	9.8	7.0	10.3	1,268	1.06	0.96
Low-Problem Units	67.8	11.8	7.9	4.8	7.8	1,442	0.95	0.72
Unrated Units	77.2	9.2	5.1	3.4	5.1	733	0.82	0.49

TABLE 6   STAFF PHYSICAL VIOLENCE

| Survey Items | Distribution of responses (%) | | | | | Number of Cases | Standard Deviation | Mean (Average) |
	0 = Not at All a Problem	1 = Small Problem	2 = Medium Problem	3 = Big Problem	4 = Very Big Problem			
Q47: Staff here have threatened women inmates with physical violence.	63.5	11.7	7.5	6.8	10.5	3,492	1.38	0.89
Q48: Staff here have used too much physical force while controlling women inmates.	49.8	13.0	10.6	10.3	16.3	3,496	1.55	1.30
Q49: Staff here have used too much force while searching women inmates.	53.6	15.2	9.8	8.8	12.7	3,497	1.45	1.12
Q50: Staff here have hit, slapped, kicked, or bitten women inmates.	69.9	11.1	5.9	4.5	8.6	3,491	1.27	0.71
Staff Physical Violence Scale (Overall):	59.2	12.8	8.5	7.6	12.0	3,479	1.25	1.00
Staff Physical Violence Scale (by Facility Type):								
Prisons	58.6	12.6	8.4	8.0	12.4	2,825	1.28	1.03
Jails	61.9	13.3	8.5	6.1	10.3	654	1.14	0.89
Staff Physical Violence Scale (by Housing Unit Rating):								
High-Problem Units	48.0	15.4	10.9	9.3	16.4	1,289	1.31	1.31
Low-Problem Units	60.0	12.6	8.0	8.1	11.3	1,452	1.25	0.98
Unrated Units	77.1	8.6	4.9	3.7	5.8	738	0.97	0.52

TABLE 7 LIKELIHOOD OF VIOLENCE

Survey Items	Distribution of responses (%)					Number of Cases	Standard Deviation	Mean (Average)
	1 = Strongly Disagree	2 = Somewhat Disagree	3 = Neither Agree nor Disagree	4 = Somewhat Agree	5 = Strongly Agree			
Q51: Women here are likely to be sexually harassed by one or more women inmates.	41.0	15.5	16.7	15.6	11.3	3,489	1.43	2.41
Q52: Women here are likely to be physically assaulted by one or more women inmates.	31.1	13.3	15.9	19.8	19.9	3,485	1.53	2.84
Q53: Women here are likely to be sexually assaulted by one or more women inmates.	50.5	14.3	19.8	9.2	6.2	3,477	1.27	2.06
Q54: Women here are likely to be sexually harassed by one or more women inmates.	50.8	13.3	19.0	10.2	6.7	3,486	1.31	2.09
Q55: Women here are likely to be physically assaulted by one or more staff.	50.3	12.0	18.5	9.8	9.3	3,488	1.38	2.16
Q56: Women here are likely to be sexually assaulted by one or more staff.	58.6	11.6	19.0	5.9	4.9	3,489	1.20	1.87
Likelihood of Violence Scale (Overall):	47.1	13.3	18.2	11.8	9.7	3,462	1.11	2.24
Likelihood of Violence Scale (by Facility Type):								
Prisons	46.6	13.3	18.0	11.9	10.3	2,811	1.12	2.26
Jails	49.1	13.7	19.0	11.2	7.1	651	1.02	2.13
Likelihood of Violence Scale (by Housing Unit Rating):								
High-Problem Units	38.1	14.3	20.0	14.1	13.4	1,281	1.12	2.50
Low-Problem Units	49.7	12.8	16.8	11.8	8.9	1,448	1.11	2.17
Unrated Units	57.4	12.6	17.6	7.6	4.8	733	0.96	1.89

TABLE 8 PHYSICAL AND SEXUAL VIOLENCE IN UNITS

Survey Items	1 = Not Violent	2	3	4	5	6	7	8	9	10 = Very Violent	Number of Cases	Standard Deviation	Mean (Average)
Distribution of responses (%)													
Q57: How physically violent is this unit?	34.3	12.9	9.2	6.9	8.1	6.5	5.9	7.6	3.1	5.5	3,467	2.91	3.80
Prisons	33.3	12.8	8.6	6.6	8.2	6.3	6.3	8.4	3.3	6.2	2,813	2.98	3.93
Jails	38.5	13.1	11.9	8.1	7.5	7.3	4.6	4.3	2.3	2.3	654	2.53	3.24
High-Problem Units	15.4	9.2	9.3	8.8	10.5	9.0	8.6	12.7	5.8	10.7	1,283	2.98	5.24
Low-Problem Units	44.1	14.6	8.9	5.1	6.8	4.8	5.2	5.5	2.0	3.1	1,448	2.66	3.12
Unrated Units	47.8	15.9	9.8	7.1	6.5	5.6	2.9	3.1	0.4	1.0	736	2.15	2.61
Q58: How sexually violent is this unit?	59.8	12.1	7.3	4.4	5.6	2.8	2.4	2.1	1.4	2.2	3,476	2.26	2.36
Prisons	58.2	12.1	7.5	4.4	5.7	3.2	2.7	2.3	1.4	2.4	2,820	2.33	2.45
Jails	66.3	12.2	6.4	4.4	4.9	1.2	1.1	1.2	1.1	1.2	656	1.88	1.98
High-Problem Units	45.7	12.7	8.9	6.7	8.2	4.2	3.4	3.5	2.3	4.3	1,288	2.66	3.07
Low-Problem Units	65.0	11.9	7.4	3.2	4.8	2.1	1.8	1.7	1.0	1.2	1,449	1.98	2.07
Unrated Units	73.9	11.4	4.3	3.0	2.6	1.6	1.8	0.7	0.4	0.4	739	1.56	1.70

TABLE 9 FACILITY PROCEDURES FOR PROTECTING WOMEN

Survey Items	Distribution of responses (%)					Number of Cases	Standard Deviation	Mean (Average)
	1 = Strongly Disagree	2 = Somewhat Disagree	3 = Neither Agree nor Disagree	4 = Somewhat Agree	5 = Strongly Agree			
Q59a: The facility's procedures are successful in protecting women inmates here from inmate physical violence.	28.4	17.2	20.3	17.9	16.2	3,493	1.44	2.76
Q59b: The facility's procedures are successful in protecting women inmates here from inmate sexual violence.	16.4	12.9	25.8	19.7	25.1	3,493	1.39	3.24
Q59c: The facility's procedures are successful in protecting women inmates here from staff sexual misconduct.	18.0	10.6	25.2	17.0	29.2	3,487	1.44	3.29
Q59d: The facility's procedures are successful in protecting women inmates here from staff physical violence.	19.2	11.4	24.2	17.0	28.2	3,487	1.46	3.24
Facility Procedures in Protecting Women Scale (Overall):	20.5	13.0	23.9	17.9	24.7	3,472	1.20	3.13
Facility Procedures in Protecting Women Scale (by Facility Type):								
Prisons	21.8	13.3	23.0	17.3	24.5	2,815	1.22	3.09
Jails	14.9	11.8	27.5	20.3	25.5	657	1.11	3.30
Facility Procedures in Protecting Women Scale (by Housing Unit Rating):								
High-Problem Units	25.1	13.5	24.9	17.7	18.8	1,282	1.15	2.91
Low-Problem Units	20.6	13.7	21.7	16.7	27.2	1,450	1.25	3.16
Unrated Units	12.2	10.9	26.3	20.5	30.0	740	1.11	3.45

TABLE 10 STAFF HARASSMENT OF INMATES WHO REPORT

Survey Items	Distribution of responses (%)					Number of Cases	Standard Deviation	Mean (Average)
	1 = Strongly Disagree	2 = Somewhat Disagree	3 = Neither Agree nor Disagree	4 = Somewhat Agree	5 = Strongly Agree			
Q60a: Staff harass women inmates who make reports about inmate physical violence.	34.6	10.4	27.0	13.3	14.6	3,494	1.44	2.63
Q60b: Staff harass women inmates who make reports about inmate sexual violence.	38.3	10.5	29.9	8.9	12.5	3,492	1.39	2.47
Q60c: Staff harass women inmates who make reports about staff sexual misconduct.	35.3	9.0	28.5	9.9	17.3	3,491	1.47	2.65
Q60d: Staff harass women inmates who make reports about staff physical violence.	33.5	7.9	26.4	11.9	20.1	3,490	1.51	2.77
Staff Harassment of Inmates Who Report Scale (Overall):	35.4	9.5	28.0	11.0	16.1	3,480	1.31	2.63
Staff Harassment of Inmates Who Report Scale (by Facility Type):								
Prisons	35.0	9.4	27.3	11.0	17.2	2,822	1.32	2.66
Jails	37.3	9.6	30.7	10.9	11.5	658	1.23	2.50
Staff Harassment of Inmates Who Report Scale (by Housing Unit Rating):								
High-Problem Units	30.6	10.2	29.2	11.5	18.6	1,288	1.28	2.77
Low-Problem Units	35.3	8.9	27.1	11.7	16.9	1,455	1.32	2.66
Unrated Units	44.1	9.2	27.5	8.8	10.3	737	1.26	2.32

TABLE II INMATE HARASSMENT OF INMATES WHO REPORT

Survey Items	Distribution of responses (%)					Number of Cases	Standard Deviation	Mean (Average)
	1 = Strongly Disagree	2 = Somewhat Disagree	3 = Neither Agree nor Disagree	4 = Somewhat Agree	5 = Strongly Agree			
Q61a: Other women harass inmates who make reports about inmate physical violence.	19.5	7.2	20.0	22.0	31.3	3,490	1.47	3.39
Q61b: Other women harass inmates who make reports about inmate sexual violence.	25.4	7.4	26.5	17.0	23.8	3,495	1.49	3.06
Q61c: Other women harass inmates who make reports about staff sexual misconduct.	30.8	8.5	28.8	13.1	18.8	3,492	1.47	2.81
Q61d: Other women harass inmates who make reports about staff physical violence.	32.4	8.7	27.9	11.5	19.5	3,493	1.49	2.77
Inmate Harassment of Inmates Who Report Scale (Overall):	27.0	8.0	25.8	15.9	23.4	3,481	1.31	3.01
Inmate Harassment of Inmates Who Report Scale (by Facility Type):								
Prisons	26.1	7.9	24.9	16.1	25.0	2,826	1.31	3.06
Jails	30.9	8.1	29.8	15.0	16.2	655	1.24	2.78
Inmate Harassment of Inmates Who Report Scale (by Housing Unit Rating):								
High-Problem Units	20.9	7.6	26.2	16.0	29.3	1,285	1.24	3.25
Low-Problem Units	28.0	8.3	24.3	16.7	22.6	1,457	1.33	2.98
Unrated Units	35.6	7.8	28.1	14.2	14.3	739	1.28	2.64

TABLE 12 STAFF REPORTING CLIMATE

Survey Items	Distribution of responses (%)					Number of Cases	Standard Deviation	Mean (Average)
	1 = Strongly Disagree	2 = Somewhat Disagree	3 = Neither Agree nor Disagree	4 = Somewhat Agree	5 = Strongly Agree			
Q62: The staff here have done a good job of handling women's complaints about sexual safety.	14.9	10.0	34.7	16.4	23.9	3,497	1.33	3.24
Q63: Staff members here are concerned about the sexual safety of women inmates.	18.6	12.8	27.7	16.5	24.5	3,495	1.41	3.15
Q64: If a woman inmate believes she will be sexually attacked, the custody housing staff here will protect her.	20.2	13.2	25.4	17.3	23.9	3,492	1.43	3.12
Q65: The custody line staff here are concerned about the sexual safety of women inmates.	20.3	12.7	29.7	15.9	21.4	3,495	1.40	3.06
Q66: The administrative staff here are concerned about the sexual safety of women inmates.	18.0	10.3	26.2	19.3	26.2	3,490	1.41	3.26
Q67: There are programs at this facility to help women inmates deal with sexual safety problems.	26.9	10.7	29.6	15.5	17.3	3,488	1.42	2.86
Q68: Staff here would report other staff who are involved sexually with women inmates.	22.0	11.3	34.5	12.4	19.8	3,493	1.38	2.97
Staff Reporting Climate Scale (Overall):	20.1	11.6	29.7	16.2	22.4	3,462	1.11	3.09
Staff Reporting Climate Scale (by Facility Type):								
Prisons	20.8	11.6	28.4	16.2	23.0	2,811	1.13	3.09
Jails	17.3	11.3	35.2	16.0	20.2	651	1.04	3.11
Staff Reporting Climate Scale (by Housing Unit Rating):								
High-Problem Units	24.9	13.1	28.8	15.4	17.8	1,279	1.12	2.88
Low-Problem Units	19.2	11.3	28.3	17.0	24.2	1,449	1.11	3.15
Unrated Units	13.6	9.3	33.9	16.0	27.2	734	1.03	3.34

TABLE 13   SUMMARY OF OPEN-ENDED COMMENTS IN
SURVEY CATEGORIES

Open-Ended Comment Category	Times Mentioned
Inmate-related	
Verbal conflict	34
Economic conflict	13
Sexual harassment	22
Physical violence	134
Sexual misconduct/violence	15
Subtotal	218
Staff-related	
Verbal conflict/harassment	240
Sexual harassment	30
Sexual misconduct	48
Physical violence	45
Subtotal	363
Class/topic suggestions	426
Other/overlapping comments	327
Total Comments	1,334

TABLE 14 DEMOGRAPHICS (NOMINAL VARIABLES)

Variable	Response	N	% of Responses[1]	% of Inmates[1]
Highest Degree of Education	Less than high school	681	12.6	19.6
	High school diploma or GED	2,711	50.1	78.1
	Vocational or trade school certificate	553	10.2	15.9
	Some college undergraduate work but no degree completed	982	18.1	28.3
	Undergraduate college degree completed	380	7.0	10.9
	Graduate work beyond completed college degree	109	2.0	3.1
Ethnicity[2]	Hispanic	288	8.5	8.5
	Not Hispanic	3,097	91.5	91.5
Race	Black or African American	835	22.7	24.5
	American Indian or Alaska Native	299	8.1	8.8
	Asian	34	0.9	1.0
	Hawaiian or Other Pacific Islander	37	1.0	1.1
	White	2,321	63.2	68.1
	Other	148	4.0	4.3
Offense History	Drug offense	1,342	34.0	38.8
	Property crime	581	14.7	16.8
	Violent crime	952	24.1	27.5
	Other crime	1,077	27.3	31.1

[1] A total of 25 Spanish surveys were collected. One was ineligible, one was incomplete to the point it was not usable for the validation analyses, and 23 were valid.
[2] Percentages may not equal 100% because of rounding and/or because participants were allowed to choose more than one response.

Glossary

BABY LIFER A person beginning a life sentence; generally someone within the first couple of years of a life sentence. This does not refer to chronological age but rather the person's stage of doing time.

BED MOVES A change of sleeping quarters.

BEING CROSSED OUT Being in jeopardy of staff or prisoner negative action; an unjust punishment; placed in a conflict not of one's making. Similar to "trick bag."

BIG BALLER A person with a considerable amount of informal power within the prison. A designation usually related to the economic position of the person but can refer to the person's status of power within the prison hierarchy. It can also refer to a prisoner who is dealing drugs inside the prison and currently has drugs available.

BON-A-ROO The best clothing style or set of clothes.

BOOKS Prisoners' accounts of prison earnings or money sent from the outside. Prisoners will say, "I have money on my books," to indicate they have funds.

BUNKIE A person in the opposite bunk (above or below) or in the same room or cell. Similar to "cellie."

CAR A clique of prisoners or staff headed by those who have some influence or power (juice); a group of people who have common interests or goals; those who join together to accomplish legitimate or illegitimate tasks.

CELLIE A person who lives in your cell or room. Similar to "bunkie."

CHILD CASE The offense of a prisoner who is incarcerated for a crime against a child. This is highly stigmatized and usually results in the prisoner being ostracized by staff as well as by most other prisoners.

CLASSIFICATION The process of being assigned to security/custody designations, privilege groups, housing, housing assignment, and program participation. Can also be shorthand for the Classification Committee and refer to prison staff who make this determination.

CO Correctional officer who works in the prison; sometimes called "the law" or "cop."

COSIGN Vouching for another's trustfulness or worth to others.

CROSSES Finding or putting oneself into a problematic situation not of her making. Typically results in some form of jeopardy. Similar to "trick bag," being set up, a Catch-22.

CRUNK Loud complaining or insulting; violent behavior; beating up another prisoner.

DO YOUR OWN TIME A prison norm that compels prisoners to "mind your own business," prohibits gossiping about other prisoners, and exhorts prisoners to avoid "backbiting" or starting trouble among others. Can also direct prisoners to "ignore things," avoid bringing attention to yourself or the bad behavior of other prisoners or staff.

DOUBLING UP The doubling of a debt in the sub rosa economy of the prison. Borrowing "two noodles" means a repayment of four. If payment is not made on time, the debt is doubled to eight. Debt continues to double until paid.

DOWN FOR YOUR PEOPLE Having a primary loyalty to your group of chosen friends. Generally, that pertains to the ethnic group you belong to (by choice or by birth).

FEATHERWOOD A white female. The male equivalent is "Peckerwood."

FISH A new prisoner or staff member; denotes low status and naïveté.

FREE WORLD The outside community.

G-ED UP Abbreviation for "Gangstered up"; dressing and behaving like a gangster.

GENERAL POPULATION Classification and living spaces that applies to most prisoners. Women in this group have the most movement and other privileges.

GET A CASE To be charged with a law violation formally.

GET BACKS Payback or retaliation for real or perceived wrongs.

GETTING OVER Avoiding detection of something one is not supposed to be doing. Usually involves direct interaction with another person, whereby a person is intentionally deceived by a person who is "getting over."

HAVE SOMETHING COMING Indicates a prisoner's worthiness or being deserving of goods, services, action, favor, or status.

HOLDING THE BAG Control or possession of drugs or other contraband inside prison.

HYGIENES Products used to keep the body clean, such as shampoo, conditioner, deodorant, toothpaste, sanitary products.

ISSUE Goods or items issued by authorities; can refer to amount of such items.

JACKED Stealing or taking. Relates to being hijacked.

JAIL (IN REFERENCE TO ADMINISTRATIVE SEGREGATION, OR AD SEG) Disciplinary housing for those accused of rule violation, under investigation, or placed in Ad Seg custody for protection. Usually a shorter term. Prisoners will say they are going to jail when sent to Ad Seg. Also see SHU.

JUICE Extraordinary influence over a situation or others; prison political power and infleunce.

KITE A written message transmitted by circumventing approved communication methods. Usually, a short note folded into a creative design and passed between prisoners without correctional staff permission or knowledge. In some systems, any written note sent to staff can be a kite.

LOCK IN THE SOCK A weapon made by dropping a combination lock into a sock to be swung; can cause serious injury.

LOSE TIME The consequence of rule violation that results in losing "good time," or sentence reduction credits earned by program partipation and other "good behavior." Typically extends time in prison. Counterintuitively, a prisoner who loses time will serve more time in prison due to loss of good time credits.

NOODLES Dry noodle packages sold in the prison commissary; often used as a unit of currency.

OG Original Gangster. Prisoner who subscribes to the more traditional prison cultural norms, such as not telling on others and not doing business with correctional staff. Related to being "old school" and doing time as a convict rather than an inmate.

PAY NUMBER Prison job with pay.

PRUNO Homemade alcohol, also known as hooch.

PUNKED A term used in women's facilities to describe economic or physical exploitation. Unlike its use in male prisons, "punked" typically does not have a sexual connotation in women's prisons and jails.

RUNNING THE YARD A prisoner who has enough influence to make decisions that should be made by correctional staff, as in controlling the activities of others; hanging out on the yard, usually engaged in nonproductive activities or interactions. Being involved in "the mix."

SHOT CALLER A prisoner with extensive prison capital; can pertain to her room, work sites, or the prison generally. Typically maintained by the threat of force or other pressures.

SHU Secure, Special, or Segregated Housing Unit. Disciplinary housing for those found guilty of a serious prison rule violation; typically a single or double cell where the prisoner is locked in 23 hours a day. Also, the "hole."

SNITCH JACKET A negative reputation for snitching.

SNITCHING Revealing confidential information about conduct to prison staff. Also known as "telling" and, somewhat less common in women's prisons, as "ratting."

STREET Outside of prison; the free world community.

STORE The prison commissary. A woman must have "money on her books" to shop legitimately.

SUB ROSA ECONOMY The informal or underground economy made up of goods outside the prison "issue."

TAKING A DATE Intentionally causing trouble for another prisoner to provoke serious disciplinary action against her, resulting in reduced "good time" or a canceled parole date.

TERM Length of a sentence; number of times sent to prison; the phase of a prison sentence.

TRICK A person who is exploited by a prisoner in order to obtain money, drugs, or some other material item. Similar to "John," or sex work client.

TRICK BAG A situation in which one person is intentionally deceived by others, resulting in a problematic situation with few options to avoid disadvantage or penalty. Similar to a Catch-22 and being between a "rock and a hard place."

TUNE UP The use of physical violence or fights to correct another's behavior.

UGLY BEDS Beds set up in nonprivate and nontraditional areas such as dayrooms, gyms, program spaces, or hallways.

USE OF FORCE Staff use of physical means to control a situation.

WALKED OFF When staff are fired, typically for serious rule-breaking behavior, they may be confronted by a team of supervisors and escorted off the facility grounds in full public view.

WEATHERING Exposure to damaging or injurious situations that undermine well-being.

THE YARD The prison or recreation yard. Most prison housing units are arranged around a large open area.

Bibliography

Abrams, L., L. Teplin, and D. Charles. 2004. "Post-Traumatic Stress Disorder and Trauma in Youth in Juvenile Detention. *Archives of General Psychiatry* 61(4): 403–410.

Abril, J. 2008. *Violent Victimization among One Native American Indian Tribe*. Saabrücken, Germany: VDM Publishing.

Adler, C., and A. Worrall. 2004. *Girls' Violence: Myths and Realities*. Albany: State University of New York Press.

Agnew, R. 2006. *Pressured into Crime: An Overview of General Strain Theory*. Los Angeles: Roxbury Publishing.

Alarid, L. 2000. "Sexual Assault and Coercion among Incarcerated Women Prisoners: Excerpts from Prison Letters." *Prison Journal* 80(4): 391–406.

Alexander, M. 2010. *The New Jim Crow: Mass Incarceration in the Age of Colorblindness*. New York: New Press.

Allard, P., and J. Greene. 2001. *Children on the Outside: The Pain and Human Costs of Parental Incarceration*. New York: Justice Strategies.

Amnesty International. 1999. *"Not Part of my Sentence": Violations of the Human Rights of Women in Custody*. London: Amnesty International.

Arnold, R. 1995. "The Processes of Victimization and Criminalization of Black Women." In R. Price and N. Sokoloff, eds., *The Criminal Justice System and Women*, 136–46. New York: McGraw-Hill.

Ataby, T., and B. Owen. 2014. *Women Prisoners and the Implementation of the Bangkok Rules*. Bangkok: Thailand Institute of Justice.

Austin, J., T. Clear, T. Duster, D. Greenberg, J. Irwin, C. McCoy, A. Mobley, B. Owen, and J. Page. 2007. *Unlocking America: Why and How to Reduce America's Prison Population*. Washington, DC: JFA Institute.

Babcock, J., S. Miller, and C. Siard. 2003. "Toward a Typology of Abusive Women: Differences between Partner-Only and Generally Violent Women in the Use of Violence." *Psychology of Women Quarterly* 27: 153–61. doi: 10.1111/14716402.00095.

Bagley, K., and A. Merlo. 1995. "Controlling Women's Bodies." In A. Merlo and J. Pollock, eds., *Women, Law, and Social Control,* 135–55. Boston, MA: Allyn and Bacon.

Baker, J., and T. Rytter. 2014. *Conditions for Women in Prison: Needs, Vulnerabilities and Good Practice.* Copenhagen: Danish Institute Against Torture.

Barberet, R. 2013. *Women, Crime and Criminal Justice: A Global Enquiry.* New York: Routledge.

Baro, A. 1997. "Spheres of Consent: An Analysis of the Sexual Abuse and Sexual Exploitation of Women Incarcerated in the State of Hawaii." *Women & Criminal Justice* 8(3): 61–84.

Baskin, D., and I. Sommers. 1998. *Casualties of Community Disorder: Women's Careers in Violent Crime.* Boulder, CO: Westview Press.

Bastick, M., and L. Townhead. 2008. *Women in Prison: A Commentary on the Standard Minimum Rules for the Treatment of Prisoners.* Geneva: Quaker United Nations Office.

Batchelor, S. 2005. "'Prove Me the Bam!' Victimization and Agency in the Lives of Young Women Who Commit Violent Offenses." *Journal of Community and Criminal Justice* 52(4): 358–75.

Batchelor, S., M. Burman, and J. Brown. 2001. "Discussing Violence: Let's Hear It from the Girls." *Probation Journal* 48(2): 125–34.

Battle, C., C. Zlotnick, L. Najavits, M. Guttierrez, and C. Winsor. 2003. "Post-Traumatic Stress Disorder and Substance Use Disorder among Incarcerated Women." In P. Ouimette and P. Brown, eds. *Trauma and Substance Abuse: Causes, Consequences, and Treatment of Comorbid Disorders.* American Psychological Association.

Beck, A. 2015. "Staff Sexual Misconduct: Implications of PREA for Women Working in Corrections." *Justice Research & Policy* 16(1): 8–36.

Beck, A., M. Berzofsky, R. Caspar, and C. Krebs. 2013. *Sexual Victimization in Prisons and Jails Reported by Inmates, 2011–2012.* Washington, DC: Bureau of Justice Statistics, U.S. Department of Justice.

Beck, A., P. Harrison, and P. Guerino. 2010. *Sexual Victimization in Juvenile Facilities Reported by Youth, 2008–2009.* Washington, DC: U.S. Department of Justice, Bureau of Justice Statistics.

Belknap, J. 2015. *The Invisible Woman: Gender, Crime, and Justice.* Belmont, CA: Wadsworth.

Belknap, J., and K. Holsinger. 2006. "The Gendered Nature of Risk Factors for Delinquency." *Feminist Criminology* 1: 48–71.

Benedict, A. 2014. *Using Trauma Informed Practice to Enhance Safety and Security in Women's Correctional Facilities.* Washington, DC: National Resource Center on Justice Involved Women.

Blackburn, A., S. Fowler, and J. Pollock. 2014. *Prisons, Today and Tomorrow.* Burlington, MA: Jones and Bartlett Learning.

Blitz, C. 2006. "Predictors of Stable Employment among Female Inmates in New Jersey: Implications for Successful Reintegration." *Journal of Offender Rehabilitation* 43(1): 1–22.

Bloom, B. 1996. "Triple Jeopardy: Race, Class, and Gender as Factors in Women's Imprisonment." PhD dissertation, University of California, Riverside.

Bloom, B., and S. Covington. 2008. "Addressing the Mental Health Needs of Women Offenders." In R. Gido and L. Dalley, eds., *Women's Mental Health Issues across the Criminal Justice System*, 160–76. Upper Saddle River, NJ: Prentice Hall.

Bloom, B., and B. Owen. 2013. *Women's Community Justice Reform Blueprint: A Gender- Responsive, Family-Focused Approach to Integrating Criminal and Community Justice*. San Francisco, CA: City and County of San Francisco, Adult Probation Department and Sheriff's Department.

Bloom, B., M. Chesney-Lind, and B. Owen. 1994. *Women in California Prisons: Hidden Victims of the War on Drugs*. San Francisco, CA: Center on Juvenile and Criminal Justice.

Bloom, B., B. Owen, and S. Covington. 2003. *Gender Responsive Strategies: Research, Practice, and Guiding Principles for Women Offenders*. Washington, DC: U.S. Department of Justice and National Institute of Corrections.

———. 2004. "Women Offenders and the Gendered Effects of Public Policy." *Review of Policy Research* 21(1): 31–48.

Bloom, S. 1997. *Sanctuary: Toward the Evolution of Sane Societies*. New York: Routledge.

Bosworth, M. 1999. *Engendering Resistance: Agency and Power in Women's Prisons*. Dartmouth, MA: Ashgate.

Bourdieu, P. 1986. "The Forms of Capital." In J. Richardson, ed., *Handbook of Theory and Research for the Sociology of Education*, 241–58. New York: Greenwood Press.

Bradley, R., and K. Davino. 2002. "Women's Perceptions of the Prison Environment: When Prison Is 'The Safest Place I've Ever Been.'" *Psychology of Women Quarterly* 26(4): 351–59.

Breitenbecher, K. 2001. "Sexual Re-Victimization among Women: A Review of the Literature Focusing on Empirical Investigations." *Aggression and Violent Behavior* 6: 415–32.

Brennan Center for Justice. 2005. *Caught in the Net: The Impact of Drug Policies on Women and Families*. New York: Brennan Center for Justice.

Brennan, T., M. Breitenbach, M. Dieterich, E. Salisbury, and P. Van Voorhis. 2012. "Women's Pathway to Serious and Habitual Crime: A Person-Centered Analysis Incorporating Gender-Responsive Factors." *Criminal Justice & Behavior* 39(11): 1481–1508.

Brent, J., K. Kraska. 2010. "Moving beyond Our Methodological Default: A Case for Mixed Methods." *Journal of Criminal Justice Education* 21(4): 412–30.

Brewer-Smyth, K. 2004. "Women Behind Bars: Could Neurobiological Correlates of Past Physical and Sexual Abuse Contribute to Criminal Behavior?" *Healthcare for Women International* 25: 835–52.

Britton, D. 2003. *At Work in the Iron Cage: The Prison as a Gendered Organization*. New York: New York University Press.

Brown, J. 2015. "Beyond Punishment: A Miami Herald Investigation of Lowell Correctional Institution." *Miami (FL) Herald*, December 13–20. www

.miamiherald.com/news/special-reports/florida-prisons/ article49175685
.html#storylink=cpy. Accessed December 29, 2015.

Brown, M. 2006. "Gender, Ethnicity, and Offending over the Life Course: Women's Pathways to Prison in the Aloha State." *Critical Criminology* 14: 137–58.

Browne, A., B. Miller, and E. Maguin. 1999. "Prevalence and Severity of Lifetime Physical and Sexual Victimization among Incarcerated Women." *International Journal of Law and Psychiatry* 22: 301–22.

Buchanan, K. 2012. "Engendering Rape." *UCLA Law Review* 59: 1630.

Burgess-Proctor, A. 2006. "Intersections of Race, Class, Gender, and Crime: Future Directions for Feminist Criminology." *Feminist Criminology* 1: 27–47.

Bush-Baskette, S. 2000. "The War on Drugs and the Incarceration of Mothers." *Journal of Drug Issues* 30: 919–28.

Butler, M. 2008. "'What Are You Looking At?' Prisoner Confrontation and the Search for Respect." *British Journal of Criminology* 48: 856–73.

Caputo, G. 2008. *Out in the Storm: Drug-Addicted Women Living as Shoplifters and Sex Workers.* Boston, MA: Northeastern University Press.

Carbone-Lopez, K., and C. Kruttschnitt. 2003. "Assessing the Racial Climate in Women's Institutions in the Context of Penal Reform." *Women & Criminal Justice* 15(1): 55–79.

Carlen, P. 1983. *Women's Imprisonment: A Study in Social Control.* London: Routledge & Kegan Paul.

Carson, E. 2014. *Prisoners in 2013.* Washington, DC: U.S. Department of Justice and Bureau of Justice Statistics.

———. 2015. *Prisoners in 2014.* Washington, DC: U.S. Department of Justice and Bureau of Justice Statistics.

Centers for Disease Control and Prevention. 2006. "Adverse Childhood Experiences Study." www.cdc.gov/nccdphp/ace/index.htm.

Chesney-Lind, M. 1991. "Patriarchy, Prisons, and Jails: A Critical Look at Trends in Women's Incarceration." *Prison Journal* 71(1): 51–67.

———. 2002. "Criminalizing Victimization: The Unintended Consequences of Pro-Arrest Policies for Girls and Women." *Criminology & Public Policy* 2(1): 81–90.

Chesney-Lind, M., and M. Eliason. 2006. "From Invisible to Incorrigible: The Demonization of Marginalized Women and Girls." *Crime, Media, and Culture* 2(1): 29–47.

Chesney-Lind, M., and K. Irwin. 2008. *Beyond Bad Girls: Gender, Violence and Hype.* New York: Routledge.

Chesney-Lind, M., and A. Merlo. 2015. "Global War on Girls? Policing Sexuality and Criminalizing Their Victimization." *Women & Criminal Justice* 25: 71–82.

Chesney-Lind, M., and M. Morash. 2013. "Transformative Feminist Criminology: A Critical Re- Thinking of a Discipline." *Critical Criminology* 21: 287–304.

Chesney-Lind, M., and L. Pasko. 2004. *The Female Offender: Girls, Women, and Crime.* Vol. 2. Thousand Oaks, CA: Sage.

Chesney-Lind, M., and N. Rodriquez. 1983. "Women under Lock and Key: A View from the Inside." *Prison Journal* 63(2): 47–65.

Clear, T. 2007. *Imprisoning Communities: How Mass Incarceration Makes Disadvantaged Neighborhoods Worse.* New York: Oxford University Press.

Clemmer, D. 1958. *The Prison Community*. New York: Holt, Rinehart and Winston.

Coates, T. 2015. *Between the World and Me*. New York: Spiegel & Grau.

Codianni, B. 2015. "What You Won't See on *Orange Is the New Black*." July 18. [Blog]. Retrieved from http://msmagazine.com/blog/2015/07/16/what-you-wont-see-on-orange-is-the-new-black/.

Comack, E. 2006. "Coping, Resisting, and Surviving: Connecting Women's Law Violations to Their Histories of Abuse." In L. Alarid and P. Cromwell, eds., *In Her Own Words: Women Offenders' Views on Crime and Victimization*, 33–45. Los Angeles, CA: Roxbury.

Commission on Safety and Abuse in American's Prisons. 2006. *Confronting Confinement*. New York: Vera Institute of Justice.

Cook, S., S. Smith, C. Tusher, and C. Railford. 2005. "Self-Reports of Traumatic Events in a Random Sample of Incarcerated Women." *Women & Criminal Justice* 16(1–2): 107–26.

Covington, S. 1998. "The Relational Theory of Women's Psychological Development: Implications for the Criminal Justice System." In R. Zaplin, ed., *Female Crime and Delinquency: Critical Perspectives and Effective Interventions*, 113–31. Gaithersburg, MD: Aspen Publishers.

———. 2012. *Becoming Trauma Informed: A Training Program for Correctional Professionals* (Facilitator Guide). La Jolla, CA: Center for Gender and Justice.

———. 2013. *Beyond Violence: A Prevention Program for Criminal Justice Involved Women*. Hoboken, NJ: John Wiley.

———. 2016a. *Beyond Trauma: A Healing Journey for Women*. Center City, MN: Hazelden.

———. 2016b. *Healing Trauma: A Brief Intervention for Women*. Center City, MN: Hazelden.

Coyle, A. 1998. *The Prisons We Deserve*. London: HarperCollins.

———. 2009. *A Human Rights Approach to Prison Management*. London: International Centre for Prison Studies.

Crenshaw, K. 2012. "From Private Violence to Mass Incarceration: Thinking Intersectionally about Women, Race, and Social Control." *UCLA Law Review* 59: 1418–72.

Crewe, B. 2009. *The Prisoner Society: Power, Adaptation, and Social Life in an English Prison*. New York: Oxford University Press.

Crouch, B. 1980. *The Keepers: Prison Guards and Contemporary Corrections*. Springfield, IL: Thomas.

Daly, K. 1992. "Women's Pathways to Felony Court: Feminist Theories of Lawbreaking and Problems of Representation." *Southern California Review of Law and Women's Studies* 2: 11–52.

———. 1994. *Gender, Crime, and Punishment*. New Haven, CT: Yale University Press.

Danner, M. 1998. "Three Strikes and It's Women Who Are Out: The Hidden Consequences for Women of Criminal Justice Policy Reforms." In S. Miller, ed., *Crime Control and Women*, 1–11. Thousand Oaks, CA: Sage.

Daye, E. 2013. "Women's Health Care within CDCR." Presentation to the Gender-Responsive Strategies Committee, Folsom, CA, July 30.

de Almeida, O., and E. Paes-Machado. 2015. "No Place to Run, No Place to Hide: Socio- Organizational Processes and Patterns of Inmate Victimization." *Australian and New Zealand Journal of Criminology* 48(2): 175–99.

Death Penalty Information Center. 2015. www.deathpenaltyinfo.org/women-and-death-penalty. Accessed June 20, 2015.

De Hart, D. 2005. *Pathways to Prison: Impact of Victimization in the Lives of Incarcerated Women.* Doc. No. 208383. Washington, DC: U.S. Department of Justice.

Deschenes, E., B. Owen, and J. Crow. 2006. *Recidivism among Female Prisoners: Secondary Analysis of the 1994 BJS Recidivism Data Set: Final Report.* Washington, DC: National Institute of Justice.

Dodge, M., and M. Pogrebin. 2001. "Collateral Costs of Imprisonment for Women: Complications of Reintegration." *Prison Journal* 81: 42–54.

Edgar, K., and C. Martin. 2003. "Conflicts & Violence in Prison, 1998–2000." Computer file. Colchester, Essex: UK Data Archive.

Edgar, K., I. O'Donnell, and C. Martin. 2003. "Tracking the Pathways to Violence in Prison." In M. Lee and E. Stanko, eds., *Researching Violence: Essays on Methodology and Measurement,* 69–87. London: Routledge.

Einat, T., and G. Chen. 2012a. "Gossip in a Maximum-Security Female Prison: An Exploratory Study." *Women & Criminal Justice* 22: 108–34.

———. 2012b. "What's Love Got to Do with It? Sex in a Female Maximum Security Prison." *Prison Journal* 92(4): 484–505.

English, K., C. Widom, and C. Brandford. 2001. *Childhood Victimization and Delinquency, Adult Criminality, and Violent Criminal Behavior: A Replication and Extension.* Washington, DC: National Institute of Justice.

Enos, S. 2012. "Mass Incarceration: Triple Jeopardy for Women in a 'Color-Blind' and Gender- Neutral Justice System." *Journal of Interdisciplinary Feminist Thought* 6(1): art. 2.

Faith, K. 1993. *Unruly Women: The Politics of Confinement and Resistance.* Vancouver: Press Gang Publishers.

Faiver, K., and D. Rieger. 1998. "Women's Health Issues." In K. Faiver, ed., *Healthcare Management in Correction,* 133–41. Lanham, MD: American Correctional Association.

Feinman, C. 1976. "Imprisoned Women: A History of the Treatment of Women Incarcerated in New York City, 1932–1975." PhD dissertation, New York University.

———. 1983. "An Historical Overview of the Treatment of Incarcerated Women: Myths and Realities of Rehabilitation." *Prison Journal* 63(2): 12–26.

Fellner, J. 2012. "The Human Rights Paradigm: A Foundation for a Criminal Justice System We Can Be Proud Of." In M. Mauer and K. Epstein, *To Build a Better Criminal Justice System,* 16–17. Washington, DC: The Sentencing Project.

Ferrenti, S. 2013. "The Gorilla Convict." *Daily Beast.* www.thedailybeast.com /articles/2013/06/02/with- cigarettes-banned-in-most-prisons-gangs-shift-from-drugs-to-smokes.html. Accessed November 11, 2015.

Fleetwood, J. 2015. "In Search of Respectability: Narrative Practice in a Women's Prison in Quito Ecuador." In L. Presser and S. Sandberg, eds., *Narrative*

Criminology: Understanding Stories of Crime, 42–68. New York: New York University Press.

Fleischer, M., and J. Krienert. 2006. *The Culture of Prison Violence*. Washington, DC: National Institute of Justice.

Flesher, F. 2007. "Cross Gender Supervision in Prisons and the Constitutional Right of Prisoners to Remain Free from Rape." *William and Mary Journal of Women and the Law* 13(Spring): 841–67.

Fletcher, B., L. Shaver, and D. Moon. 1993. *Women Prisoners: A Forgotten Population*. Westport, CT: Praeger.

Flower, S. 2010. *Employment and Female Offenders: An Update of the Empirical Research*. Washington, DC: U.S. Department of Justice and National Institute of Corrections.

Fogel, C. 1991. "Health Problems and Needs of Incarcerated Women." *Journal of Prison and Jail Health* 10(1): 43–57.

———. 1995. "Pregnant Prisoners: Impact of Incarceration on Health and Healthcare." *Journal of Correctional Healthcare* 2: 169–90.

Freedman, E. 1981. *Their Sister's Keepers: Women's Prison Reforms in America, 1830–1930*. Ann Arbor: University of Michigan Press.

Frost, N., J. Greene, and K. Pranis. 2006. *Hard Hit: The Growth in the Imprisonment of Women, 1977–2004*. New York: Institute on Women & Criminal Justice.

Gabel, K., and D. Johnston, eds. 1995. *Children of Incarcerated Parents*. New York: Lexington Books.

The GAINS Center. 2001. *Integrated Services Reduce Recidivism among Homeless Adults with Serious Mental Illness in California*. Rockville, MD: Substance Abuse and Mental Health Services Administration (SAMHSA).

Garcia, C. and J. Lane. 2010. "Looking in the Rearview Mirror: What Incarcerated Women Think Girls Need from the System." *Feminist Criminology* 5(3): 227–243.

Geertz, C. 1983. "Thick Description: Toward an Interpretive Theory of Culture." In R. Emerson, ed., *Contemporary Field Work: A Collection of Readings*, 19–36. Boston: Little, Brown.

Georges-Abeyie, D. 2015. "Sex, Gender, Multidimensional Value Space, and Social Cultural Resistance: Afrocentrism." *Women & Criminal Justice* 25: 100–119.

Geronimus, A. 2001. "Understanding and Eliminating Racial Inequalities in Women's Health in the United States: The Role of the Weathering Conceptual Framework." *Journal of American Medicine* 56(4): 133–50.

Giallombardo, R. 1966. *Society of Women: A Study of a Women's Prison*. New York: Wiley.

Giordano, P., S. Cernkovich, and J. Rudolph. 2002. "Gender, Crime, and Desistence: Toward a Theory of Cognitive Transformation." *American Journal of Sociology* 107: 990–1064.

Girls Study Group. 2008. *Violence by Teenage Girls: Trends and Context*. Washington, DC: Office of Juvenile Justice and Delinquency Prevention.

———. 2010. *Causes and Correlates of Girls' Delinquency*. Washington, DC: Office of Juvenile Justice and Delinquency Prevention.

Girshick, L. 1999. *No Safe Haven: Stories of Women in Prison.* Boston, MA: Northeastern University Press.

Glaze, L., and L. Maruschak. 2010. *Parents in Prison and Their Minor Children.* Washington, DC: U.S. Department of Justice and Bureau of Justice Statistics.

Gobeil, R., K. Blanchette, and I. Stewart. 2016. "A Meta-Analytic Review of Correctional Interventions for Women Offenders: Gender-Neutral versus Gender-Informed Approaches." *Criminal Justice and Behavior* 43(3): 301–22.

Goffman, E. 1961. *Asylums: Essays on the Social Situation of Mental Patients and Other Inmates.* New York: Anchor Books.

Goldenson, J., M. LaMarre, and M. Puisis. 2013. *Central California Women's Facility Health Care Report.* Sacramento: California Department of Corrections and Rehabilitation.

Goleman, D. 1995. *Emotional Intelligence.* New York: Bantam Books.

Goodkind, S., I. Ng, and R. Sari. 2006. "The Impact of Sexual Abuse in the Lives of Young Women Involved or at Risk of Involvement with the Juvenile Justice System." *Violence Against Women* 12(5): 456–77.

Green, B., J. Miranda, A. Daroowala, and J. Siddique. 2005. "Trauma Exposure, Mental Health Functioning, and Program Needs of Women in Jail." *Crime & Delinquency* 51(1): 133–51.

Greenfield, L., and T. Snell. 1999. *Special Report: Women Offenders.* Washington, DC: U.S. Department of Justice.

Greer, K. 2000. "The Changing Nature of Interpersonal Relationships in a Women's Prison." *Prison Journal* 80(4): 442–68.

———. 2002. "Walking an Emotional Tightrope: Managing Emotions in a Women's Prison." *Symbolic Interaction* 25(1): 117–39.

Hagan, J., and H. Foster. 2012. "Children of the American Prison Generation: Student and School Spillover Effects of Incarcerating Mothers." *Law & Society Review* 46(1): 37–69.

Haney, C. 2006. "The Wages of Prison Overcrowding: Harmful Psychological Consequences and Dysfunctional Correctional Reactions." *Washington University Journal of Law & Policy* 22: 265–93. http://openscholarship.wustl .edu/law_journal_law_policy/vol22/iss1/22

Harlow, C. 1999. *Selected Findings: Prior Abuse Reported by Inmates and Probationers.* Washington, DC: U.S. Department of Justice and Bureau of Justice Statistics.

Hartnagel, T., and M. Gillan. 1980. "Female Prisoners and the Inmate Code." *Pacific Sociological Review* 23: 85–104.

Heffernan, R. 1972. *Making It in Prison: The Square, the Cool, and the Life.* New York: Wiley.

Heney, J., and C. Kristiansen. 1998. "An Analysis of the Impact of Prison on Women Survivors Of Childhood Sexual Abuse." In J. Harden and M. Hill, eds., *Breaking the Rules: Women in Prison and Feminist Therapy,* 29–44. New York: Haworth Press.

Henriques, Z. 1995. "African American Women: The Oppressive Intersection of Gender, Race, and Class." *Women & Criminal Justice* 7(1): 67–80.

Henriques, Z., and E. Gilbert. 2000. "Sexual Abuse and Sexual Assault of Women in Prison." In R. Muraskin, ed., *It's a Crime: Women and Justice*, 253–68. Upper Saddle River, NJ: Prentice-Hall.

Holtfreter, K., and M. Morash. 2003. "The Needs of Women Offenders: Implications for Correctional Programming." *Women & Criminal Justice* 14: 137–60.

Holtfreter, K., M. Reisig, and M. Morash. 2004. "Poverty, State Capital, and Recidivism among Women Offenders." *Crime and Public Policy* 3(2): 185–208.

Hughes, R. 1987. *The Fatal Shore*. New York: Knopf.

Human Rights Watch. 1998. *Nowhere to Hide: Retaliation against Women in Michigan's State Prisons*. New York: Human Rights Watch.

Human Rights Watch Women's Project. 1996. *All Too Familiar: Sexual Abuse in U.S. State Prisons*. New York, NY: Human Rights Watch.

Irwin, J. 1970. *The Felon*. Englewood Cliffs, NJ: Prentice-Hall.

———. 2005. *The Warehouse Prison: Disposal of the New Dangerous Class*. Los Angeles, CA: Roxbury.

Irwin, J., and J. Austin. 2001. *It's about Time: America's Imprisonment Binge*. Belmont, CA: Wadsworth.

Irwin, J., and D. Cressey. 1962. "Thieves, Convicts, and Inmate Culture." *Social Problems* 10: 142–55.

Isaac, A., L. Lockhart, and L. Williams. 2014. "Violence against African American Women in Prisons and Jails." *Journal of Human Behavior in the Social Environment* 4: 129–53.

Islam-Zwart, K., and P. Vik. 2004. "Female Adjustment to Incarceration as Influenced by Sexual Assault History." *Criminal Justice and Behavior* 31(5): 521–41.

Jenness, V. 2010. "From Policy to Prisoners to People: A 'Soft Mixed Methods' Approach to Studying Transgender Prisoners." *Journal of Contemporary Ethnography* 39(5): 517–53.

Johnston, D. 1995. "Effects of Parental Incarceration." In K. Gabel and D. Johnston, eds., *Children of Incarcerated Parents*, 259–63. New York: Lexington Books.

Jordan, B., W. Schlenger, J. Fairbank, and J. Caddell. 1996. "Prevalence of Psychiatric Disorders among Incarcerated Women: Convicted Felons Entering Prison." *Archives of General Psychiatry* 53(6): 513–19.

Joseph, J. 2006. "Intersectionality of Race/Ethnicity, Class, and Justice: Women of Color." In A. Merlo and J. Pollock, eds., *Women, Law, and Social Control*, vol. 2, 292–315. Boston, MA: Pearson Publishing.

Just Detention International. 2009. *Prisoner Rape Is Torture under International Law*. Los Angeles, CA: JDI.

Kempfner, C. 1995. "Post-Traumatic Stress Reactions in Children of Imprisoned Mothers." In K. Gabel and D. Johnston, eds., *Children of Incarcerated Parents*, 89–100. New York: Lexington Books.

Kerman, P. 2010. *Orange Is the New Black: My Year in a Women's Prison*. New York: Random House.

Keys, D. 2002. "Instrumental Sexual Scripting: An Examination of Gender-Role Fluidity in the Correctional Institution." *Journal of Contemporary Criminal Justice* 18(3): 258–78.

Kilgore, J. 2015. "Mass Incarceration: Examining and Moving beyond the New Jim Crow." *Critical Sociology* 41(2): 283–95.

Krabill, J., and R. Aday. 2005. "Exploring the Social World of Aging Female Prisoners." *Women & Criminal Justice* 17(1): 27–53.

Kruttschnitt, C. 1981. "Prison Codes, Inmate Solidarity, and Women: A Re-Examination." In M. Warren, ed., *Comparing Male and Female Offenders*, 123–41. Beverly Hills, CA: Sage.

———. 1983. "Race Relations and the Female Inmate." *Crime and Delinquency* 29(4): 577–92.

Kruttschnitt, C., and K. Carbone-Lopez. 2006. "Moving beyond Stereotypes: Women's Subjective Accounts of Their Violent Crime." *Criminology* 44: 321–51.

Kruttschnitt, C., and R. Gartner. 2005. *Marking Time in the Golden State.* Cambridge: Cambridge University Press.

Kruttschnitt, C., R. Gartner, and K. Ferraro. 2002. "Women's Involvement in Serious Interpersonal Violence." *Aggression and Violent Behavior* 7: 529–65.

Kubiak, S., J. Hanna, and M. Balton. 2005. "'I came to prison to do my time—Not to get raped': Coping within the Institutional Setting." *Stress, Trauma, and Crisis* 8: 157–77.

Kubiak, S., W. Kim, D. Bybee. 2013. "Differences among Incarcerated Women with Assaultive Offenses: Isolated versus Patterned Use of Violence." *Journal of Interpersonal Violence* 28(12): 2462–90.

Labelle, D. 2013. *Criminal Justice and Human Rights in the United States.* Atlanta, GA: Human Rights Network.

Lahm, K. 2015. "Predictors of Violent and Non-Violent Victimization behind Bars: An Exploration of Women Inmates." *Women & Criminal Justice* 25: 273–91.

Lambert, E., K. Minor, J. Wells, and N. Hogan. 2015. "Leave Your Job at Work: The Possible Antecedents of Work-Family Conflict among Correctional Staff." *Prison Journal* 95(1): 114–34.

Langan, N., and B. Pelissier. 2001. "Gender Differences among Prisoners in Drug Treatment." *Journal of Substance Abuse* 13(3): 291–301.

Leahy, J. 2014. "The Power of Perception: The Impact of Age, Race, and Previous Experiences on Women's Perception of Safety in Prison." Master's thesis, California State University, Fresno.

Lee, H., T. McCormick, M. Hicken, and C. Wildeman. 2015. "Racial Inequalities in Connectedness to Imprisoned Individuals in the United States." *Du Bois Review* 12(2):269–82. http://dx.doi.org/10.1017/S1742058X15000065.

Leigey, M., and J. Hodge 2012. "Gray Matters: Gender Differences in the Physical and Mental Health of Older Inmates." *Women & Criminal Justice* 22: 289–303.

Leigey, M., and K. Reed. 2010. "A Woman's Life before Serving Life: Examining the Negative Pre-Incarceration Life Events of Female Life-Sentenced Inmates." *Women & Criminal Justice* 20: 302–23.

Light, I. 2005. "Cultural Capital." In *New Dictionary of the History of Ideas.* www.encyclopedia.com/topic/Cultural_capital.aspx.

Lipsitz, G. 2012. "'In an avalanche, every snowflake pleads not guilty': The Collateral Consequences of Mass Incarceration and Impediments to Women's Fair Housing Rights." *UCLA Law Review* 59: 1746–1809.

Lynch, S., D. De Hart, J. Belknap, and B. Green. 2012. *Women's Pathways to Jail: The Roles and Intersections of Serious Mental Illness & Trauma.* Washington, DC: U.S. Department of Justice and Bureau of Justice Assistance.

Maeve, M. 2000. Speaking Unavoidable Truths: Understanding Early Childhood Sexual and Physical Violence among Women in Prison." *Issues in Mental Health Nursing* 21: 473–98.

Mahan, S. 1984. "Imposition of Despair: An Ethnography of Women in Prison." *Justice Quarterly* 1: 357–85.

Makarios, M. 2007. "Race, Abuse, and Female Criminal Violence." *Feminist Criminology* 2(2): 100–116.

Mandraraka-Sheppard, A. 1986. "The Dynamics of Aggression in Women's Prisons in England." *Howard Journal of Criminal Justice* 25(4): 317–19.

Marcus-Mendoza, S., and E. Wright. 2003. "Treating the Woman Prisoner: The Impact of a History of Violence." In S. Sharp, ed., *The Incarcerated Woman: Rehabilitative Programming in Women's Prisons,* 107–18. Upper Saddle River, NJ: Prentice Hall.

Marksamer, J., and H. Tobin. 2015. *Standing with LGBT Prisoners: An Advocate's Guide to Ending Abuse and Combating Imprisonment.* Washington DC: National Center for Transgender Equality.

Martin, S., and N. Jurick. 2007. *Doing Justice, Doing Gender.* Thousand Oaks, CA: Sage.

Maruschak, L. 2008. *Medical Problems of Prisoners.* Washington, DC: U.S. Bureau of Justice Statistics.

Mauer, M. 2013. *The Changing Racial Dynamics of Women's Incarceration.* Washington, DC: The Sentencing Project.

Mauer, M., and M. Chesney-Lind, eds. 2002. *Invisible Punishment: The Collateral Consequences of Mass Imprisonment.* New York: New Press.

Mauer, M., and K. Epstein. 2012. *To Build a Better Criminal Justice System.* Washington, DC: The Sentencing Project.

Mauer, M., C. Potler, and R. Wolf. 2000. "The Impact of the Drug War on Women: A Comparative Analysis in Three States." *Women, Girls, and Criminal Justice* 1(2): 21–22, 30–31.

McDaniels-Wilson, C., and J. Belknap. 2008. "The Extensive Sexual Violation and Sexual Abuse Histories of Incarcerated Women." *Violence Against Women* 14(10): 1090–1127.

McGuire, M. 2005. "Violence as a Routine Feature of Prison Life for Women: A Qualitative Study." *Corrections Compendium* 30(4): 36–38.

———. 2011. "Doing the Life: An Exploration of the Connection between the Inmate Code and Violence among Female Inmates." *Journal of the Institute of Justice and International Studies* 11: 145–58.

McKenry, P., J. Serovich, T. Mason, and K. Mosack. 2006. "Perpetration of Gay and Lesbian Partner Violence: A Disempowerment Perspective." *Journal of Family Violence* 21: 233–43.

Messina, N. 2011. "TOWAR: Training for Women's Addiction and Recovery." UCLA Integrated Substance Abuse Programs. www.uclaisap.org/html /research%20projects%202010–2012/womens-substance-use-disorders-issues.html#towar.

Messina, N., S. Calhoun, and J. Braithwaite. 2014. "Trauma-Informed Treatment Decreases Post-Traumatic Stress Disorder among Women Offenders." *Journal of Trauma & Dissociation* 15(1): 6–23.

Messina, N., and C. Grella. 2006. "Childhood Trauma and Women's Health Outcomes in a California Prison Population." *American Journal of Public Health* 96(10): 1842–48.

Messina, N., C. Grella, W. Burdon, and M. Prendergast. 2007. "Childhood Adverse Events and Current Traumatic Distress: A Comparison of Men and Women Drug-Dependent Prisoners." *Criminal Justice & Behavior* 34(11): 1385–1401.

Messina, N., C. Grella, J. Cartier, and S. Torres. 2010. "A Randomized Experimental Study of Gender-Responsive Substance Abuse Treatment for Women in Prison." *Journal of Substance Abuse Treatment* 38: 97–107.

Messman-Moore, T., and P. Long. 1994. "Child Sexual Abuse and Its Relationship to Re-Victimization in Adult Women: A Review." *Clinical Psychology Review* 16: 397–420.

———. 2000. "Child Sexual Abuse and Re-Victimization in the Form of Adult Sexual Abuse, Adult Physical Abuse, and Adult Psychological Maltreatment." *Journal of Interpersonal Violence* 15: 489–502.

Middlebrooks, J., and N. Audage. 2008. *The Effects of Childhood Stress on Health across the Lifespan.* Atlanta, GA: Centers for Disease Control and Prevention, National Center for Injury Prevention and Control.

Miller, J. 2002. "Reconciling Feminism and Rational Choice Theory: Women's Agency in Street Crime." In A. Piquero and S. Tibbetts, eds., *Rational Choice and Criminal Behavior,* 219–39. New York: Routledge.

Miller, J., and N. White. 2003. "Gender and Adolescent Relationship Violence: A Contextual Examination." *Criminology* 41(4): 1207–48.

Millson, B., D. Robinson, and M. Van Dieten. 2010a. *Women Offender Case Management Model: The Connecticut Project.* Washington, DC: National Institute of Corrections.

———. 2010b. *Women Offenders Case Management Model: Outcome Evaluation.* Washington, DC: National Institute of Corrections.

Moe, A., and K. Ferraro. 2003. "Malign Neglect or Benign Respect: Women's Health Care in a Carceral Setting." *Women & Criminal Justice* 14(4): 53–80.

Morash, M. 2010. *Women on Probation and Parole: A Feminist Critique of Community Programs and Services.* Boston, MA: Northeastern University Press.

Morgan, R., and L. Freeman. 2009. "The Healing of Our People: Substance Abuse and Historical Trauma." *Substance Use & Misuse* 44(1): 84–98.

Moss, A. 2007. "The Prison Rape Elimination Act: Implications for Women and Girls." *Corrections Today* 69(4): 47–52.

Moyer, I. 1984. "Deceptions and Realities of Life in Women's Prisons." *Prison Journal* 64(1): 45–56.

Mullings, J., J. Marquart, and D. Hartley. 2003. "Exploring the Effects of Childhood Sexual Abuse and Its Impact on HIV/AIDS Risk-Taking Behavior among Women Prisoners." *Prison Journal* 83(4): 442–63.

Mumola, C. 2000. *Incarcerated Parents and Their Children*. Washington, DC: U.S. Department of Justice and Bureau of Justice Statistics.

National Center on Addiction and Substance Abuse at Columbia University (CASA). 2010. *Behind Bars II: Substance Abuse and America's Prison Population*. www.casacolumbia.org/templates/Publications_Reports.aspx? keywords=prison.

National Resources Center on Justice Involved Women. 2014. "Innovator: Lynn Bissonnette, Massachusetts Correctional Institution–Framingham." www.cjinvolvedwomen.org.

National Scientific Council on the Developing Child. 2005. *Excessive Stress Disrupts the Architecture of the Developing Brain, 3*. Cambridge: The Council. www.developingchild.net/pubs/wp/Stress_Disrupts_Architecture_ Developing_Brain.pdf.

Negy, C., D. Woods, and R. Carlson. 1997. "The Relationship between Female Inmates' Coping and Adjustment in a Minimum-Security Prison." *Criminal Justice and Behavior* 24(2): 224–33.

Nickel, J., C. Garland, and L. Kane. 2009. *Children of Incarcerated Parents: An Action Plan for the Federal Government*. New York: Council of State Governments, Justice Center.

Nowacki, J. 2016. "An Intersectional Approach to Race/Ethnicity, Sex, and Age Disparity in Federal Sentencing Outcomes: An Examination of Policy across Time Periods." *Criminology and Criminal Justice* 1: 1–20.

Nuytiens, A., and J. Christiaens. 2015. "Female Pathways to Crime and Prison: Challenging the (US) Gendered Pathways Perspective." *European Journal of Criminology* (July): 1–19.

O'Brien, P. 2014. "We Should Stop Putting Women in Jail. For Anything." *Washington Post*, Editorial, November 6.

Office of the High Commissioner for Human Rights. 2012. *The United Nations Human Rights Treaty System*. Geneva and New York: United Nations.

Owen, B. 1988. *The Reproduction of Social Control: Prison Workers at San Quentin*. Westport, CT: Praeger Press.

———. 1998. *In the Mix: Struggle and Survival in a Women's Prison*. Albany: State University of Albany Press.

———. 2003. "Differences with a Distinction: Women Offenders and Criminal Justice Practice." In B. Bloom, ed., *Gendered Justice*, 4–25. Hendersonville, NC: Carolina Press.

———. 2005. "Gendered Harm in the Contemporary Prison." In J. Irwin, ed., *The Warehouse Prison*, 240–60. Los Angeles: Roxbury Press.

Owen, B., and B. Bloom. 1995. "Profiling Women Prisoners: Findings from National Surveys and a California Sample." *Prison Journal* 75(2): 165–85.

Owen, B., and A. Mobley. 2012. "Realignment in California: Policy and Research Implications." *Western Criminology Review* 13(2): 46–52.

Owen, B., and A. Moss. 2009. "Sexual Violence in Women's Prisons and Jails: Results from Focus Group Interviews." In *Staff Perspectives Sexual Violence in Adult Prisons & Jails.* Washington, DC: U.S. Department of Justice, National Institute of Corrections.

Owen, B., and J. Wells. 2005. *Staff Perspectives on Sexual Violence in Adult Prisons and Jails: Results from Focus Group Interviews.* Washington, DC: National Institute of Corrections.

Owen, B., J. Wells, J. Pollock, B. Muscat, and S. Torres. 2008. *Gendered Violence and Safety: A Contextual Approach to Improving Security in Women's Facilities.* Washington, DC: National Institute of Justice.

Petersilia, J., and R. Rosenfeld. 2007. *Parole, Desistance from Crime, and Community Integration.* Washington, DC: National Academy Press.

Pettit, B., and B. Western. 2004. "Mass Imprisonment and the Life Course: Race and Class Inequality in U.S. Incarceration." *American Sociological Review* 69: 151–69.

Pleydon, A., and J. Schner. 2001. "Female Adolescent Friendship and Delinquent Behavior." *Adolescence* 36: 189–205.

Pollack, S. 2007. "'I'm Just Not Good in Relationships': Victimization Discourses and the Gendered Regulation of Criminalized Women." *Feminist Criminology* 2(2): 158–74.

Pollock, J. 1984. "Women Will Be Women: Correctional Officers' Perceptions of the Emotionality of Women Inmates." *Prison Journal* 64(1): 84–91.

———. 1986. *Sex and Supervision: Guarding Male and Female Inmates.* New York: Greenwood Press.

———. 1998. *Counseling Women in Prison.* San Francisco, CA: Sage.

———. 2002. *Women, Prison, and Crime.* Vol. 2. Belmont, CA: Wadsworth Thomson Learning.

———. 2013. *Prisons and Prison Life: Costs and Consequences.* Los Angeles, CA: Roxbury Publishing. New ed. Boston, MA: Oxford Publishing.

———. 2014. *Women's Crimes, Criminology, and Corrections.* Downers Grove, IL: Waveland Press.

Pollock, J., and S. Davis. 2005. "The Continuing Myth of the Violent Female Offender." *Criminal Justice Review* 30(1): 5–29.

Pollock, J., J. Mullings, and B. Crouch. 2006. "Violent Women: Findings from the Texas Women Inmates' Study." *Journal of Interpersonal Violence* 21(4): 485–502.

Potter, H. 2013. "Intersectional Criminology: Interrogating Identity and Power in Criminological Research and Theory." *Critical Criminology* 21: 305–8.

———. 2015. *Intersectionality and Criminology.* London: Routledge.

Proctor, J. 2009. "The Impact Imprisonment Has on Women's Health and Healthcare from the Perspective of Female Inmates in Kansas." *Women & Criminal Justice* 19: 1–36.

Propper, A. 1982. "Make-Believe Families and Homosexuality among Imprisoned Girls." *Criminology* 20: 127–39.

Rabuy, B., and D. Kopf. 2015. *Prisons of Poverty: Uncovering the Pre-Incarceration Incomes for the Imprisoned.* North Hampton, MA: The Prison Policy Initiative.

Rafter, N. 1985/1990. *Partial Justice: State Prisons and Their Inmates, 1800–1935.* Boston, MA: Northeastern Press. Republished as *Partial Justice:*

Women, Prisons, and Social Control. New Brunswick, NJ: Transaction Books.

Raphael, J. 2013. *Freeing Tammy.* Boston, MA: Northeastern University Press.

Rasche, C. 2000. "The Dislike of Female Offenders among Correctional Officers: Need for Specialized Training." In R. Muraskin, ed., *It's a Crime: Women and Justice,* 3rd ed. 237–252. Upper Saddle River, NJ: Prentice-Hall.

Reisig, M., K. Holtfreter, and M. Morash. 2002. "Social Capital among Women Offenders." *Journal of Contemporary Criminal Justice* 18(2): 167–87.

———. 2006. "Assessing Recidivism Risk across Female Pathways to Crime." *Justice Quarterly* 23: 384–403.

Renzetti, C. 1992. *Violent Betrayal: Partner Abuse in Lesbian Relationships.* Newbury Park, CA: Sage.

Rhodes, L. 2004. *Total Confinement: Madness and Reason in Maximum Security Prison.* Berkeley: University of California Press.

Richie, B. 1996. *Compelled to Crime: The Gender Entrapment of Battered Black Women.* New York: Routledge.

———. 2001. "Challenges Incarcerated Women Face as They Return to Their Communities: Findings from Life History Interviews." *Crime & Delinquency* 47: 368–89.

———. 2004. "Feminist Ethnographies of Women in Prison." *Feminist Studies* 30(2): 438–50.

———. 2012. *Arrested Justice: Black Women, Violence, and America's Prison Nation.* New York: New York University Press.

Rierden, A. 1997. *The Farm: Life inside a Women's Prison.* Amherst: University of Massachusetts Press.

Rigby, M. 2006. "Michigan's Dirty Little Secret: Sexual Abuse of Female Prisoners Pervasive, Ongoing." *Prison Legal News,* January 15, 6–15.

Rizzo, E., and M. Hayes. 2011. "Struggling for Healthcare on the Inside." *Correctional Healthcare Report,* 3–14.

Roeder, O., L. Eisn, and J. Bowling. 2015. *What Caused the Crime Decline?* New York: Brennon Institute.

Rosenbaum, J. 1987. "Social Control, Gender, and Delinquency: An Analysis of Drug, Property, and Violent Offenders." *Justice Quarterly* 4: 117–32.

———. 1989. "Family Dysfunction and Female Delinquency." *Crime & Delinquency* 35(1): 31–44.

Rosenbaum, M. 1981. *Women on Heroin.* New Brunswick, NJ: Rutgers University Press.

Ross, M. 2011. "Pedagogy for Prisoners: An Approach to Peer Health Education for Inmates." *Journal of Correctional Health Care* 17(1): 6–18.

Ross, R., and A. Fabiano. 1986. *Female Offenders: Correctional After-Thoughts.* Jefferson, NC: McFarland.

Sabo, D., T. Kupers, and W. London, eds. 2001. *Prison Masculinities.* Philadelphia, PA: Temple University Press.

The Saguaro Seminar. 2016. "About Social Capital." The Saguaro Seminar, Harvard University, Cambridge, MA. www.hks.harvard.edu/programs/saguaro/about-social-capital.

Salisbury, E., and P. Van Voorhis. 2009. "Gendered Pathways: A Quantitative Investigation of Women Probationers' Paths to Incarceration." *Criminal Justice & Behavior* 36(6): 541–66.

Sassoon, D. 2015. *Five to Fifteen: A Woman, a Prison, a Redemption.* San Diego: Kandon Publishing.

Saylor, W., and G. Gaes. 1999. *The Differential Effect of Industries and Vocational Training on Post Release Outcome for Ethnic and Racial Groups: Research Note.* Washington, DC: Office of Research and Evaluation and Federal Bureau of Prisons.

Schneider, R. 2014. *Battered Women Doing Time: Injustice in the Criminal Justice System.* Boulder, CO: First Forum Press.

Selling, L. 1931. "The Pseudo-Family." *American Journal of Sociology* 37: 247–53.

The Sentencing Project. 2005. *Women in the Criminal Justice System: Briefing Sheets.* Washington DC: The Sentencing Project.

———. 2007. *Women in the Criminal Justice System: Briefing Sheets.* Washington, DC: The Sentencing Project.

Sered, S., and M. Norton-Hawk. 2014. *Can't Catch a Break.* Oakland: University of California Press.

Sharma, E., N. Mazar, A. Alter, and D. Ariely. 2013. "Financial Deprivation Selectively Shifts Moral Standards and Compromises Moral Decisions." *Organizational Behavior and Human Decision Processes* 123(2): 90–100.

Sharp, S. 2014. *Mean Lives, Mean Laws: Oklahoma's Women Prisoners.* New Brunswick, NJ: Rutgers University Press.

Siegel, J., and L. Williams. 2003. "The Relationship between Child Sexual Abuse and Female Delinquency and Crime: A Prospective Study." *Journal of Research in Crime and Delinquency* 40(1): 71–94.

Silverman, J. and R. Caldwell. 2008. "Peer Relationships and Violence among Female Juvenile Offenders." *Criminal Justice and Behavior* 35:333–343.

Simkins, S., and S. Katz. 2002. "Criminalizing Abused Girls." *Violence Against Women* 8(12): 1474.

Simon, J. 2007. *Governing through Crime.* New York: Oxford University Press.

———. 2014. *Mass Incarceration on Trial: A Remarkable Court Decision and the Future of Prisons in America.* New York: New Press.

Slocum, L., S. Simpson, and D. Smith. 2005. "Strained Lives and Crime: Examining Intra- Individual Variation in Strain and Offending in a Sample of Incarcerated Women." *Criminology* 43: 1067–1110.

Smith, B. 2005. "Sexual Abuse of Women in United States Prisons: A Modern Corollary of Slavery." *Fordham Urban Law Journal* 33: 571.

———. 2006. "Rethinking Prison Sex: Self-Expression and Safety." *Columbia Journal of Gender & Law* 15: 185.

Smith, B., and J. Yarussi. 2009. "Legal Responses to Sexual Violence in Custody: State Criminal Laws Prohibiting Staff Sexual Abuse of Individuals under Custodial Supervision." http://ssrn.com/abstract=1517350.

———. 2015. *Policy Review and Development Guide: Lesbian, Gay, Bisexual, Transgender, and Intersex Persons in Custodial Settings.* 2nd ed. Washington DC: National Institute of Corrections.

Snell, T., and D. Morton. 1994. *Women in Prison: Special Report.* Washington, DC: U.S. Department of Justice and Bureau of Justice Statistics.

Sommers, I., and D. Baskin. 1993. "The Situational Context of Violent Female Offending." *Journal of Research in Crime and Delinquency* 30(2): 136–62.

Sotero, M. 2006. "A Conceptual Model of Historical Trauma: Implications for Public Health Practice and Research." *Journal of Health Disparities Research and Practice* 1(1): 93–108.

Special Litigation Section of the Civil Rights Division. 2014. Letter re: *Investigation of the Julia Tutwiler Prison for Women and Notice of Expanded Investigation.* Washington, DC: U.S. Department of Justice.

Steffensmeier, D., and D. Haynie. 2000. "Gender, Structural Disadvantage, and Urban Crime: Do Macrosocial Variables Also Explain Female Offending Rates?" *Criminology* 38: 403–38.

Steiner, B., and J. Wooldredge. 2009. "Individual and Environmental Effects on Assaults and Nonviolent Rule Breaking by Women in Prison." *Journal of Research in Crime and Delinquency* 46: 437–67.

Stohr, M. 2015. "The Hundred Years' War: The Etiology and Status of Assaults on Transgender Women in Men's Prison." *Women & Criminal Justice* 25: 120–29.

Stuckman-Johnson, C., & Struckman-Johnson, D. 2002. "Sexual Coercion Reported by Women in Three Mid-Western Prisons." *Journal of Sex Research, 39(3),* 217–227.

Substance Abuse and Mental Health Services. n.d. *Creating a Trauma-Informed Criminal Justice System for Women.* Rockville, MD: Substance Abuse and Mental Health Services.

Sykes, G. 1958. *The Society of Captives.* Princeton, NJ: Princeton University Press.

Sykes, G., and S. Messinger. 1960. "The Inmate Social System." In R. Cloward, ed., *Theoretical Studies in the Social Organization of the Prison,* 5–19. New York: Social Science Research Council.

Teague, R., P. Pazerolle, M. Legosz, and J. Sanderson. 2008. "Linking Childhood Exposure to Physical Abuse and Adult Offending: Examining Mediating Factors and Gendered Relationships." *Justice Quarterly* 25: 313–48.

Teplin, L., K. Abrams, and G. McClelland. 1996. "Prevalence of Psychiatric Disorders among Incarcerated Women." *Archives of General Psychiatry* 53(2): 505–12.

Tjaden, P., and N. Thoennes. 2006. *Extent, Nature, and Consequences of Rape Victimization: Findings from the National Violence against Women Survey.* Washington, DC: National Institute of Justice.

Torres, S. 2007. "Women's Pathways to SHU: Serious Rule Violations in the Security Housing Units of California Prisons." Thesis, California State University, Fresno.

Trammell, R. 2009. "Relational Violence in Women's Prison: How Women Describe Interpersonal Violence and Gender." *Women & Criminal Justice* 18: 267–86.

———. 2012. *Enforcing the Convict Code: Violence and Prison Culture.* Boulder, CO: Lynne Rienner.

Travis J., and B. Western, eds. 2014. *The Growth of Incarceration in the United States.* Washington, DC: National Academies Press.

United Nations. 1988. *Body of Principles for the Protection of All Persons under Any Form of Detention or Imprisonment.* General Assembly Resolution 43/173 (9 December). New York: United Nations.

———. 2010. *United Nations Rules for the Treatment of Women Prisoners and Non-Custodial Measures for Women Offenders* (Bangkok Rules). New York: United Nations.

———. 2015. *United Nations Standard Minimum Rules for the Treatment of Prisoners* (Mandela Rules). New York: United Nations.

United Nations, Office of Drugs and Crime (UNODC). 2012. *UNODC and the Promotion and Protection of Human Rights: Position Paper.* Geneva: United Nations.

———. 2015. *Women and Imprisonment: The Handbook for Prison Managers and Policy-Makers.* Vienna: United Nations.

Van Dieten, M., N. Jones, and M. Randon. 2014. *Working with Women Who Perpetuate Violence.* Washington, DC: National Resource Center for Justice-Involved Women.

Van Voorhis, P. 2005. "Classification of Women Offenders: Gender-Responsive Approaches to Risk/Needs Assessment." *Community Corrections Report* 12(2): 19–20.

———. 2012. "On Behalf of Women Offenders: Women's Place in the Science of Evidence-Based Practice." *Criminology and Public Policy* 11(2): 111–45.

Veysey, B. 1998. "Specific Needs of Women Diagnosed with Mental Illnesses in U.S. Jails." In B. Levin, A. Blanch, and A. Jennings, eds., *Women's Mental Health Sources: A Public Health Perspective,* 368–89. Thousand Oaks, CA: Sage.

Veysey, B., and J. Heckman. 2006. *It's My Time to Live: Journeys to Healing and Recovery.* Rockville, MD: Substance Abuse and Mental Health Services.

Wagner, P. 2013. *The Prison Index.* Northampton, MA: Prison Policy Initiative.

Walmsley, R. 2015. *World Female Imprisonment List.* 3rd ed. London: Institute for Criminal Policy Research.

Walters, K. 2010. *Historical Trauma and Microaggressions: A Framework for Culturally Based Practice.* Minneapolis: University of Minnesota Extension, Child, Youth, and Family Consortium.

Ward, D., and G. Kassebaum. 1965. *Women's Prison: Sex and Social Structure.* Chicago, IL: Aldine-Atherton.

Watterson, K. 1996. *Women in Prison: Inside the Concrete Womb.* Boston, MA: Northeastern University Press.

Weiss, K. 2010. "Too Ashamed to Report: Deconstructing the Shame of Sexual Victimization." *Feminist Criminology* 5(3): 286–310.

Wells, J., K. Minor, E. Angel, A. Matz, and N. Amato. 2008. "Predictors of Job Stress among Staff in Juvenile Correctional Facilities." *Criminal Justice and Behavior* 25(3): 245–58.

Wells, J., B. Owen, and S. Parson. 2013. *Development and Validation of the Women's Correctional Safety Scales (WCSS): Tools for Improving Safety in Women's Facilities.* Washington, DC: National Institute of Corrections.

Wesely, J. 2006. "Considering the Context of Women's Violence: Gender, Lived Experiences, and Cumulative Victimization." *Feminist Criminology* 1(4): 303–28.

———. 2012. *Being Female: The Continuum of Sexualization.* Boulder, CO: Lynne Rienner.

West, C., and D. Zimmerman. 1987. "Doing Gender." *Gender & Society* 1: 125–51.

Western, B. 2006. *Punishment and Inequality in America.* New York: Russell Sage Foundation.

Widom, C. 1989a. "Child Abuse, Neglect, and Violent Criminal Behavior." *Criminology* 27: 251–366.

———. 1989b. "The Cycle of Violence." *Science* 244: 160–66.

———. 1989c. "Does Violence Begat Violence? A Critical Examination of the Literature." *Psychological Bulletin,* 1063–28.

———. 1991a. "Avoidance of Criminality in Abused and Neglected Children." *Psychiatry* 54: 162–74.

———. 1991b. "Childhood Victimization: Risk Factor for Delinquency." In M. E. Colten and E. Gore, eds., *Adolescent Stress: Causes and Consequences,* 201–21. New York: Aldine de Gruyter.

———. 1995. *Victims of Childhood Sexual Abuse—Later Criminal Consequences.* Washington, DC: U.S. Department of Justice, National Institute of Justice.

———. 1996. "Childhood Sexual Abuse and Criminal Consequences." *Society* 33(4): 47–53.

———. 2000. "Childhood Victimization and the Derailment of the Girls and Women to the Criminal Justice System." In *Research on Women and Girls in the Criminal Justice System,* 27–35. Washington, DC: National Institute of Justice.

Widom, C., and M. Ames. 1994. "Criminal Consequences of Childhood Sexual Victimization." *Child Abuse & Neglect* 18(4): 303–18.

Widom, C., and M. Maxfield. 2001. *An Update on the "Cycle of Violence."* Research in Brief (NIJ 20531). Washington, DC: U.S. Department of Justice, National Institute of Justice.

Williams, M., and R. Rikard. 2004. "Marginality or Neglect: An Exploratory Study of Policies and Programs for Aging Female Inmates." *Women & Criminal Justice* 15(3–4): 121–41.

Winfree, T., and C. De Jong. 2015. "Police and the War on Women: Examination Behind and in Front of the Blue Curtain." *Women & Criminal Justice* 25: 50–70.

Winterfield, L., M. Coggeshall, M. Burke-Storer, V. Correa, and S. Tidd. 2009. *The Effects of Post-Secondary Correctional Education: Final Report.* Washington, DC: Urban Institute.

Wolff, N., D. Blitz, J. Shi, R. Bachman, and J. Siegel. 2006. "Sexual Violence inside Prisons: Rates of Victimization." *Journal of Urban Health: Bulletin of the New York Academy of Medicine* 83(5): 835–48.

Wolff, N., J. Shi, D. Blitz, and J. Siegel. 2007. "Understanding Sexual Victimization inside Prisons: Factors That Predict Risk." *Criminology & Public Policy* 6(3): 535–64.

Wolff, N., J. Shi, and J. Siegel. 2009. "Understanding Physical Victimization inside Prisons: Factors That Predict Risk." *Justice Quarterly* 26: 445–75.

Wooldredge, J., and B. Steiner. 2016. "Assessing the Need for Gender-Specific Explanations of Prisoner Victimization." *Justice Quarterly* 33(2): 209–38.

Wright, E., E. Salisbury, and P. Van Voorhis. 2007. "Predicting the Prison Misconduct of Women Offenders: The Importance of Gender-Responsive Needs." *Journal of Contemporary Criminal Justice* 23: 310–40.

Wright, E., P. Van Voorhis, E. Salisbury, and A. Bauman. 2012. "Gender-Responsive Lessons Learned and Policy Implications for Women in Prison: A Review." *Criminal Justice & Behavior* 39(12): 1612–32.

Young, V., and R. Reviere. 2006. *Women Behind Bars: Gender and Race in Prisons*. Boulder, CO: Lynn Rienner.

Zaitzow, B., and J. Thomas, eds. 2003. *Women in Prison: Gender and Social Control*. Boulder, CO: Lynne Reinner.

Zupan, L. 1986. "Gender-Related Differences in Correctional Officers' Perceptions and Attitudes." *Journal of Criminal Justice* 14: 349–61.

———. 1992. "Men Guarding Women: An Analysis of the Employment of Male Correctional Officers in Prisons for Women." *Journal of Criminal Justice* 20: 297–309.

Index

Abrams, K., 25
Abril, J., 28
adaptive strategy, 76, 89, 135, 141
Aday, R., 58
Adler, C., 25
administrative segregation (Ad Seg), 46–47;
  "jail," 224
Adoption and Safe Families Act (1977), 27
Adverse Childhood Experience (ACE)
  Study, 28–29, 59
advocacy groups, 86, 87
African American women, 10, 25, 28, 105;
  and cumulative disadvantage, 38; and
  domestic violence, 34–35; health care
  inequalities of, 38, 59; housing
  discrimination and, 37–38; violence in
  prison and, 104–105. *See also*
  intersectional inequalities; race and
  ethnicity
agency, 5, 33, 35, 179; female violence as,
  95, 96, 173; male violence as, 94–95.
  See also constrained choice
aging women prisoners: health problems of,
  58, 59–60; and violence, 99–101; as
  vulnerable to exploitation, 59–60,
  110–112. *See also* younger women
  prisoners
Agnew, R., 28, 36
Alabama prison conditions, 172
Alexander, M., 20, 21, 23, 185
Allard, P., 27, 39

Ames, M., 25
Amnesty International, 152
Arnold, R., 28
arrest rates, 21, 24, 29
Ataby, T., 176
Audage, N., 39
Austin, J., 48, 176
Australia, as prison colony, 44–45

Babcock, J., 96
baby lifer, 223
Bagley, K., 11, 44
Baker, J., 176
Balton, M., 167
Bangkok Rules (*United Nations Rules for
  the Treatment of Women Prisoners and
  Non-Custodial Measures for Women
  Offenders*) (United Nations 2010), 3,
  70, 177–178, 183n; development of,
  x–xi, 12, 182–183; as ignored in U.S.
  prisons, 136
Barberet, R., 19, 24, 176
Baro, A., 152
Baskin, D., 8, 21, 40
Bastick, M., 176
Batchelor, S., 5, 26, 94
Battle, C., 28
Beck, A., 18, 70, 106, 121, 138, 152–153,
  165–166
bed moves, 223
being crossed out, 223

"being messy" (gossiping), violence and, 113–114
Belknap, J., 2, 4, 5, 21, 24, 26, 27, 29, 30, 32, 33, 34, 58, 63
Benedict, A., 64–65, 69, 179
big baller, 223
Big House style of prison, 45, 136
Blackburn, A., 87, 88–89
Blanchette, K., 178, 179
Blitz, C., 31
Bloom, B., 3, 5, 8n, 20, 21, 24, 25, 26, 27, 29, 30, 49, 58, 63, 70, 81, 147, 177–178, 178
Bloom, S., 177
bonaroo, 73, 73n, 223
books, 223
Bosworth, M., 5, 8n, 87, 137, 174
Bourdieu, P., 87
Bowling, J., 19
Bradley, R., 72
Braithwaite, J., 179
Brandford, C., 26
Breitenbecher, K., 168
Brennan, T., 33
Brent, J., 12
Brewer-Smyth, K., 58
Britton, D., 1, 8n, 42–43
Brockway, Z., 45
Browne, A., 27
Brown, J., 26, 47, 94
Brown v. Plata, 65, 66
bunkie, 223
Burgess-Proctor, A., 6, 12
Burman, M., 26, 94
Bush-Baskette, S., 21
Butler, M., 90
Bybee, D., 96

Caldwell, R., 26
Calhoun, S., 179
California prisons, 65–66, 77, 172
canteen whores (gold-diggers), 76
capital (free world): community justice model and, 177–178, 183; cumulative disadvantage and, 9–10, 36; gender difference in, 32; gender-responsive practice and, 179; leveraged to build prison capital, 75–76, 86, 91; as pathway, 34, 35, 36. See also disadvantaged communities
capital, prison. See prison capital
Caputo, G., 36
car, 86, 223
Carbone-Lopez, K., 33, 96–97, 104

Carlen, P., 8n
Carlson, R., 79
Carson, E., 1, 20, 23
cellie, 223
Cernkovich, S., 26
Charles, D., 25
Chen, G., 113, 130
Chesney-Lind, M., 6, 7–8, 8n, 10, 20, 21, 24, 26, 27, 35, 36, 44, 94–95
child cases (crimes against children), 223; as stigmatized offense, 87, 115–116
children, 25–26, 52n6; toxic stress for, 39. See also child cases; children of imprisoned parents; families; violent victimization in childhood
children of imprisoned parents, 27, 176, 178, 183; fathers in prison, 26–27; mothers in prison, 24, 26–27; toxic stress, 39
Christiaens, J., 5n
class, 45, 135–136; and "cult of true womanhood," 44n; intersectionality and, 4, 22
classification, 51–52, 106–107, 223–224; overclassification, 52
cleanliness, 43–44, 56, 75, 75n3, 224; as human rights issue, 171–172; as safety issue, 56, 171; sanitary products, 75n2, 171–172
Clear, T., 21, 38, 82, 169
Clemmer, D., 8, 42
clothing, 73, 73n, 75n3, 223, 224
CO (correctional officer), 224
Coates, T., 119
Codianni, B., 84
Coleman v. Schwarzenegger, 65–66
Comack, E., 29, 69
commissary, 75n; as status marker, 75. See also economic exploitation
communicable diseases, 30, 56, 60–61
communities of causality, 40
community: free world and prison, similarities of, 8–9. See also disadvantaged communities
community capacity, 38–39
community justice model, 176, 177–178, 183, 184
conditions of confinement, 43–52, 52n6, 90; architecture, 43, 45, 46–47; crowding, 48–52, 60, 226; as human rights violations, 170–172; litigation of, 65–66; overview, 42–43, 66–67; punishment principles and, 43, 45, 47, 63, 184–185; as safety risk, 46, 69;

summer heat, 47–48, 48n, 77–78; vermin problems, 47. *See also* health care in prison, as inadequate; mental health and care (in prisons)
constrained choice, 5, 33, 35, 110; staff sexual misconduct and, 154, 159–160; and violence initiated by females, 96, 97, 173
contraband, trafficking and trading in, 78–79, 78n, 111
convict strategy, 89, 105, 115, 135, 138
Cook, S., 27
cosign, 224
"cottage"-style of prison, 45, 46
Covington, S., 3, 5, 10, 21, 24, 27, 29, 30, 49, 58, 63, 64–65, 70, 81–82, 147, 178, 179–180
Coyle, A., 169, 171
Crenshaw, K., 2, 4, 6, 36
Cressey, D., 8, 87, 88
Crewe, B., 90
crime: decriminalization of, 185; falling rates of, and increasing incarceration rates, 19–20; gender differences in offense categories, 21, 23–24; women's vulnerabilities to, 2. *See also* criminalization; drug crimes; property crimes; stigmatized offenses; violent crime
criminalization: of abused girls, 26; of poverty, 22; of victimizaton, 35. *See also* mass incarceration
crosses, 224
Crouch, B., 135
crowding, 48–52, 60, 226
Crow, J., 22
crunk, 224
"cult of true womanhood," 43–44, 44n
cultural capital, 87–91; outside sources of, 86. *See also* prison capital
cumulative disadvantage as context, 27, 106–107, 176, 178, 183; constrained choice caused by, 33, 35; cumulative victimization and female-initiated violence, 96–97, 172–173; pathways and, 36–41, 81, 172–173
cutting (self-harm), 102

Daly, K., 32–33, 94, 99, 173
Danner, M., 20, 169
Davino, K., 72
Davis, S., 21
Daye, E., 58
de Almeida, O., 9, 69–70, 175
death row, 47

debts, 206; banker-inmates, 111; for drugs and tobacco, 111; racial dynamics involving, 105; violence sparked by, 98, 111, 120
De Hart, D., 5, 8n
De Jong, C., 21, 35
dental care, 30
Deschenes, E., 22
dignity, 178, 180, 186; human rights approach based in, 170, 171, 181; Mandela Rules and, 182; prison conditions and damage to, 42, 47, 49, 69; trauma-informed practice and, 180
disadvantaged communities, 34–35, 38–40, 67; disinvestment in, 170; housing discrimination and, 37–38; mass incarceration and creation of, 169–170; reentry into, 35, 38–39, 40, 169–170
disciplinary housing (SHU), 129, 161, 164, 225
disciplinary reports, 91, 117–119, 145–146, 161
disenfranchised grief, 36–37
disrespect. *See* respect
Dodge, M., 20
dog programs in prison, 52n
domestic violence. *See* intimate partner violence
doubling, 224
down for your people, 224
do your own time, 72, 74, 88, 91, 128, 224; women's prison code and, 89, 98–99, 128
drug crimes, 21, 35, 40, 185; gendered offense patterns, 23–24, 29–30. *See also* "war on drugs"
drugs: debts for, 111; "drug mix," 90
drug treatment programs, 79–80
dynamic security, 184

economic capital, 74–79, 225; hustles, 76, 77–78; prison job assignments (pay number) as, 75–78, 225; trafficking and trading, 78–79, 78n, 111. *See also* economic exploitation; prison capital
economic exploitation, 206; extortion of the materially advantaged, 109–111, 122; intimate relationships and, 110, 130; staff inattention to safety and, 141
Edgar, K., 97–98
education (in prison), 76, 81. *See also* programs
Einat, G., 113, 130
Eisen, L., 19
Eliason, M., 21

emotional capital, 24, 79–82; and prison violence, 98. *See also* prison capital
emotional labor, 80
employment, 31, 39; prison job assignments (pay numbers), 75–78, 225
English, K., 26
English prison system, 43–45; respect in men's prisons, 90
Enos, S., 5, 21
European Committee for the Prevention of Torture and Inhuman or Degrading Treatment or Punishment, 172

Fabiano, A., 8n, 147
Faith, K., 8n
Faiver, K., 58
families (outside), support from, 76–77, 86, 109. *See also* families, disordered; families, prison/play
families, disordered, 24–26, 85; historical trauma and, 36–37. *See also* children; violent victimization in childhood
families, prison/play, 84–85
featherwood, 224
Feinman, C., 8n, 43–44
Fellner, J., 172, 181
female staff: and approach to job, 146–147; history of punishment and, 136; name calling by, 142; physical violence by, 149–150; searches and abuses by, 159; sexual misconduct with female prisoners, 70, 122, 155, 174; sexual misconduct with male prisoners, 165–166; transport of female prisoners and, 174–175. *See also* staff
feminist criminology, 7–8. *See also* intersectional inequalities
Ferraro, K., 21, 62, 95
Ferrenti, Seth, 78
fish, 224
Fleetwood, J., 90
Fleischer, M., 125
Flesher, F., 152
Fletcher, B., 8n
Florida women's prisons, 47, 62–63
Flower, S., 31
Fogel, C., 58
foster care, 25, 27
Foster, H., 27
Fowler, S., 87, 88–89
Freedman, E., 8n, 43–44
freedom, deprivation of: gender differences in experience of, 88, 169; as pain of imprisonment, 70, 88

Freeman, L., 36
free world, 224; education and gender differences in, 31; emotional capital and, 24, 81–82; human capital disproportionality, 71; intimate partnerships in, 26; social capital disproportionality, 2, 9–10, 28. *See also* capital (free world); community; health care (free world); intimate partner violence (free world); mental health (free world); pathways; poverty; property crimes; recidivism; release/reintegration to free world; violent crime
friends and friendships: economic support from, 76–77, 109; healthy relationships in prison as, 82–83. *See also* families, prison/play; intimate partnerships
Frost, N., 20, 21
Fry, Elizabeth, 45

Gabel, K., 27
Gaes, G., 77
gangs, 79, 104, 111–113, 121; men's prisons and, 78–79, 111
Garcia, C., 26
Garland, C., 27
Gartner, R., 8n, 21, 49, 71, 76, 85, 87, 88, 89, 92, 95, 105, 117, 135, 138, 141
G'ed up, 73n, 224
Geertz, C., 12, 188
gender, definition of, 3–4, 6
gender differences: in arrest rates, 21, 24; and capital, vulnerability to harm for lack of, 32; in convict code, 87–89, 114–115; in deprivation of freedom, experience of, 88, 169; in drug offenses, 23–24, 29–30; education in free world, 31; in intimate partnerships (prison), 126; in mental health (free world), 24, 30; and offenders with childhood violent victimization, 25–26, 29–30; in offenders with disordered families, 24–25; in offense categories, 21, 23–24; in pre-prison employment status, 31; and relationships, importance to emotional health, 81–82; of staff approach to job, 146–147; staff gender, inmate preferences for, 146–147, 159; in thefts in prison, 97; in violence among inmates, 2, 15–16, 93; in violent crime perpetrators, 21. *See also* gender inequality; gender-neutral policies; gender-responsive practice; intersectional inequalities; pathways

gender entrapment, 37
gender inequality, 12–13; definition of, 6;
and women committing violent crime,
94–97, 172–173. See also intersectional
inequalities
gender-neutral policies, 3, 147–148,
170–171
gender-nonconforming persons, 11, 73,
75n3, 105–107
gender-responsive practice, 80, 173,
177–179, 184; definition of, 178–179;
human rights approach and, 175, 179,
186; training in, 147–148, 180
Gender-Responsive Strategies: Research,
Practice and Guiding Principles for
WOmen Offenders (NIC report), 178
general population, 224
Georges-Abeyie, D., 7
Geronimus, A., 38, 59
get a case, 224
get backs, 224
getting over, 224
Giallombardo, R., 8n, 88–89
Gilbert, E., 152
Gillan, M., 8n
Giordano, P., 9–10, 26
girls and young women as offenders, 25–26
Girls Study Group, 25, 26
Girshick, L., 8n, 126
Glaze, L., 24, 25, 26
glossary, 223–226
Gobeil, R., 178
Gobell, R., 179
Goffman, Erving, 42
gold-diggers, 76
Goldenson, J., 66
Goodkind, S., 25
gossiping ("being messy"), 113–114
governance, prisoner, 87
Green, B., 30
Greene, J., 20, 21, 27, 39
Greenfield, L., 23, 27
Greer, K., 80, 85
Grella, C., 27, 29–30
Guerino, P., 18, 106, 138, 165–166

Hagan, J., 27
Haney, C., 48, 175
Hanna, J., 167
Harlow, C., 27
Harrison, P., 18, 106, 138, 165–166
Hartley, D., 27
Hartnagel, T., 8n
have something coming, 75, 224

Hayes, M., 59, 63
Haynie, D., 21
health care (free world), as inadequate, 30,
38, 58, 59
health care (in prison): as civil rights issue,
172; crowding and, 60; dental care, 30;
as human rights issue, 171, 172, 182;
and illness seen as personal flaw, 59;
reproductive health, 30, 84, 182; as
safety issue, 58–60; staff dismissal or
neglect of requests for care, 59, 61–63;
staff sexual misconduct during, 158. See
also mental health and care (in prisons)
health problems, 30; communicable
diseases, 30, 56, 60–61; disabilities, 101;
inequality for black women, 38, 59; and
lack of prison capital, 59, 71; toxic
stress for children and, 39; and violence,
escalation of, 61; weathering, and cumulative disadvantage, 38, 226. See also
health care
Heckman, J., 80–81
Heffernan, R., 8n
Heney, J., 69
Henriques, Z., 8n, 37, 152
Her Royal Highness, Princess Bajrakitiyabha of Thailand, x–xi. See also Bangkok
Rules
historical grief, 36–37
historical trauma, 36–37
HIV/AIDS, 56, 61, 62
Hodge, J., 58, 60
holding the bag, 224
Holsinger, K., 26
Holtfreter, K., 9–10, 178
housing change requests, 128–130
housing discrimination, 37–38
Hughes, R., 44
human capital (free world) disproportionality, 9–10, 24
human capital (in prison), 9–10, 59, 70–74;
abuse and victimization reducing, 28,
73, 74. See also prison capital
human rights: community justice model
(noncustodial), 176, 177–178, 184;
conditions of confinement and violations
of, 170–172; conflict and violence
among women and violations of,
172–173; constructive ways for women
to do time, 173; dynamic security, 184;
gender and gender equality, definitions
of, 6; gender-based special measures not
discriminatory, 180; gender-neutral
policies as violation of, 3, 170–171;

human rights *(continued)*
 gender-responsive approach compatible
 with, 175, 179, 184; health care, 171;
 Mandela Rules, 2n, 166–167, 182; as
 precluding strip searches by officers of
 opposite sex, 166; reform of system and,
 176–177, 180–186; sanctuary principle,
 177; sanitary conditions, 171–172; staff
 misconduct/sexual misconduct and, 153,
 166–167, 174–175; state-sponsored
 suffering as violation of, 175–176;
 Universal Declaration of (UNDHR),
 11–12; vs. civil rights approach, 172,
 181. *See also* Bangkok Rules; United
 Nations
Human Rights Watch, 70, 152, 166–167
hustles, 76, 77–78
"hygienes," 75, 75nn2–3, 81, 171–172,
 224. *See also* cleanliness

identity, 81, 88; spoiled, as "former
 prisoner," 175. *See also* intersectional
 inequalities
Ignatieff, M., 141
incarceration rates, 1, 5, 20, 23; of death
 row, 47; growth rate in, despite falling
 crime rates, 19–20; reform initiatives,
 185; of U.S., as highest in world, 19;
 women's rate of, as increasing, 20–22.
 See also mass incarceration; sentences
individual pathologies vs. structural inequalities: and cumulative disadvantage, 36;
 economic inequalities blamed on,
 39–40, 185; as explanations of prison
 conflict and violence, 3, 6, 16; and
 pathways to prison, 24, 34; and sickness
 and disability, 59
individual responsibility in prison: for debts,
 111; safety and, 71–72
inmate-on-inmate assaults. *See* reporting
 misconduct; sexual violence among
 female inmates; violence among female
 inmates
institutional trauma, 64–65
intersectional inequalities: analysis of, 1–3;
 and critique of white feminism, 22;
 definition of, 4, 6–8; domestic violence
 and, 34–35; historical and collective
 trauma and, 36–37, 38; inside prison
 and, 7, 34; nonconforming gender
 identity and, 11, 106–107; pathways
 approach enhanced by, 32, 41; and
 policy initiatives, 185; prison capital as
 response to, 68, 91–92; state-sponsored

suffering produced by, 170; violence in
 prison and, 93–94, 97, 134. *See also*
 class; gender inequality; individual
 pathologies vs. structural inequalities;
 pathways; poverty; race and ethnicity;
 safety
intimate partnerships (prison), 126–133;
 disrespect in, 127–128; economic
 exploitation and, 110, 130; gender
 differences in, 126; gold-diggers, 76; as
 healthy, 82–83, 85; intensity of, 127,
 129; living together, 128–130; and social
 capital, 85. *See also* families, prison/
 play; friends and friendships; intimate
 partner violence (prison); solidarity
intimate partner violence (free world): as
 control of male over female behavior,
 95; economic dependence and inability
 to end relationship, 173; female-initiated, 95–96; rate of in women offenders,
 27; in same-sex relationships, 95; and
 structural inequalities, 34–35
intimate partner violence (prison), 130–133,
 207–208; and dysfunctional relationships of pathways, 126, 131–133; living
 together and, 128–129; and medical
 needs, 58; as most common source of
 violence, 121, 133; as risk, 85; and
 sexuality as prison capital, 11; snitching
 and, 115; staying single to avoid
 victimizing, 133
Irwin, J., 8, 45, 46, 48, 76, 84, 87, 88, 88n,
 113, 136, 184–185
Irwin, K., 10, 21, 26, 94–95
Isaac, A., 104
Islam-Zwart, K., 26
isolate strategy, 71, 89, 105, 117, 135, 138
"issue," 75, 75n2, 75n3, 224. *See also*
 commissary; contraband

jacked, 224
jail (in reference to administrative
 segregation, or Ad Seg), 224
jails, 30–31, 46, 52n6, 77, 115
jealousy: staff sexual misconduct and,
 153–154; violence among inmates and,
 98, 127–128
Jenness, V., 12
job assignments, 75–78, 225
Johnston, D., 27
Jones, N., 95–96
Joseph, J., 1, 4, 6, 36
juice (informal power), 86–87, 225
Jurick, N., 4, 72

Just Detention International (JDI), letters describing assaults by staff, 14–15, 152, 153, 156, 157, 160–161, 163–165, 192–193

Kane, L., 27
Katz, S., 25, 26
Kempfner, C., 27
Kerman, P., 83–84
Keys, D., 107
Kilgore, J., 22
Kim, W., 96
kite, 225
Kopf, D., 31
Krabill, J., 58
Kraska, K., 12
Krienert, J., 125
Kristiansen, C., 69
Kruttschnitt, C., 8n, 21, 33, 49, 71, 76, 85, 87, 88, 89, 92, 95, 96–97, 104, 105, 117, 135, 138, 141
Kubiak, S., 96, 167
Kupers, T., 42, 88

Labelle, D., 152, 171, 172, 181–182
Lahm, K., 97
Lamarre, M., 66
Lambert, E., 169
Lane, J., 26
Langan, N., 24, 29
language barrier as vulnerability, 102–103
Latinas: and family members concurrently imprisoned, 25; housing discrimination and, 37–38; incarceration rates of, 23. *See also* race and ethnicity
"la vida loca," 29, 33
Leahy, J., 105
"learning how to do time," 26, 71, 91. *See also* do your own time; prison capital
Leigey, M., 58, 60
LGBT persons, 4, 95, 106, 107, 159. *See also* gender nonconforming persons; intimate partnerships
life-term prisoners. *See* long-term prisoners
Lipsitz, G., 8, 37
litigation, 65–66, 70, 165–167, 172
Lockhart, L., 104
lock in the sock, 225
London, W., 42, 88
Long, P., 27, 168
long-term prisoners: and clean record, need to maintain, 91, 117–119; and crowding, effect of, 50, 51; and job assignments, 77; mentor-protégée

relationships among, 83; and outside economic support, erosion of, 76; and prison capital, building of, 116; and staff-inmate relationship, 139–140; and violence, 116–119
lose time, 225
Lynch, S., 5, 29, 30–31

McDaniels-Wilson, C., 27
McGuire, M., 47, 49, 70, 87, 88, 98–99, 113, 119
McKenry, P., 96
Maeve, M., 26
Maguin, E., 27
Mahan, S., 8n
Makarios, M., 26, 96
male gaze, 70, 175
mandatory minimum laws, 20, 20n, 22
Mandela, Nelson, 182, 186
Mandela Rules, 2n, 166–167, 182
Marcus-Mendoza, S., 27
Marksamer, J., 106
Marquart, J., 27
Martin, C., 97–98
Martin, S., 4, 72
Maruschak, L., 24, 25, 26
masculine roles: appearance, 73, 75n3; male pronoun used, 120n; prison/play families and, 85; and violence between women, 107
masculinity, men's prisons and, 42, 88
Massachusetts, trauma-informed practice, 65
mass incarceration, 19–20, 20n; collateral consequences of, 169–170, 175–176; global, and harm to women in prison, 175–176; as the "new Jim Crow," 185; and purpose of prisons, 169, 185. *See also* crime; criminalization; incarceration rates; sentences; war on drugs
Matza, D., 33
Mauer, M., 20, 23
Maxfield, M., 25
"mean laws," 5
medical staff, 62nn
men. *See* gender differences
men's prisons: assaults on staff, 138; convict code of, 14, 87–88; gendered experience of male prisoners, 2n; gender-neutral operational practices, 3, 170–171; male definition of prisoners, 42, 42n; and masculinity, 42, 88; nonconforming gender identities and, 11; offense categories of inmates, 23; poverty as

men's prisons (continued)
disproportional among inmates, 2;
prison capital and, 1–2n; racial
dynamics in, 52, 97, 104; relationships
and, 126; respect and, 90; and snitching,
114; stigmatized offenses and, 115–116;
tobacco trafficking, 78–79; and
trauma-informed corrections, need for,
65n; and violence, 2, 15–16, 93, 97–98,
108; and weapons, use of, 121
mental health (free world): childhood
experiences of victimization and effect
on, 25–26, 29, 30–31; gender differences
in, 24, 30; need for care, vs. imprisonment, 184; as predictive of offending
history, 31; self-medicating, 29; toxic
stress for children and, 39
mental health and care (in prisons):
dismissal of need for care as "manipulation," 63; and emotional capital,
development of, 79–80; fragility of, and
lack of prison capital, 71; institutional
trauma/trauma-informed environments,
64–65, 65n, 177, 179–180, 186; jails
and, 30–31; lack of care found to be
cruel/unusual/inhumane, 65–66; neglect
by staff of need for, 63, 65–66, 102;
reentry to free world compromised by
lack of, 173; reinforcement of symptoms
by lack of, 173; self-harm, 102; and
victims/victimizers of violence, 101–102.
See also trauma
Merlo, A., 11, 35, 44
Messina, N., 27, 29–30, 59, 179
Messinger, S., 88
Messman-Moore, T., 27, 168
methodology, 13–15, 187–204; focus
groups, 46, 104, 163, 187–188, 189,
190; inductive methods and, 46; mixed
methods as feminist methods, 12;
sampling, 9, 187–188, 190; sources of
narrative data, 15; verbal conflict,
measurement of, 108; Women's
Correction Safety Scales (WCSS) survey,
12, 15, 55, 190–193, 193–204. See also
tables of findings
Michigan, litigation for staff sexual
misconduct in prisons, 70, 165–167, 172
Middlebrooks, J., 39
Miller, B., 27
Miller, J., 5, 26, 81
Miller, S., 96
Millson, B., 179
the mix, "in the mix": definition of, 9, 89,
90; drug mix, 90; fighting mix, 89; and
"good officer" definitions by inmates,
138; as source of prison capital, 9, 90;
strategies for negotiation of, 89;
transformation out of, 81. See also
prison culture
Mobley, A., 65
Moe, A., 62
Moon, D., 8n
Morash, M., 6, 7–8, 9–10, 36, 178, 179
Morgan, R., 36
Morton, D., 29
Moss, A., 12, 13, 122–123, 153
Moyer, I., 8n
Mullings, J., 27
Mumola, C., 27
mutual aid, 84

Native American women, 25, 28
Negy, C., 79
neighborhoods in prison, 8–9, 115; "good"
vs. "bad," 52–55, 57–58
Ng, I., 25
Nickel, J., 27
noise, 51, 64
noodles, 225
Norton-Hawk, M., 5, 8, 34, 35, 37–38,
39–40, 59, 71, 75
Nuytiens, A., 5n

O'Brien, P., 169
O'Donnell, I., 97
OG (original gangster), 139, 225
Oklahoma prisons, 5, 23
operational practices: and Big House prison
model, 45, 136; community justice
model, 176, 177–178, 183, 184;
definition of, 46n; disciplinary housing
(SHU), 129, 161, 164, 225; disciplinary
reports, 91, 117–119, 145–146, 161;
gender-neutral, 3, 147–148, 170–171;
gender nonconforming individuals and,
106–107; and human rights approach,
182; reentry to community, preparation
for, 177; trauma-informed practice, 65,
65n, 177, 179–180, 186; as undermining women's safety, 3, 66–67; and
women's perception of safety, 17, 43,
46. See also classification; gender-
responsive practice; health care (in
prison); mental health and care (in
prison); programs; staff
Orange Is the New Black (Kerman,
television), 83–84, 84n

Paes-Machado, E., 9, 69–70, 175
pains of imprisonment: deprivation of
    freedom as, 70, 88; indigenous prison
    subcultures as response to, 87; lack of
    privacy as, 70; policy makers as having
    principal obligation for reducing, 185;
    prison capital as alleviated by, 87–88;
    rejection by society as, 88; and staff
    sexual misconduct, 157
parole, 91, 117–119; "short and shitty,"
    118–119
Parson, S., 9, 12, 13, 15, 55
Pasko, L., 27
pathways: away from crime, gender-respon-
    sive practice and, 178, 179; away from
    prison, recovery and, 81; cumulative
    disadvantage as context for, 36–41, 81,
    172–173; inside prison, culture arbi-
    trating, 69; intersectional analysis added
    to, 32, 41; intimate partner violence
    and, 126, 131–133; as more predictive
    than confinement factors, 16; multiple,
    35; overview, 5; quantitative research
    and, 33, 33nn; shared characteristics of,
    24–32; social capital disproportionality,
    28; as theory, 5, 32–34; three-category
    conceptualization of pathways, 33–34.
    See also cumulative disadvantage as
    context; gender-responsive practice
pay number (prison jobs), 75–78, 225
Pelissier, B., 24, 29
personal responsibility. See individual
    pathologies vs. structural inequalities;
    individual responsibility in prison
Petersilia, J., 38–39
Pleydon, A., 26
Pogrebin, M., 20
policing in communities of color, 21–22, 35,
    74–75
popular conceptions about women's
    prisons: Orange Is the New Black,
    83–84; of sexual violence, 74, 122
post-traumatic stress disorder (PTSD),
    30–31, 38
Potler, C., 20
Potter, H., 1, 2, 4, 6–7, 20, 32, 36
poverty: as compounded in prison, 75;
    criminalization of, 22; disproportional-
    ity of incarcerated women, 2, 31; LGBT
    persons and, 106; mirrored in prison
    capital, 71; offenses of women due to,
    173, 176, 184, 185; pre-prison incomes,
    31; social capital eroded by, 28; social
    control of the poor, 74–75

Pranis, K., 20, 21
prison(s): Big House style of, 45, 136;
    community justice model (noncustodial
    care) as alternative to, 176, 177–178,
    183, 184; "cottage"-style of, 45, 46;
    history of philosophy of punishment
    and, 42–45, 136; industry jobs, 77; as
    political reaction to social problems,
    175; punishment principles, 43, 45, 47,
    63, 184–185; as total institution, 42, 93,
    136. See also conditions of confinement;
    human rights; incarceration rates; men's
    prisons; neighborhoods in prison; pains
    of imprisonment; prison capital; prison
    culture; staff
prison capital: confidence and self-assurance
    as, 72–73; controlling reactions to
    inequalities, 68; definition of, 2, 9–10;
    free-world capital leveraged to produce,
    75–76, 86, 91; intersectional inequalities
    and safety via, 68, 91–92; men's prisons
    and, 1–2n; the mix as source/cultural
    context of, 9, 90; pains of imprisonment
    as alleviated by, 87–88; reform of prisons
    and increase of, 177; rejection of honor
    block and, 54; and release to free world,
    as disadvantage, 170; sexual capital,
    44–45, 159–161; social networking as
    facilitating, 82; staff sexual misconduct
    and, 11, 154, 158, 159–161; violence as,
    97, 119–120; vulnerability as determined
    by access to, 69–70, 91, 99–107. See also
    cultural capital; economic capital; emo-
    tional capital; human capital; safety;
    social capital
prison culture: convict code, 87–89, 98–99,
    114–115, 128; formal and public rules
    vs. informal and private normative
    demands, 69; indigenous vs. imported
    origins of, 87–88, 88n6; normative
    framework of, 69, 87; and pathways
    within prison, 69. See also "mix, the"
prison nation, 22
prison population. See incarceration rates
Prison Rape Elimination Act (PREA, 2003),
    12–13, 122, 155, 164
privacy: human rights and staff sexual
    misconduct, 166, 167, 175; lack of, as
    gendered pain of imprisonment, 70
Proctor, J., 58
programs: adaptive strategy and use of, 76;
    education, 76, 81; and emotional
    capital, development of, 80–81;
    "gleaning" as taking advantage of, 76;

programs: adaptive strategy *(continued)*
international standards calling for, 173;
and noncustodial care, 183; overclassification and restriction from, 52; reentry
to free world and need for, 173; safety
inside prison and, 173; trauma-informed
practice, 65, 65n, 177, 179–180, 186;
women-centered, and emotional capital,
80. *See also* gender-responsive practice
property crimes, 21, 35; decriminalization
of, 185
pruno, 225
Puisis, M., 66
punishment, principles of, 43, 45, 47, 63,
172, 181, 184–185. *See also* human
rights; pains of imprisonment
punked, 225

"rabbits" (vulnerable women), 103–104
Rabuy, B., 31
race and ethnicity: black staff and racial
discrimination, 104; and custodial vs.
Reformatory Era prison conditions, 45;
disproportionality of problems for black
women, 104–105; and family members
concurrently imprisoned, 25; and health
care inequalities, 38, 59; intrastaff
conflict and, 148; and isolate- or
convict-strategy, 105; men's prisons and
dynamics of, 52, 97, 104; and
methodology of study, 104; and
pathways, 37–38; policing in communities of color, 21–22, 35, 74–75; and
staff, problems with, 105, 168; as
subtext vs. organizing principle in
women's prisons, 52, 97, 104–105; and
victimization, 28; and violence
perpetrated by women, 95, 97; work
experience/training and post-release
outcomes, 77. *See also* intersectional
inequalities; racial discrimination in
criminal justice
racial discrimination in criminal justice: as
conversation, 20–21; mass incarceration
as "the new Jim Crow," 185; and
overrepresentation of people of color in
prisons, 23
Rafter, N., 8n, 45
Randolph, J., 26
Randon, M., 95–96
rape. *See* sexual violence among female
inmates; staff sexual misconduct; violent
victimization
Rasche, C., 147

recidivism: community justice model and
reduction of, 177–178; high rates of,
21–22; improvement of capital and
reduction of, 10; jobs/training, and
reduction of, 77, 173. *See also* release/
reintegration to free world
recovery, as development of emotional
capital, 80–81
re-entry. *See* release/reintegration to free
world
Reformatory Era, 45, 136
Reiger, D., 58
Reisig, M., 9–10, 178
relational pathway, 34
relationships: healthy, importance of,
82–83; loss of freedom and deprivation
of, 88. *See also* families; friends and
friendships; intimate partnerships; social
capital; solidarity
release/reintegration to free world:
alternatives to prison and, 176,
177–178, 183; community capacity to
support, 38–39, 169–170, 185;
education/vocational training in prison
and, 77, 173; inverse relationship of
prison capital and success following,
170; post-conviction barriers unique to
women, 21; reform initiatives, 185; and
spoiled identity as "former prisoner,"
175; and worldview of unfairness and
distrust, 170. *See also* recidivism
Renzetti, C., 95, 127
reporting misconduct, 218–220; inmate
harassment of inmates who report, 165,
219; staff harassment of inmates who
report, 162, 163–165, 167, 218; staff
reporting climate, 153, 220; treated as
snitching, 164, 165
reputation: establishment of, 108; for
getting things done, as juice, 86–87
respect, 90, 98, 108; asymmetry of, in
staff-inmate relationship, 141–146;
disrespect, 90–91, 113, 127–128; as
human right, 90; as prison capital,
90–91. *See also* dignity
Reviere, R., 8n, 37
Rhodes, L., 141
Richie, B., 4, 6, 10, 12, 21, 22, 23, 34–35,
37, 69, 75
Rierden, A., 8n
Rigby, M., 167
Rikard, R., 60
Rizzo, E., 59, 63
Robinson, D., 179

Rodriquez, N., 8n
Roeder, O., 19
room/cell/dorms, 56–58
Rosenbaum, J., 26
Rosenbaum, M., 35
Rosenfeld, R., 38–39
Ross, M., 58
Ross, R., 8n, 147
running the yard, 81, 86, 225
"running your mac," 76
Rytter, T., 176

Sabo, D., 42, 88
safety, 217; advice on seeking, 73–74, 84; confidence and self-assurance and, 72–73; defined as the product of having one's needs met, 68–69; defined as the state of being protected from harm/danger/threats, 68, 177; deprivation of freedom and risks to, 70; "doing safety" as daily effort, 72; facility procedures for, 217; fragility of, 69; personalized strategies for securing, 71–73; prison conditions as risk to, 46, 69; reform initiatives, 186. See also human rights; reporting misconduct; solidarity
Saguaro Seminar (Harvard Kennedy School), 82
Salisbury, E., 7, 9–10, 18, 25, 32, 33, 34, 38
same-sex orientation. See LGBT persons. See also gender-nonconforming persons; intimate partnerships
sanitation. See cleanliness
Sari, R., 25
Saylor, W., 77
Schneider, R., 8n, 69, 79
Schner, J., 26
searches: female staff and, 159; prohibitions on male staff performing, 70; as staff sexual misconduct, 158–159, 166, 174
Selling, L., 8n
sentences: indeterminate, and need to maintain a clean prison record, 91; length of, and increasing prison population, 20, 20n, 22; mandatory minimum laws, 20, 20n, 22; reform of policy, 176, 177, 185; Three Strikes laws, 20; truth-in-sentencing laws, 20n. See also long-term prisoners; short-term prisoners
Sentencing Project, 21, 181
Sered, S., 5, 8, 34, 35, 37–38, 39–40, 59, 71, 75

serious mental illness (SMI), 30
sexual capital, 11, 44–45, 159–161
sexuality, 10, 44
sexualization, 10, 28, 29, 157
sexual orientation. See LGBT persons
sexual pressure, 123–124
sexual violence among female inmates, 121–126, 207–208, 216; and and "good" vs. "bad" prison neighborhoods, 55; continuum of types of, 123–126; invisibility of, 122–123; physical violence as much more common than, 125, 126, 133; popular image of, vs. reality, 74, 122; prevalence of, 121–122; protective pairings and, 122; rape, prevalence of, 125–126; in retaliation for reporting staff sexual misconduct, 165; staff concern about, 141; verbal threats of, 122. See also reporting misconduct; staff sexual misconduct
Sharp, S., 5, 8n, 25, 28, 32, 36, 59
Shaver, L., 8n
short-term prisoners: "short and shitty," 118–119; and violence, 116–119
shot caller, 57, 225
SHU (disciplinary housing), 129, 161, 164, 225
Siard, C., 96
Siegel, J., 25
Silverman, J., 26
Simkins, S., 25, 26
Simon, J., 20, 65–66, 171, 172
Simpson, S., 36
sisterhood. See solidarity
Slocum, L., 36
Smith, B., 11, 44, 106–107
Smith, D., 36
Snell, T., 23, 27, 29
snitching, 225; "dry snitching," 108; norm of prohibition on, 87, 114–115; reporting of staff sexual misconduct treated as, 164, 165; "snitch jacket," 115, 225; violence and, 114–115
social capital (in prison), 81–87; families (play/prison) as, 84–85; healthy relationships as developing, 82–83, 85; hustles and jobs as developing, 77; intimate relationships as, 85; and juice, 86–87, 225; outside sources of, 86; sisterhood and solidarity as, 83–84. See also prison capital
social services, 21–22, 74–75
solidarity: with aging inmates, 110–111; constructive relationships, 82–83;

solidarity: with aging inmates *(continued)* interpretation for non-English speakers, 102–103; mental health challenges and, 102; mutual aid, 84; popular representations of, 83–84; welcome wagon gifts, 84

Sommers, I., 8, 21, 40

spouses: concurrent imprisonment of, 25. *See also* families

staff: approach to job, gender differences in, 146–147; assaults on, by inmates, 65, 138, 151; as "being messy" (gossiping), 114; black, and racial discrimination, 104; conflicts among staff, 148–149, 162; dependence of inmates on, 136; diversity of, 135–136; gender composition of, 136; hierarchy and inequality shaping lives of, 91n7; job assignments by, 77; male gaze, 70, 175; male, prohibitions on, 70, 136, 182; men's prison code of antipathy toward, 88; prison as toxic to, 169; quality and preparation of, 144–145; respect and empathy for inmates, and recovery/transformation, 81; and respect from inmates, investment in, 91, 144; substance use/abuse by, 144. *See also* female staff; staff inattention to women's safety; staff-inmate relationship; staff physical violence; staff sexual misconduct; staff verbal abuse

staff inattention to women's safety, 49, 106, 108, 141; and "good" vs. "bad" officer definitions by inmates, 138–139, 168

staff-inmate relationship: active and overt harming behaviors by staff, 138–139; adaptive strategy and, 135, 141; challenging staff, 135, 140; decision-makers from outside the facility, 86, 137; gender of staff, inmate preferences for, 146–147, 159; gender-responsive policies, need for, 147–148; "good" and "bad" officers, wide-ranging inmate definitions of, 138–140, 143, 146–147; inconsistency of staff as problem in, 139, 145–146; and intrastaff conflict, 148–149; isolate- and convict-strategy of women and avoidance of, 89, 135, 138; long-termers and, 139–140; manipulation of staff, 135, 140; power of staff as absolute, 136–138, 167–168, 174; power of staff, inmate management of, 137; protection by staff, 141; and respect, assymetry of, 141–146; types of relationships, 135–136

staff physical violence, 149–152, 214–215; as ever-present threat, 138, 151–152. *See also* reporting misconduct

staff sexual misconduct, 152–167, 211, 212–213, 215–216; African American women and, 105; awareness of by staff and management, 153; collateral consequences of, 164–165; consensuality/illegality issues, 152–153, 154, 155, 156, 159–160; fatalistic acceptance by inmates, 158, 167; female staff and, 70, 122, 155, 174; human rights approach to, 174–175; inmate initiation of, 154–155, 162; inmate reporting of, retaliation for and dismissal of, 162, 163–165, 167; international human rights laws defining as torture, 153, 174; jealousy and, 153–154; litigation and investigations regarding, 70, 165–167, 172; and male staff duties, prohibitions on, 70, 136, 182; physical violence by staff and, 153–154; prior abuse and vulnerability to, 27; prison capital and, 11, 154, 158, 159–161; Prison Rape Elimination Act (PREA), 12–13, 122, 155, 164. *See also* reporting misconduct; staff sexual misconduct, types of behaviors

staff sexual misconduct, types of behaviors: flashing, voyeurism, and touching, 157–158; grooming, 162; intimidation, 161; love and seduction, 154, 156; searches, abuse of authority for, 158–159, 166, 174; sexual assault, 157, 158; sexual exchange, 159–161; sexual requests, 157; sex without physical violence, 162; sex with physical violence, 163–164, 166–167; verbal sexual harassment, 156–157, 166, 211

staff verbal abuse, 117, 137, 168, 211; assymetry of respect and, 141–146; by female officers, 142; human rights approach to, 174; staff members not intervening against, 143; trauma-informed practice and training to avoid, 180

stalking, in prison, 124–125

standing your ground, 90, 108

state jobs (prison job assignments), 75–78, 225

state-sponsored suffering: as human rights violation, 175–176; intersectional inequalities producing, 170. *See also* human rights

Steffensmeier, D., 21

Steiner, B., 2, 16, 49, 52, 97, 104

Stewart, I., 178, 179
stigmatized offenses: prison culture and norms of, 87, 115–116; violence and, 115–116
Stohr, M., 11
Stop Prison Rape. *See* Just Detention International (JDI)
store, 225
street, 225
sub rosa economy, 77–79, 225
substance abuse: as gendered pathway to prison, 24, 29–30, 38; need for care for, vs. imprisonment, 184; prevalence of, 30
Sykes, G., 87, 88

tables of findings, 205–222
"take your date," 118–119, 225
Teague, R., 26
Teplin, L., 25
term, 225
Thailand Institute of Justice, x–xi
thefts in prison, 97, 105, 108, 206. *See also* economic exploitation
Thoennes, N., 168
Thomas, J., 8n
Three Strikes laws, 20
Tjaden, P., 168
tobacco, 78–79, 78n, 111
Tobin, H., 106
Torres, S., 47
torture: Mandela Rules on, 182; staff sexual misconduct defined as, 153, 174
touching, undesired, 123, 157–158
Townhead, L., 176
trafficking and trading, tobacco, 78–79, 78n, 111
Trammell, R., 85, 87
transgender women and men. *See* gender-nonconforming persons
trauma: historical and collective, 36–37, 38; institutional, 64–65; reactions to, and reduction of human capital, 28; trauma-informed practice, 65, 65n, 177, 179–180, 186. *See also* violent victimization
Travis, J., 20, 22
trick, 226
trick bag, 226
truth-in-sentencing laws, 20n
tune up, 226

ugly beds, 50–51, 226
United Nations: Body of Principles for the Protection of All Persons under Any Form of Detention or Imprisonment, 180; Convention on the Elimination of All Forms of Discrimination against Women (CEDAW), 180–181; Convention on the Rights of the Child, 181; Declaration on the Elimination of Violence against Women, 181; International Convention Against Torture and Other Cruel, Inhuman and Degrading Treatment or Punishment (Torture Convention), 166; International Covenant on Civil and Political Rights (ICCPR), 166–167, 180, 181–182; International Covenant on Economic, Social and Cultural Rights, 180; Mandela Rules (*Standard Minimum Rules for the Treatment of Prisoners*), 2n, 166–167, 182; Tokyo Rules, 183; Universal Declaration of Human Rights (UNDHR), 11–12; *Women and Imprisonment: The Handbook for Prison Managers and Policy-Makers* (UNODC 2015), 6, 171–172, 173, 176, 179, 180, 184. *See also* Bangkok Rules
U.S. Constitution, and prisoner rights, 167, 181
use of force, 226
U.S. Supreme Court, prison rights, 171, 172

Van Dieten, M., 95–96, 179
Van Voorhis, P., 3, 7, 9–10, 18, 25, 32, 33, 34, 38, 52, 52n7, 178
verbal conflict, 107–108, 121, 122
Veysey, B., 80–81
victimization. *See* violent victimization
Vik, P., 26
violence among female inmates, 209–210, 215–216; crowding as promoting, 49, 50, 51; cumulative disadvantage and, 172–173; duality of vulnerability, 99; escalation model for, 97–98, 107, 108; "fighting mix," 89–90; gender differences in, 2, 15–16, 93; and "good" vs. "bad" prison neighborhoods, 52–55, 58; health problems as escalating, 61; inmate explanations of catalysts for, 98–99; instrumental vs. expressive, 93–94, 96; prison capital as, 97, 119–120; prison capital inequalities and vulnerability to, 99–107, 172–173; in "public" vs. "private" spaces, 57; pushing back against, 110–111; staff reaction to, as varying, 120–121, 141; trauma-informed correctional practice

violence among female inmates *(continued)*
lowering rates of, 65; victim "mentality"
and, 103–104; weapons as uncommon
in, 121. *See also* staff physical violence;
violence among female inmates, types of
violence among female inmates, types of:
"being messy" (gossiping), 113–114;
debt, 111; economic exploitation,
109–111; gangs, 111–113; intimate
relationships, 108, 126–133; long-termers vs. short-terms and relationship to
time, 116–119; sexual violence,
121–126; snitching, 114–115;
stigmatized offenses, 115–116; verbal
conflict, 107–108, 121; violence
embraced as capital, 119–120
violent assaults on staff, 65, 138, 151
violent crime, 21, 94–97; reform initiatives,
185; systemic gender inequality and,
94–95, 96–97, 172–173
violent victimization: criminalization of, 35;
cumulative, and female-initiated
violence, 96–97, 172–173; as disproportionate for women offenders, 27, 29;
mental health problems and, 30–31; and
revictimization, 27, 103, 168; and safety
in prison as problematic, 69; sexualization through, 28; as shaping pathways,
33, 38; staff misconduct as triggering
trauma of, 150, 158–159; and strain/
negative emotionality, 28; systemic
gender inequality and, 34–35
violent victimization in childhood: drug
abuse/crimes and history of, 29–30; and
earlier onset of criminal behavior, 29;
gender differences in association
between offending and, 25–26, 29–30;
and girls and young women as
offenders, 26–27; and health/mental
health, 25–26, 29, 30–31, 59; as
pathway to prison, 29, 33; prisons as
triggering trauma of, 64; rates of,
among women offenders, 27; revictimi-

zation as adults, 27, 168; as risk factor
(ACE Study), 28–29, 59; and violence
perpetrated by women as adults, 94

Wagner, P., 77
walked off, 226
Walmsley, R., 1, 19
Walters, K., 36–37
"war on drugs," 20–22, 20n; as war on
women, 20
Watterson, K., 8n
weakness, appearance of, 80
weathering, 38, 226
Wesely, J., 4, 10, 11, 26, 28, 94, 96, 119
West, C., 3, 4
Western, B., 20, 22
White, N., 26
Widom, C., 25, 26
Williams, L., 25, 104
Williams, M., 60
Winfree, T., 21, 35
Winterfield, L., 76
Wolff, N., 27
Wolf, R., 20
Women's Correctional Safety Scales
(WCSS), 12, 15, 55, 190–193, 193–204
Woods, D., 79
Wooldredge, J., 2, 16, 49, 52, 97, 104
Worrall, A., 25
Wright, E., 27, 178

the yard, 226
Yarussi, J., 11, 107
younger women prisoners: and gangs,
112–113; disapproval of, 139; and
violence, 99–101. *See also* aging women
prisoners
Young, V., 8n, 37
Yurussi, J., 106–107

Zaitzow, B., 8n
Zimmerman, D., 3, 4
Zupan, L., 147